Defending Freedom:
American Labor and Foreign Affairs

by PHILIP TAFT

With a Foreword by
Robert D. Murphy

NASH PUBLISHING, LOS ANGELES

1973

TO JOHN, NANCY, and DOUGLAS BLAKE

Copyright © 1973 by Philip Taft

Library of Congress Catalog Card Number: 73-3083.
Standard Book Number: 8402-4623-4.

Published simultaneously in the United States and Canada
by Nash Publishing Corporation, 9255 Sunset Boulevard,
Los Angeles, California 90069.

Printed in the United States of America.

First Printing.

Contents

32228

Foreword

PROFESSOR PHILIP TAFT has succeeded in producing a long-needed, comprehensive account of American Labor's influence on foreign affairs. It is both timely and readable.

What shines forth from this history of American Labor's involvement abroad is the consistency of its attitude toward and abhorrence of totalitarianism. At the same time Labor's policy line consistently hews to a line avoiding unacceptable intervention, or meddling in the internal affairs of other countries. This is a highly sensitive area of demarcation which the author fully recognizes and understands.

It is clear, too, that by and large there is a persistent desire to demonstrate loyalty to our government's policies even though inevitably there are situations where strong differences of judgment and viewpoint occur. In time of war as well as peace, Labor's leadership as well as its rank and file reveals a determined and intelligent sense of national values avoiding extreme chauvinism and narrow isolationism.

During the many years I was privileged to serve as a member of the United States Foreign Service in a number of countries abroad, I count as highly valued opportunities my contacts with American Labor's representatives. This was true in Paris before World War II with the controversial development of French labor in the *Force Ouvrière* and the *Confédération Generale du Travail.* It was a time when acquaintance with many American leaders was possible— George Meany, David Dubinsky, Walter Reuther, Matthew Woll, Jay Lovestone, Irving Brown—to mention a few. The soundness of their views and their energetic courage made a deep impression. They developed a comprehensive grasp of European affairs which from time to time was of inestimable value to our government in a political sense.

Of course the postwar years in Germany provided the most colorful experience in the struggle for the establishment of an independent, democratic Central European labor organization. When the Russians torpedoed the Potsdam Agreement, and the division of Germany crystallized, the fate of the East German labor organization under Soviet auspices was sealed. Before that, the illusion of the World Federation of Trade Unions so ardently promoted by Moscow had a seductive impact. Those were the days of Franklin Roosevelt's "grand design"—his hope of cooperation between the West and the USSR. His reasoning, of course, was simple. If cooperation failed, the result inevitably would be war between the USSR and the United States. Therefore, every effort and concession promoting understanding and cooperation had to be tried. Before Mr. Roosevelt died, I believe he understood that his grand design had failed.

As the true character of the Russian objective emerged, those in the West who had initially been attracted to the thought of a universal labor organization were disappointed. But it was a close tift with totalitarianism, and American labor leaders, even those initially enthusiastic, were quicker to detect the dangers than some of our European friends and allies. I recall the dramatic defection from U.S. Military Government at Berlin by George Shaw Wheeler, who renounced his American citizenship, publicly acknowledged his membership in the Communist Party, and fled to Prague; it illuminated the pitfalls which had developed.

Quite naturally Professor Taft is oriented more toward labor problems in Europe, Latin America, and Africa, than in Asia. After all, so much of American action in the labor field found its inspiration in the history of European workers' earlier struggles, one effect of which was to stimulate immigration to the United States. There they found—as did my own Grandfather—elbow room and freedom to promote so many ideas for the improvement of labor's participation in our social structure. In the days of Samuel Gompers, of course, this was more pronounced and perhaps more urgently necessary than later.

Professor Taft's treatment of the Asian labor complex is more sketchy. Perhaps there is room for subsequent analysis of that important field of labor evolution.

"Defending Freedom; American Labor and Foreign Affairs" merits attention. I congratulate Professor Taft on a vigorous and stimulating contribution to Labor's best interests.

ROBERT D. MURPHY

Preface

THIS STUDY aims to describe the attitudes and activities of American labor in what can be broadly described as foreign affairs. It includes efforts by the labor movement of the United States to influence the foreign policy of the United States government. It also includes the relationship between the labor organizations and the central bodies they have established with labor movements of foreign countries, as well as those with the international organizations which the labor movements of the world have jointly created. In addition, the financial and material assistance to unions and labor federations provided after World War II, the views of American labor on colonialism, communism, fascism and other subjects which impinge upon the above, have been examined. Discussions of tariffs and trade have been omitted as these questions do not appear vital, at this time, to the central purpose of the study.

My principal sources have been the archives of the old American Federation of Labor (AFL) and of the American Federation of Labor-Congress of Industrial Organizations (AFL-CIO). I am greatly indebted to President George Meany who gave me unrestricted access to records of the two federations. President Meany has been a leading participant in the development and execution of the major labor policies in the international area during the last 30 years. I have greatly profited from my discussions with him.

In addition to the cooperation of AFL-CIO Secretary-Treasurer Lane Kirkland, I have had the aid of the AFL-CIO department of international affairs. I wish to thank Jay Lovestone, the chief of the department, for sharing his knowledge with me on many of the topics covered in the study, and for providing many necessary documents not available elsewhere. His comments and criticisms of several versions of the material have been invaluable. I have also benefited from the assistance of other members of the department: Irving Brown, Andrew McClellan, Ernest Lee, Harry Goldberg and Elly Borochowicz were generous with their time and knowledge. In addition to the labor archives, I have relied on the papers of the late Matthew Woll. I have also used the papers of Henry Rutz, one of the first representatives of the old AFL in Europe after World War II and a member of the AFL and AFL-CIO departments of international affairs.

In addition, a number of libraries were used: the Rockefeller Library at Brown University, the Regenstein Library at the University of Chicago, the main branch of the New York Public Library, the Congressional and the U.S. Department of Labor libraries in Washington, and the industrial relations division of the Littauer Library at Harvard University, whose librarian, Mrs. Claire Brown, was especially helpful in scouring up a number of scarce items. All have my sincere thanks.

My colleague, Professor Jerome Stein, took time off from his labors to read my manuscript, and I am indeed grateful for his sharp eye and unmerciful criticism. Theresa Taft has acted as editorial guide, proofreader, and general aide.

Much of the work was done at the Graduate School of

Business of the University of Chicago, and I wish to express my thanks for the assistance of the secretarial and the copying services and for their many kindnesses to me. At Brown University, Mrs. Jeanne Clark, Miss Marion Anthony, and Mrs. Sally Deslauriers aided with the typing of versions of the manuscript. My thanks to them. Finally, I express my gratitude to the Ford Foundation, whose grant aided this study.

However, I alone am accountable for the contents and opinions expressed.

PHILIP TAFT
Brown University
Providence, Rhode Island

Introduction

THE CONCERN of the old American Federation of Labor (AFL) with foreign affairs was more limited than that of its successor, the American Federation of Labor-Congress of Industrial Organizations (AFL-CIO). To some extent this attitude reflected the isolationist mood of the country, although some leaders consistently favored more active cooperation with the international labor movement being fashioned in Europe in the late nineteenth century. Even while abstaining from such affiliations and favoring a policy of isolation by the government of the United States, the AFL did more than take note of injustice and oppression in other parts of the world. In the 1880's it protested the signing of an extradition treaty with czarist Russia, and later denounced the execution of the Spanish anarchist/educator Francesco Ferrer as a crime. It aided workers and unions facing assaults by employers in other lands, and deviated from its isolationist policy by cooperating with the British Trades Union Congress.

The degree of interest in the affairs of foreign labor and its organizations has, of course, varied over time. There were always those who wanted to withdraw into a sort of "fortress America" and sever all connections with the European

1

homeland. Others were more sensitive to affairs outside the United States, and favored a more permanent cooperation with labor groups in other lands. However, a movement as large as the AFL-CIO, operating in the last third of the twentieth century, is likely to regard events abroad somewhat differently than did its predecessors. The older federations would not have invested both funds and energy in international enterprises on the scale of either the AFL (after World War II) or of the AFL-CIO.

Who determines the views and activities of organized labor? Some who are opposed to the positions taken by the AFL-CIO attribute its stress on anti-communist policies to Jay Lovestone. One need not doubt his influence, but anti-communist policy has a long history: it was promulgated by Samuel Gompers and eventually became the official view of the AFL. Soon after the overthrow of the Czar, Gompers telegraphed his congratulations to the Russian people for the "splendid proclamation of your provisional government, declaring for free speech and press and the right of workers to organize and if necessary to strike. . . ."[1] Gompers was anxious that Russia remain in the war, but he was also gratified that the Russian provisional government was a democratic one.

His views about the Russian government changed drastically with the victory of the Bolsheviks in November of 1918. In a statement to President Woodrow Wilson, Gompers warned against encouraging the Bolsheviks.[2] In a memorandum to the Peace Commission (American members), Gompers protested the

> policy of favoring both directly and indirectly the Bolshevist, revolutionary and anti-democratic movements which aim to overthrow the democratic governments associated with America in the war. . . . I know as you know that no such policy can bear the light of

day before the American people. ... There are now
present in Paris a number of American citizens who are
continually giving proof that they enjoy the confidence
of the administration and of your Commission; who
constantly and openly express agreement with the
Bolsheviki, satisfaction at the success of the Bolsheviki
regime, and who are now working with every means in
their power for the success of the Bolsheviki in Russia
and the growth of the movement in other countries. ...
I am not guessing at these matters, I know that he who
temporizes with Bolshevism or assists those who are
helping the Bolshevist cause by agreeing with them are
committing an unspeakable crime against civilization
itself.[3]

The American Federation of Labor opposed recognition of
the Soviet Union at every convention during which the issue
was considered, and Gompers wrote innumerable letters
defending his and the AFL's position. In a typical letter to
Secretary of State Charles Evans Hughes, Gompers wrote:

I have stated many times that so far as my viewpoint is
concerned, I am not able to see where good crops, or an
improving economic condition, or any one of a number
of things, including an acknowledgement of Russia's
financial obligations, could change the American position regarding recognition, as long as the principle of
tyranny remains. It has been urged that the so-called
New Economic policy, modifying the practice of
communism, removed some of the objection to recognition, but we have held that any policy that was changed
one way by edict could well be changed another way by
edict—and we are opposed to the whole autocratic
principle under which people are governed by fiat, edict
and military command.[4]

Gompers was succeeded by William Green, a coal miner

who had served on the AFL executive council for ten years. Green was an internationalist and defended the League of Nations. The first convention over which he presided reiterated opposition to the recognition of the Soviet Union and praised the United States government's "adherence to ... democracy and ... refusal to ... barter and sale for diplomatic advantage and capitalist exploitation." Not all organizations of labor accepted the AFL's views on this issue. A number of dissidents, led by Albert Coyle, editor of the journal of the Brotherhood of Locomotive Firemen and Enginemen, decided to organize a commission to visit the Soviet Union and to report on conditions in that country. Coyle sought to gain Green's support and asked him to appoint a member of the group that would make the investigation. Green rejected the request, and wrote to Coyle that the commission "would lack authority to speak for or to represent the American labor movement. The absence of such representative authority would ... nullify the work of a self-constituted committee and render its mission fruitless."[5] The executive council subsequently endorsed Green's views.[6]

The commission returned with a favorable report on conditions within the Soviet Union, and recommended an end to the non-recognition policy by the United States government. Its views had no influence on the outlook of the AFL, which continued to disapprove of governmental recognition. When, in 1933, the administration of President Franklin D. Roosevelt took steps to recognize the Soviet government, Green, speaking for the AFL, submitted a brief in opposition. The AFL, he said, continued to support the conditions and principles enunciated by President Wilson and restated by subsequent administrations as "prerequisites to Russian recognition."[7] He acknowledged the right of the Russian people to "adopt the Soviet form of government and to administer their own political and governmental affairs

free from interference by any other nation." He asked
President Roosevelt for an appointment in order to discuss
the issue, but failed in his mission to halt recognition.[8]

The fight against recognition may have been ended, but
the AFL did not relent in its opposition to collaboration with
Soviet labor organizations. The old AFL and the AFL-CIO
took the position that Soviet labor unions were neither free
nor autonomous; that they were controlled by the government and thus incapable of developing their own policies. As
a result the AFL threatened to withdraw from the
International Federation of Trade Unions (a group of
national federations) if Soviet labor organizations were
admitted to membership (see Chapter 3). Despite pressure
from the United States government, the AFL rejected a 1942
invitation to join in a cooperative venture with the British
Trades Union Congress and the Soviet trade unions. In both
instances the AFL argued that Soviet unions were dissimilar
to those found in the United States and England, and that
they were in fact agencies of their own government (see
Chapter 4).

Refusal to cooperate with labor unions in other totalitarian countries followed: the AFL showed the same hostility
to fascist Italy,[9] Hitler's Germany and Franco's Spain; and
did so for the same reason that led it to oppose the policies
of the Soviet Union—the absence of freedom.

Domestic policies and foreign affairs.

The American labor movement is primarily an economic
one in that its principal activities are to deal with an
employer over terms of employment. It is also engaged in
two kinds of political activity—lobbying in state capitals and
in Congress for favorable legislation, and supporting candidates for public office who hold opinions favorable to
labor's objectives and who are willing to support these

objectives with their votes. Endorsement of such candidates is based upon their entire past record, though the real test is how they have voted on domestic issues.

In September 1970, AFL-CIO President George Meany stated that a candidate's position on the Vietnam war would not be the basis for making a political endorsement in the 1972 presidential elections. "The determining factor," said President Meany, "is going to be the position of congressmen and senators on domestic issues, on the issue of civil rights, and all of the things we think should be done, on the domestic scene."[10]

Since Meany made this statement, Senator George McGovern (Dem.-S.D.) has been a presidential candidate to whom President Meany and the AFL-CIO denied endorsement. It seems to me virtually certain that McGovern's views on war and peace had little to do with the AFL-CIO's position or with that of George Meany. This has always been the policy of the American labor movement, and any other would be suicidal.

CHAPTER ONE

In Search of
International Cooperation

International relations.

As with other issues, there was no agreement among early American labor leaders on a desirable policy toward European workers and their organizations. Some favored complete disregard of the problems of Europe, and others a policy of cooperation. Mutual help, regulation of the flow of immigrants across the borders of states, and prevention of the recruitment of strike-breakers from one country to serve in another, were visualized as some of the advantages of cooperation. In addition, a large number of American unions in the late ninteenth century held the British labor movement in high esteem, and hoped its American counterpart would follow its example. This respect accounts for the greetings sent by the founding convention of the Federation of Trade and Labor Unions of the United States and Canada to the Parliamentary Committee of the British Trades Union Congress in 1881.[1] This federation did not, however, become an effective body, and was swallowed by the newly formed American Federation of Labor (AFL) in 1886.

A year after the founding of the AFL Gompers recommended that the Federation, in response to a request for attendance, send two delegates to the convention of the

International Labor Congress scheduled for 1888. Opposition to the proposal, led by Peter McGuire, was able to defeat it.[2] The executive council of the AFL, of which both Gompers and McGuire were members, explained that the failure to send delegates was due to the fact that "work at home requires the active presence of all our available men." It also noted: "The late war of slave emancipation has added to the ranks of our class more than 4,000,000 people who stand in direct necessity of organization and education." The remainder of the document was taken up in extolling the virtues of free trade unions, and "regretting our enforced absences from your councils."[3]

As Gompers was most sympathetic to and active in behalf of international cooperation, his views on the subject are of interest. Late in 1888, William Liebknecht, a follower and collaborator of Karl Marx and a founder of the German labor movement, asked whether he could use Gompers' name in calling an international labor congress for the following year. Gompers informed him of the convention's refusal and told him that "the expression of the convention of the organization is binding upon its president and since no distinction can be made between my position as president and my individuality I am constrained by my sense of duty to decline the honor you wish to confer."[4]

The emerging labor movements of Europe were seeking wider unity, and while they got no active cooperation from the AFL, their efforts always received friendly encouragement from Gompers, who would have preferred closer relations. When André Gily invited Gompers to an international congress in Paris in 1889, his invitation was rejected because a campaign for the eight hour day would not allow leaders of American labor to divide their energies.[5] Gompers assured him that it was not due to the absence "of a fraternal feeling and recognition of the identity of interest of the workingmen of all countries that we are not represented."[6]

In his early years, Gompers was always interested in promoting closer relations with the labor movements of Europe. He reacted favorably to a suggestion of Eleanor Marx Aveling, the daughter of Karl Marx, and Will Thorne, a British trade union leader, that England and the United States devise a plan for inhibiting the movement of strike-breakers between the two countries. Gompers asked that the plan be enlarged to include "the trade unions of Great Britain and Ireland, Continental Europe, Australia, and the American Federation of Labor."[7]

In responding to a request for a representative to the International Labor Congress, at Brussels, Belgium, in 1891, Gompers expressed the view that where the right to organize exists, "all energies, political and social, should be directed to secure the utmost freedom of coalition and combination."[8] His plea was based upon the belief that "when the economic movement has sufficiently developed so as to produce a unity of thought on all essentials, . . . a political Labor Movement will be the result. In fact, there is not and cannot be any economic action taken by organized labor unless it has its political and social influence."[9] When a representative of the German trade unions came to the United States to collect funds for the printers on strike, he was given a credential by Gompers to visit affiliated unions and make his plea.[10]

Aware of opposition to entangling alliances with continental labor movements, Gompers informed the 1895 AFL convention of the planned International Socialist and Trade Union Congress at London in August 1896, but the convention rejected a resolution to send delegates by a vote of 52 to 11.[11]

During this period, Gompers sought to have unions in the United States adopt a system whereby members of European organizations could transfer their memberships to the union of their trade in the United States if they emigrated; it was adopted by only a few. In the meantime, the British Trades Union Congress initiated its long relationship with the American labor movement by sending two delegates to the 1894 AFL convention. Upon Gompers' return to the presidency of the AFL after his one-year "sabbatical," he again requested the executive council to enter into fraternal relationships with labor movements on the Continent. He believed that if "these fraternal visitations can be conducted successfully, . . . they should develop into a holding of bona fide International Trade Congresses every few years, and thus take the place of the fraternal delegations." The suggestion was rejected by the executive council.[12]

Gompers continued to remain in touch with European labor leaders, and on occasion offered advice upon request. He advised August Keufer, secretary of the French Typographical Union and an opponent of militant syndicalism, then at the peak of its power, on how to promote a federation of trade unions. Gompers urged that unions be allowed to affiliate immediately and not wait until they had existed for five years. Otherwise, the newly organized would lose the benefit of being attached to a federation of unions. Gompers emphasized the need for building up the financial base of unions through adequate dues and assessments, urged that all sections of the country should be represented on the governing boards (instead of only Paris), argued against three-year terms of office as too long, and found the idea of rotating secretaries objectionable. Gompers also spoke against dependence upon volunteers for doing the work of the organization. In his view, a worker would neglect either his work or his union if he were not paid for his services and, moreover, an organization could not require work over long periods of time without compensation.[13]

The International Secretariat of National Trade Union Centers.

The trade union federations of the European countries were, during the latter part of the nineteenth century, trying to establish closer and more formal relationships with each other. While they were largely unsuccessful until 1901, they *were* able — beginning with the tobacco workers' unions, which set up an international organization in 1889 — to establish federations of unions in the same trade or industry, or *international trade secretariats,* as they are called.[14] Closer relations between the AFL and the organized workers of Europe were advocated, and Gompers wrote that American labor could not be "indifferent to the movement and struggles of peoples of all countries for justice and right."[15] The executive council of the AFL went along, and approved a program for promoting the transfer of workers from the unions of their native lands to those of the host country when they emigrated. Some unions found the proposal acceptable and helpful, but the desire to limit entry (a common policy among unions of skilled workers) discouraged others from accepting it.[16]

Although attempts to build an international labor movement of national labor federations were not successful, a limited cooperative arrangement of Norway, Sweden, and Denmark was established in 1886. It was J. Jensen, head of the Danish trade unions, who initiated the broader effort of uniting national centers into an international federation. While attending a meeting of the British Trade Union Federation as a fraternal delegate, Jensen proposed the setting up of an international organization, and won approval from Isaac Mitchell, secretary of the federation. The idea also found support in Karl Legien, president of the general committee of the German trade unions. A socialist who was also a great labor leader, Legien understood that to be effective and meaningful, an international organization of national trade union federations had to allow for the independent views of each national central organization.

Legien was elected president and secretary of the International Secretariat, established in Denmark at a conference in Copenhagen in 1901. The AFL did not join immediately, although Gompers would have preferred to do so. Opposition to affiliation came from two sources within the AFL — one wanted to be completely free of European influences, and the second was opposed to the revolutionary philosophy and militant tactics which some branches of European labor espoused. Legien, aware of the reasons for the AFL's reluctance to join the International Secretariat, believed that the labor movement of each country must be free to work out its own views without pressure from other lands.

It was for these reasons that Legien, at the conference of 1905, opposed the radical proposals of the French Confederation of Labor. Unions in France were, at that time, dominated by the philosophy of revolutionary syndicalism, which advocated the use of the general strike, sabotage of industry, and anti-militarism. Legien argued that the conference was not the place for discussion of these tactics which were the business of French labor.[17] The conference agreed and decided that its purpose was to promote closer relations between the trade unions of all countries, the collection of uniform trade statistics, the provision of mutual support in industrial conflicts, and deal with all other questions directly relating to the trade union organization of the working class. At the same time, the conference decided: "All theoretical questions and questions affecting the tendencies and tactics of the trade union movement in the various countries shall be excluded from treatment by the Conference."[18]

The AFL had not yet affiliated, but relations between the

organizations were cordial; correspondence relative to the AFL's participation had taken place from the beginning. Even so, Gompers requested that the 1907 AFL convention not ask him to accept an invitation to attend the International Trade Union Conference of 1908 because of pending national elections. At the 1908 convention, Gompers' recommendation that he attend the next meeting of the International Trade Conference of Trade Unions was unanimously endorsed. He was to attend the conference after the close of the British Trades Union Congress to which he had been appointed a fraternal delegate. The conference took place in Paris in 1909, not, as was originally proposed, a year later in Stockholm.[19]

International Federation of Trade Unions.

Gompers attended the 1909 conference as a fraternal delegate and proposed, although denying that he was a voting delegate, that

> The International Conference recommends the National Trade Union Centers of every country to study the question of the formation of an "International Federation of Labor," the autonomy of the trade union movement in each country being ordained and guaranteed. The purpose of the Federation is for the protection and the advancement of the rights and interests of the wage-earners of every land and the establishment of international fraternity and solidarity.[20]

There were several attacks upon the American trade union movement. Gompers said:

> Even supposing that with respect to several of the International Secretaries the foregoing queries bring a disappointing answer, will it not be helpful to international trade-unionism to send a delegate to the

Conference two years hence? My answer must be an emphatic "Yes."
The 1911 conference was held in Budapest.

According to Sassenbach, the secretary in 1921-1927 and general secretary in 1927-1930, a particularly gratifying event to be recorded was the affiliation of the American Federation of Labor, the first non-European national center.[21] Gompers was aware of differences between the majority of trade union leaders in the United States and their opposite numbers in Europe, and he insisted that "One thing . . . was to be understood: every country is to decide upon its own policy, tactics, and tendencies."[22] He had expected to work with leaders who represented different viewpoints, and as long as these leaders did not attempt to impose their ideals upon the American labor movement, Gompers would not be concerned. He truly believed that cooperation among international organizations was possible only if each avoided controversies over the principles or tactics of the others.

Legien shared this view, and criticized Léon Jouhaux, head of the French General Workers' Confederation (CGT), who had unfavorably commented on the Spanish labor movement. Gompers agreed with Legien, and said that such action led to

controversial correspondence calculated to mar rather than harmonize international relations of organized labor. If my opinion were asked, I should express a difference from the tactics and methods of the organization of the working people of Spain, as I might differ from certain phases of the workingmen's movement of other countries; but claiming for the workers of America the right of our activities as judgment dictates, I can only yield to the movements of other countries the right we ask for ourselves.[23]

The AFL regarded the international organization of labor as one which would perform limited but important tasks. The 1909 convention of the AFL voted to affiliate, but, in selecting a delegate to the 1911 conference, the executive council gave instructions that their delegate inform the conference that the AFL did not favor the general strike, anti-militarism, or anti-patriotism as understood by the French Labor Confederation. As the AFL saw it, the principal activities of an international organization should be prevention of the exporting of strike-breakers from one country to another, uniform legislation governing hours of labor for both men and women in dangerous trades, restriction of the labor of children under 14 years in gainful occupation, the regulation of dangerous occupations, and housing reform. In addition, the AFL recommended that the International Federation publish a journal in several languages covering the state of trade, conditions of labor, progress in labor legislation, and all other matters affecting the lives of workers in the various countries.[24]

James Duncan, a vice president of the AFL, was appointed as delegate to the 1911 conference at Budapest. At the same time, the Industrial Workers of the World (IWW) appointed William Z. Foster, thus challenging Duncan's right to represent American labor. The chief point in the controversy was that Duncan was a member of the National Civic Federation, a group made up of labor union officials, businessmen, industrialists, and members of the public interested in developing an understanding between unions and their employers through promoting industrial peace and the trade agreement. The attack upon Duncan was joined by the leader of the French labor movement, Jouhaux, who charged that the Civic Federation was an organization which "aimed at obscuring the class struggle, whose activities were directed against the workers."[25] Jouhaux announced he would not vote for Duncan's admittance as a delegate if he belonged to the National Civic Federation.

Legien, in contrast, believed that Duncan's membership in any organization could not be a subject of discussion and that raising such a question was improper: Duncan represented the AFL and therefore had to be recognized as a delegate; Foster could not be admitted as a representative of the IWW as only one trade union national center from each country was eligible. After a long and somewhat irrelevant discussion, Duncan was seated and the IWW was denied membership.[26]

A proposal for changing the name of the conference was not adopted until the Zurich meeting of 1913 when, at the motion of the American delegate, George Perkins, the name of International Federation of Trade Unions was unanimously endorsed. The next meeting (the first under the new name) was scheduled for San Francisco. Unfortunately, the war made the meeting impossible.[27]

World War and isolation.

The outbreak of World War I disrupted relations between the labor movements of Europe and the United States, created a division between labor organizations of the warring nations, and broke the connections between the American Federation of Labor and the labor movements of Europe — with the exception of England with which the AFL continued to have fraternal relations. At the outbreak of the war, Legien, head of the International Federation of Trade Unions and also of the free German trade union movement, assured Gompers that Germany had done everything possible to "preserve the peace and prevent war."[28] Gompers replied that he regretted the "terrible monstrous war," and expressed the hope that it would be "speedily ended and peace established."[29]

The 1914 AFL convention authorized the calling of a meeting, to be held during the peace conference at the end of the war, of representatives of labor federations of different countries for purposes of restoring fraternal relations among workers and devising policies which could be useful to the working people of all the countries.[30] A copy of the proposal was sent to President Wilson for his consideration "in the event that a Peace Congress shall be ultimately called."[31] The plan, however, failed to receive the approval of labor representatives of the belligerent countries who were faced at the time with the problem of steering their organizations through a difficult course in a war of increasing violence, and could not then concern themselves with the making of peace.

Transfer of headquarters of the International Federation of Trade Unions.

Legien, who headed the International Secretariat and the International Federation of Trade Unions when it succeeded the Secretariat, could see no conflict in his retention of office after the outbreak of war. He found no reason "for distrusting the management of the IFTU in Germany."[32] He therefore rejected the suggestion of the Dutch National Labor Center that a correspondence bureau be established in a neutral country for the duration of the war, and instead suggested that Jan Oudegeest act as an intermediary between him and those national labor centers whose countries were at war with Germany.

Legien's plan was not acceptable to the leaders of the French and English trade unions; W. A. Appleton, secretary of the General Federation of Trade Unions, and Léon Jouhaux, secretary of the Confédération du Travail. They believed that the chief office should be transferred to a neutral country; that its personnel should be neutral; and that the office should be in Berne, Switzerland. The AFL executive council approved of these suggestions.[33]

Because Gompers transmitted both the view of the allied

labor leaders and its endorsement by the AFL executive council, he was criticized in the *Weekly Report of the International Transport Workers Federation.* The criticism came from Oudegeest, who questioned whether Gompers' statement reflected the view of his organization on this issue, and charged that the plan to transfer IFTU headquarters was an attempt "to break up the German trade union movement." In rebuttal, Gompers pointed out that he had acted as an intermediary, and that the suggestion for moving the headquarters to a neutral country had been duly endorsed by the AFL executive council.

Leeds Conference.

Legien would not agree to the transfer of the headquarters. He insisted that he had not tried to use the IFTU in behalf of Germany in the war and that he had already established Oudegeest to act as an intermediary, from his post at Amsterdam, between trade union centers of the warring powers. This state of affairs was not regarded as satisfactory by the trade union centers in the allied countries. In Leeds, England, on July 5, 1916, at a conference attended by delegates from the British, French, Italian and Belgian labor movements, a program for presenting the demands of labor to the peace conference at the end of the war was drawn up and a correspondent bureau for issuing information to the trade union centers was established in Paris. Legien, who continued to act as the head of the IFTU, thereupon called for a conference of trade union representatives in Switzerland to take place in Berne on December 11, 1916. At the request of the Scandinavian national trade union centers, the plan for this meeting was cancelled.[34]

The United States becomes a belligerent.

Gompers' role as an intermediary between the labor

movements of Germany and the allied countries came to an end with the entry of the United States into the war. As the break between Germany and the United States approached, Gompers appealed to Legien and to the German ambassador to help prevent war between the two countries.[35] On April 2, 1917, he wrote to Legien appealing for aid in preventing a break. He defended the right of the United States to protect its citizens and told Legien: "We are doing our level best to avert actual war and we have a right to insist that the men of labor of Germany exert their last ounce of effort to get your government to make an immediate and satisfactory avowal that shall save all from America's entrance into universal conflict."[36]

Legien was powerless to change the policies of his government, and Gompers' letter virtually forced him to defend its behavior. "No intervention with government on my part [he cabled] has any chance of success unless America prevails upon England to discontinue starvation war as being contrary to law of nations. I appeal to American labor not to allow themselves to be made catspaws of warmongers by sailing into war zone and thus contribute to extending conflict."[37]

Wartime policies of the AFL.

As war approached, Gompers recognized the need for formulation of a policy for protecting labor standards. He noted that the organizations of labor in the belligerent countries had been swept "away from their moorings" in their efforts to contribute to national defense.[38] He urged avoidance of the same errors in the United States. He pointed to the effort (which eventually failed) by the AFL "to prevail upon Congress to avoid compulsory military service."[39] He was most concerned that labor should be given a voice "in the determination of defense plans," and warned that if labor remained aloof from the defense effort, it would be forced to accept the decisions of others – even those who might be hostile to the organized workers of the United States.[40]

The executive council of the AFL agreed with this assessment and endorsed the calling of a conference of both affiliated and unaffiliated national organizations which was held on March 12, 1917, and was attended by delegates from 79 AFL unions and five trade departments (five independent organizations were also represented). The conference asserted the necessity for labor organizations to continue their defense of workers' rights during wartime, and demanded labor representation on government boards dealing with war production.[41]

Labor missions.

Gompers was always on the alert lest labor's importance be overlooked. When he learned that the British and French governments were sending missions to the United States, he cabled both prime ministers, asking that the heads of trade union movements in their respective countries be included so as to inform American labor on the handling of wartime labor issues.[42] This marked the beginning of several exhanges of labor delegations among the three countries; exchanges which in time were expanded to include other countries.

Conference of national union centers proposed at Stockholm.

Legien's attempt to convoke a meeting of the IFTU had failed, but a new effort was initiated by the Swiss Trade Union Federation. It suggested that a delegate conference meet to discuss the proposals of the Leeds conference.[43] At the same time, two conferences were being proposed for June 8, 1917, at Stockholm. In a cablegram, Oudegeest notified Gompers that delegates from the affiliated trade union centers would meet for "discussion, and establishment of trade unionists at peace negotiations. . . . The Dutch Federation of Trade Unions in charge."[44]

Gompers replied immediately and called attention to the AFL's unsuccessful attempt to have the IFTU approve of a conference of trade union centers at the place and time of the eventual peace conference. "Now," he said, "after the United States is in the war you propose a conference be held in Stockholm at the same time and place when the so-called International Socialist Conference is to be held and this proposition too without the consultation with trade union centers of the United States and other countries."[45]

The Stockholm conference met as scheduled, but only the Scandinavian countries, neutral Holland, Finland, and Germany and her allies sent delegates. Another conference was proposed for September 17, 1917, and the AFL was invited to send delegates.[46] The invitation was rejected by the AFL executive council as "premature and untimely" and "to no good purpose. . . . If an international trade union conference is to be held it should be at a more opportune time than the present or the immediate future."[47]

The conference of the neutrals and Germany and her allies was held in Berne in October 1917. The Belgian, British and American trade unions refused to attend, and the French were prevented by their government from being present. The Germans would not agree to the transfer of the headquarters of the IFTU to a neutral country and regarded the temporary bureau established at Amsterdam under the administration of Oudegeest as sufficient to meet the criticisms from allied labor leaders.

As the war continued, the leaders and the labor movements of France, England, and the United States drew closer together. This was shown in a number of labor commissions sent by the respective labor movements to other allied countries as visitors and for the purpose of investigating conditions. In the course of time, efforts were made to hold inter-labor conferences where the definition of war aims, the representation of the labor movement at the peace conference, and other questions would be considered. An invitation sent on behalf of the British Trades Union Congress and the Labor Party, in January 1918, did not reach the AFL in time for the appointment of delegates. The reply was cordial.[48]

Inter-allied labor conference.

Delegates of the AFL were present at the inter-allied labor conference held in London in September, 1918. Showing an increasing sensitivity to all things with a socialist label, Gompers complained that the credentials were headed "Inter-Allied Socialist Conference" and he and the other American delegates refused to sign them. Arthur Henderson explained that the word "labor" had been inadvertently omitted and the protest was withdrawn. The conference endorsed the 14 points laid down by President Wilson as the basis for peace, and approved the holding of an international labor conference at the time and place of the meeting for preparing a peace treaty.[49]

The American delegates were satisfied with the results of the inter-allied conference, but they appeared to have been irritated by the criticism of Jean Longuet, a leader of the majority socialists in France.[50] He complained of the AFL's opposition to allowing United States socialists to be represented at the conference. When an invitation for a meeting of delegates from labor and socialist parties was received by the AFL, Gompers replied that he had been instructed by his executive council to meet with the delegations from the trade union national centers but to avoid conferences with political parties. "We propose," wrote Gompers, "to help at conferences not only upon peace treaty terms but to build a bona fide International Trade Union Movement."[51]

This position has been held by the AFL ever since its formation, on both the domestic and the international level. It is not unusual for an organization to exclude those it does not believe ideologically or organizationally compatible: one need only recall the fight of the Marxists, led by Marx and Engels, for the exclusion of Bakunin and his anarchist followers from the International Workingmen's Association (First International), and the ousting of the anarchists by the international socialist (Brussels) congress in 1896. F. Domela Niewenhuis, a founder of the Dutch labor movement, was among the excluded because of failure to endorse political action.

Exclusion is not exercised only by moderates, but is even more forcefully practiced by the communists on the international as well as the domestic plane. The launching of the Communist (Third) International was accompanied by a list of 21 points which would be the basis for the exclusion of non-conforming applicants and also of certain individuals mentioned by name.[52] Some commentators appeared to believe that both the AFL and its successor federation were committing an egregious sin by refusing to cooperate with political organizations. The AFL never refused to cooperate with any union center because it was led by socialists or syndicalists or anarchists. Gompers' relations with Jouhaux, a one-time militant syndicalist, were always friendly. Bowerman and Ben Tillet, among other labor leaders in England, were socialists, as was Legien.

Gompers was willing to offer advice only when asked for it. When the Christian Trade Union of Belgium appealed to the American delegation to be allowed representation before the peace conference, Gompers, speaking on behalf of the

American delegates, said that the purpose of the American delegation was to present to the peace conference the views of organized labor in America, and to participate in the establishment of a "Federation of the trade centers of the different countries of the world." Outside of "these duties" the delegation felt that it "should not interfere in the contentions of factional portions of organized labor in the different countries of Europe. ... It believes that each country should have its one complete organization so that the different national centers might then properly federate for the common good, and to that end will apply such influence as it may have, believing in doing so it will be acting for the general welfare of all the workers of the world."[53]

Meeting at Berne.

Soon after the armistice in Europe, Arthur Henderson, secretary of the British Labor Party, and Charles Bowerman, secretary of the British Trades Union Congress, invited the AFL to send a delegation to a meeting for reestablishing the labor international and to discuss the terms of peace that would be presented to the chiefs of allied governments meeting in Paris. After some discussion Berne was fixed as the site for the labor conference.[54]

The American delegation arrived in London on January 17, 1919, and informed their English hosts that they were willing to confer with representatives of labor of the allied countries, but not with delegates from enemy countries or with those mainly interested in partisan political movements.

Reconstituting the IFTU at Amsterdam, Holland.

Leaving London, Gompers and his associates met with trade union delegations from Belgian, French and Canadian organizations. The Belgians supported the American view, but the French believed they were under an obligation to attend the Berne meeting. At the meeting Jouhaux and Oudegeest were authorized to call a conference of trade union national centers in Amsterdam on July 25, 1919. It was agreed that the first two days would be spent in winding up the old IFTU, and then in establishing a new international labor organization. Three AFL delegates, including Gompers, were present. Gompers seemed annoyed at the decision of the British Trades Union Congress, which had heretofore not been concerned with international problems, to enter the international arena. British labor had been represented by the British Federation of Trade Unions, an alliance for defensive purposes. Most of its affiliates also belonged to the British Trades Union Congress, which now took on responsibility in the international field and was allowed to appoint half the members of the British delegation.

When the Amsterdam conference opened on July 23, the Belgian delegates demanded that the Germans acknowledge the wrongs inflicted on their country and its people by the German armies. At first the Germans refused but, in time, Johann Sassenbach recognized the cruel acts committed by the German armies during the Belgian occupation. He assured the conference that the German trade unions always condemned the ruthless conduct of German troops and the deportation of Belgian civilian workers to Germany.[55] Sassenbach also informed the delegates that German labor had been misled into believing that its country was fighting a defensive war. Gompers was not satisfied with the explanation, and sponsored a resolution castigating German labor for its failure "to perform their duties."[56]

The Sassenbach statement provoked a threat of withdrawal from the conference by the German delegation. Jouhaux offered a conciliatory declaration which was accepted by the delegates. Legien favored the spirit of Sassenbach's statement, and repeated that the German workers had been convinced that their country was fighting a defensive war.[57] He alluded to the efforts of the unions in his country to prevent the conflict but said that, once it had started, nothing else could be done but to side with their own government as the unionists of all countries had done.[58] After the debate on war guilt had ended, the conference went on with its regular business. It ended the life of the old IFTU and established a successor under the same name.

The AFL delegation showed no enthusiasm for the deliberations and the decisions of the IFTU conference. They complained about the rate of contributions that had been set, and grumbled about the radicalism of some of the discussions. On the plus side was the election of W. A. Appleton as president. This man was a long time friend of Gompers and a man of conservative instincts, all of which must have influenced Gompers' conciliatory speech in the closing session. He assured the delegates that the AFL wanted to be a member of the IFTU, but warned that it must be allowed to pursue its own policies.[59]

The AFL's emphasis on radicalism appears to have been misplaced. In fact, the IFTU's aims were very modest. It sought to promote the interests of both affiliated and non-affiliated national labor centers, encourage cooperation of unions in different countries on problems of mutual concern, and prevent international blacklegging or strike-breaking. It nevertheless aroused resistance to affiliation by the AFL. Gompers appeared concerned, and told Appleton that the executive council "feels strongly that unless the situation be clearly met and the solution reached, the AFL would not join the IFTU."[60]

The predominant sentiment among the leaders of the AFL was against entangling alliances with the labor movements of Europe. Gompers, William Green, and several others high in the councils favored cooperation, but the majority were for "splendid" isolation. On the other hand, Europeans did not make the position of those who favored cooperation easier. For example, Walter Schevenels claimed that Gompers and those close to him favored exclusion of the leaders of the Austrian and German labor movements from the international labor conference to be held under the covenant of the League of Nations in the fall of 1919.[61] The opposite was the case. Gompers cabled to George Barnes, a member of the British War Cabinet, that "unless the German and Austrian delegates are admitted to the International Labor Conference at Washington the conference would be a failure in advance."[62]

Although the conduct of Schevenels and others like him exacerbated differences between the AFL and the European movements, sentiment within the AFL was overwhelmingly against affiliating with the IFTU. In refusing to join, the 1920 AFL convention pointed to a circular issued by the IFTU which called for May Day demonstrations and the general strike. Gompers challenged the right of the IFTU to issue such circulars, although he conceded that national trade union centers were free to espouse whatever views were congenial to them. However, for the IFTU to express itself on these questions was, according to Gompers, acting in an "outrageously high-handed manner."[63] When Appleton resigned the presidency of the IFTU, the suspicions and fears of the AFL that the IFTU was sponsoring radical programs and tactics were confirmed.[64] An old friend, C. W. Bowerman, secretary of the British Trades Union, tried to assure Gompers that the IFTU was not a militant organization, but did not manage to affect his views.[65]

In fact, all efforts of assurance were to no avail. In March, 1921, the AFL executive council, while "anxious to be part of an international trade union movement," said that it "must decline to be part of a movement which undertakes the destruction of the American labor movement or the overthrow of the democratic government of the Republic of the United States."[66] Later the council claimed the IFTU had committed itself to revolutionary policies. These allegations were untrue, but the AFL did not wish to make public the real reason for non-affiliation; the growing isolationist views among the leadership and the rank and file. For the next several years, the two organizations continued their correspondence with each repeating its position and neither able to make the concessions which would have made affiliation by the AFL possible.

This isolationist feeling was clearly apparent in the treatment accorded the appeal for help by the German General Federation of Trade Unions. Its funds decimated by the hyper-inflation which held German economy in its grip during the first years of the decade, the labor movement asked the AFL for assistance. Three members of the AFL executive council voted to reject the plea, and two supported it because of the urging of Gompers. In calling upon the American labor movement to assist an organization of another country, Gompers said the aid was "a distinctive relief work that devolves solely upon American Workers . . . confident that the cry for assistance will appeal to your judgment and heart."[67]

As if to demonstrate that opposition to aid for workers of foreign lands was influenced by a general principle and not by prejudice against those of a particular country, three members of the AFL executive council voted not to issue an appeal on behalf of the British coal miners. Their need for assistance was the result of a long struggle, begun almost immediately after the end of World War I and lasting until the miners' defeat in 1926. William Green, who succeeded Gompers, was himself a coal miner and was anxious that

American trade unionists provide financial help.[68] In addition to the refusal of a minority to endorse the appeal, William Hutcheson, head of the Carpenters' Union, qualified his support by "strenuously" objecting to the use of funds in behalf of the general strike which had been called by the British Trades Union Congress because of his conviction that the mine operators were seeking to destroy the Miners' Union.[69] Hutcheson must have known that the funds would not be used for this purpose, and that the AFL had always proclaimed the right of the labor movements of different countries to devise their own principles and tactics.

CHAPTER TWO

American Labor
and the Mexican Revolution

COOPERATION BETWEEN organized labor in Mexico and
the United States was based on a desire to work out common
policies in those instances where workers of the two
countries competed in the same labor and product markets.
Support within the United States, however, went beyond
that simple level. The sympathy of American organized labor
was enlisted in behalf of political refugees who, in fleeing
from the Mexican dictator, Porfirio Diaz, began to use the
United States as a base for fomenting revolt at home. Finally,
the American Federation of Labor threw its weight against
demands by concessionaires in the mining and oil industries
and leading newspaper publishers, for armed intervention by
the United States against the Mexican revolutionary republic
during the critical years of storm and stress.

When the United States government seized Ricardo
Flores Magon and a number of his associates, charging them
with violating the laws of the United States and threatening
deportation to Mexico, the 1908 AFL convention protested.
(Magon was the leader of the outlawed Mexican Liberal
Party, and the Mexican government sought his return for
trial.[1]) The convention directed President Gompers to take
up the issue of the arrest and deportation of political refugees

with President Taft, with an eye toward preventing Magon's return to Mexico.

Gompers was assured that the laws guaranteeing asylum would be applied to the Mexican insurgents, if the facts warranted such action. The convention of the following year, while satisfied with this assurance, called for "a ceaseless watch" over the authorities charged with enforcing the laws governing the right of asylum.[2] In Gompers' opinion, it was the pressure of labor which forced the Roosevelt and Taft administrations to discontinue acting as "Mexican man-hunters."[3]

Intervention in Mexico.

A more serious challenge confronting the labor movement came from threats of American intervention in Mexico as a result of the disorders that followed efforts to replace the Mexican dictator. Pressure for active interference in the affairs of our sister republic came from a variety of sources. Powerful mining and oil interests which had received lucrative concessions and owners of potent journalistic empires who had profited from the generosity of Mexican politicians were among those demanding intervention. The 1912 convention of the AFL not only declared: "We believe in a determined policy of 'hands off' on the part of our government," but extended its cordial greetings and best wishes to those in Mexico who were "fighting to eliminate ancient wrongs and abolish land tenure."[4]

This was only the beginning of a counter-attack upon the powerful contingent which sought to destroy the embryonic Mexican revolution. The AFL was among the staunchest defenders of the right of the Mexican people to determine their own government, by revolution if necessary: at no time was there the slightest question of where the AFL stood. In

1913, the AFL again condemned American and foreign corporations and "jingo newspapers" (Hearst) which favored armed intervention in Mexico, and called for a peaceful adjustment of differences. The president and secretary of the Federation were directed to transmit its position to the President of the United States.

Madero government and usurper.

The overthrow of the long Diaz dictatorship did not bring peace and tranquility to the people of Mexico. Francesco Madero, who had become president, was overthrown and he and his vice president were murdered in a revolt led by Victoriano Huerta. The United States then refused recognition and Huerta faced a successful revolt. The new revolutionary forces, under Venustiano Carranza, split as soon as victory had been achieved, although Carranza became the head of state.

Insurgent forces under Pancho Villa continued the war — now directed against Villa's former leader. This split among the revolutionary forces strengthened the agitation in the United States for armed intervention. Anxious to prevent what it regarded as a calamitous step, the AFL executive council sent its "felicitations to the Constitutionalist cause" and expressed hope for an end to the fighting. In a letter to the Mexican representative in Washington, Gompers reviewed both the position of the AFL, and its efforts to prevent interference in the internal affairs of the Mexican people.

He said that the AFL had sought to aid, especially by providing information to the public, the revolutionary forces seeking to depose Diaz; it had supported the government of Madero; and it had used its influence with the United States government to prevent recognition of Huerta. "We helped," said Gompers, "in sustaining the attitude of the government

of the United States in its refusal to recognize Huerta up to
the present hour and for the success of the revolutionary
movement headed by General Carranza."[5]

Opposition to President Carranza in the United States.

President Carranza came to power as a reformer who
promised to seek solutions for the age-old problems of his
country. Foreign investors saw him only as a menace to their
concessions, and demanded that the United States government take steps to protect them. As the demand for armed
intervention again mounted, the AFL directed Gompers to
express its opposition to it. Gompers was glad to do so and,
in a letter to President Wilson, told him that the struggle
across the border was part of the "old struggle for freedom."
He wanted the President to realize that a revolution might
bring excesses, but that "these are the first crude efforts of a
people long accustomed to despotism and denial of rights."
He praised General Carranza as a "friend of the working
people . . . the real leader of the people generally in Mexico."
Finally, he pleaded with the President to "aid those who are
less fortunate," stating that "as representatives of the labor
movement of America we urge upon you recognition of
General Carranza as the head of the Mexican government."[6]

Criticism of Gompers.

Gompers' activity on behalf of the Mexican revolutionary
government evoked sharp criticism from Frank Duffy, a
member of the AFL executive council and secretary of the
United Brotherhood of Carpenters and Joiners of America,
one of its largest and most powerful affiliates. Duffy did not
approve of Gompers' letters or of his conduct on behalf of
the Mexican government, with the focus of his complaint the
anti-religious (anti-Catholic) policy of the revolutionary
regime. Duffy attributed an attack upon the AFL by the

Archbishop of Quebec to the federation's support of the Mexican revolution. He charged the Mexican government with "pursuing priests and martyrizing the Sisters and causing death everywhere."[7] The executive council directed an investigation, but no change in policy was ordered.

Duffy's protests were against religious persecution and not against social or economic changes. When he received a letter from a Catholic clergyman decrying the AFL's support of the Mexican revolution because of its "oppression . . . in the dearest right to worship God as 'conscience dictates,' " Duffy assured him that the AFL did not countenance religious or political persecution. Religion, Duffy said, "has no standing in our movement. . . . What I mean is that religion has no part in the labor movement, neither has nationality or party politics."[8]

The objections raised by Duffy did not stop Gompers' efforts to bring about better relations between the governments of the United States and Mexico, nor between the labor movements of the two countries. Incursions by Mexican irregulars did not help the situation, even though there was widespread suspicion that these intrusions were financed by "concessionaires, the American trusts and the foreign capitalists" to arouse opposition within the United States to the revolutionary government of General Carranza.[9]

Meeting with the Mexican representative.

Gompers called a meeting of representatives of Mexico's *Casa del Obrero Mundial* with the executive council to discuss methods for easing tensions between the two countries. Frank Duffy claimed that the calling of the meeting was improper since, under similar circumstances, the members of the executive council had always been consulted and provided with correspondence between the AFL and foreign labor movements.[10]

Gompers did not believe he was exceeding his authority. In reviewing the activity of the AFL on behalf of the Mexican revolution, he informed the Mexican delegates of the necessity for a "still closer understanding between the workers of all the Americas, particularly in this crisis in the world's history."[11]

The Mexican delegation met the members of the AFL executive council on June 26, 1916, in Washington. Gompers expressed his satisfaction at changes across the border. He reviewed the AFL's efforts on behalf of the Mexican revolution and said: "When the situation became critical," with great pressure upon the United States government to send troops across the border, "we were helpful in prevailing upon the President not to intervene in that conflict. Colonel Martinez called upon me and I placed what he had to say before President Wilson. . . . The Executive Council decided to ask the President to recognize the Carranza government, and he did so, much to the surprise of many people."[12]

Cementing closer relations with Mexican labor.

There was hope on both sides that closer understanding between the two labor movements would be helpful in maintaining peace. Hope was also expressed that the union would serve as the beginning of a wider federation of labor of North and South America. For the time being, a general conference of the AFL and the Latin American labor movements was regarded as untimely, but an arrangement for periodic exchanges of views between heads of the Mexican and United States labor organizations was made. Such an arrangement, it was hoped, would make it possible to confer quickly when an international crisis threatened. Two members from each country were commissioned to meet whenever it appeared desirable.[13]

The value of this joint arrangement became evident after a clash between United States troops and a detachment of the Mexican army. A number of Americans were killed, and others captured. Release of the prisoners was demanded by President Wilson, and the failure of the Mexican government to act expeditiously raised a war fever in the United States. Urged to act by the Mexican labor representatives, Gompers wired President Carranza asking for the release of the imprisoned Americans "in the name of common justice and humanity." The order for the release of the soldiers was immediately issued and the president of Mexico swiftly informed Gompers of his action.[14]

Plans to unify the labor movements of the Americas.
For the AFL, closer relations with the labor movement of Mexico were only the first step in a broader program of uniting all organized labor into an international federation. In a report to the 1915 convention, the executive council suggested that such a project might be feasible and should be undertaken by the AFL.[15] The time was not propitious until the summer of 1916, when Gompers sent an invitation for a meeting of delegates to labor movements of the Latin American countries. "The realization of an alliance between the labor movements of all Pan-American countries," in Gompers' opinion, would "constitute a genuine parliament of men, one of the highest purposes to which all mankind has aspired."[16]

As usual in such situations, Gompers emphasized the right of workers of every country to devise the kinds of organizations and to espouse the principles that were congenial to themselves. Reporting to the 1916 convention on his invitation, Gompers said: "the AFL will yield to no other organization authority over the affairs of the economic movement in this country. We stand for the right of workers of every country to work out their own problems in accord with their ideals and highest conception."[17]

Issuance of invitations for a Pan-American labor meeting.

Gompers, Santiago Iglesias from Puerto Rico, Carlos Loveira from Mexico, and John Murray, a trade unionist from the United States, invited the labor movements to attend a conference to establish wider unity of Pan-American labor.[18] Plans for the new federation moved slowly. In the meantime Gompers appointed a mission of three labor people, including John Murray, to Mexico. Labor missions were achieving their first popularity at the time, and the one to Mexico was sent in hope of creating better feeling in that country towards the United States, which was then at war in Europe. The commission found considerable anti-American sentiment, some of it fueled by German propaganda, but believed that closer relations between labor movements would lead to better understanding as well as to a better life for the working population.[19]

Pan-American Federation of Labor.

The promoters had hoped that the presidents of both Mexico and the United States, and the governors of the border states, would be present at the opening session. Instead, each country sent a high official to convey the greetings of its chief executive. The meeting opened in Laredo, Texas, on November 18, 1918, with 72 delegates present. However, 46 of them came from the United States, only 21 from Mexico, and the remainder from only three Central American countries. The course of the conference was not a completely smooth one: a number of Mexican delegates raised the question of the imprisonment of members of the Industrial Workers of the World (IWW), who had been convicted for violating the espionage law. The issue was debated and then withdrawn. Gompers was elected chairman; John Murray, English secretary; and C. A. Varga, Spanish secretary. Washington, D.C., was chosen as the headquarters city.

The Dominican conflict.

The Pan-American Federation of Labor did not have many resources. Moreover, the Latin American countries, except Mexico, seemed to show only sporadic interest. The federation nevertheless served as an effective channel through which abuses of power by the American government or private enterprises of United States origin operating in Latin America could be called to the attention of the labor movement of the United States. Gompers and his successor, William Green, were always willing to bring abuses and violation of rights to the attention of American officials.

At the second conference of the Pan-American Federation of Labor, representatives of the Dominican labor movement presented evidence of grave abuses practiced by the military government imposed by the United States. After submitting a bill of complaint to President Wilson, Gompers told him that "such conduct does not conform to the principles of modern civilization, they are not compatible with the doctrine that men are born free and equal and must be accorded full opportunity to life, liberty and pursuit of happiness."[20]

Secretary of State Robert Lansing acknowledged "the complaints." Gompers was advised that censorship had been abolished, and that the other charges would be discussed with the American minister to Santo Domingo.[21] The AFL nevertheless appointed a commission of two members to investigate.

These two, in their report, denounced the miserable conditions and recommended that the import of workers be

limited, and that the "sugar interests" should not be allowed
to secure additional land, at least "during the military
occupation of the United States." In addition, they advised
that steps be taken to raise wages and improve working
conditions, that food prices be lowered, that education be
made compulsory, and that the right of workers to organize
and strike be granted. Finally, the commission believed that
American military personnel should be removed from the
properties of the sugar planters, as their presence tended to
intimidate the work force.[22]

The Pan-American Federation of Labor made demands
upon the government of the United States, but the burden of
convincing the State Department always fell upon the AFL.
Gompers again demanded the removal of troops from Santo
Domingo, but they were not withdrawn until 1924.[23]

Recognition of the Obregón government of Mexico.

In 1921, the United States' recognition of the government
of Alvaro Obregón was in question. Obregón had come into
office after Carranza had been killed in a popular uprising,
and had widespread support among both the army and the
masses. Carranza had been a disappointment as a reformer,
but Obregón promised to follow another route. Opposition
to recognition was based in part on the view that he *was* a
serious reformer.

The AFL again took up the cause of the Mexican
government. Gompers told Secretary of State Charles E.
Hughes that the reported kidnapping of several Americans
"no wise changed the position of the American Federation of
Labor on the question of recognition."[24] Gompers believed
that as long as recognition was denied, the enemies of the
Obregón government would be "emboldened to create
trouble and embarassment" for the government.

When the Mexican government was recognized, Gompers

expressed his "sincere pleasure" at the reestablishment of "full diplomatic relations with the government of the Republic of Mexico."[25]

Pan-American Federation of Labor Meetings.

Conferences of the Pan-American Federation were held periodically, and they usually adopted resolutions calling for reforms of labor practices or changes in laws. The Federation's major advantage was that it provided Latin American labor leaders with a forum in which they could bring complaints against the North American colossus. Gompers strongly believed that the relationship between the labor movements of the Americas could grow into a virile movement for the mutual protection and advancement of the workers in both North and South America.

Criticism of Secretary of State Kellogg.

William Green, who succeeded Gompers as president of the AFL (Gompers died in 1924; he became ill while attending a conference in Mexico City), followed his example by protesting against American officials who expressed hostility to the Republic of Mexico. After Secretary of State Frank B. Kellogg threatened the Mexican government, Green told him that he had read his statement "with most startling surprise," and that he regarded it as a very serious matter that the government of the United States should even think of supporting a movement against the constitutional government of Mexico.[26]

Opposition to friendship toward Mexican government.

The friendship shown by AFL leaders toward the Mexican government did not always meet with universal approval in AFL ranks, mainly because the revolution had brought changes in the status of the Mexican Roman Catholic Church, which had been rich and powerful. The laws of the liberator, Benito Pablo Juárez, sought to reduce religious influence through disentailment and confiscation of church property. Some of the Church's rights were restored by the Diaz regime. The Mexican revolution of 1910 sought to limit property holding and also affected the right of the Church to engage in educational and other activities.[27]

This struggle had repercussions on Catholics in the United States, and the AFL executive council felt constrained to defend its position in its report to the 1926 convention: "The principle of tolerance is so firmly embedded in our trade union practices, regardless of creed, nationality or race, wage earners can unite for the promotion of their economic interests."[28] It advised that the steps taken in Mexico with regard to religious matters were decisions that affected only the Mexican Federation of Labor, and pleaded that American workers and their unions should avoid becoming involved in this dispute.

The statement of the executive council was attacked by James Fitzpatrick, a member of the White Rats Actors and Artists and a delegate from the Waterbury, Connecticut, General Labor Union. He labeled the statement "deception," and urged that "this Federation should clear its skirts of the slime. . . ."[29] Fitzpatrick was answered by two members of the executive council, Matthew Woll and Daniel Tobin, both practicing Catholics. Tobin told him that the executive council had no right to tell the Mexican people "what they are going to do on their religious situation." Woll defended the statement and policy of the executive council and pleaded for understanding of the problems facing the government of Mexico.[30]

Last meeting of the Pan-American Labor Federation.

In 1927, at the last congress of the Pan-American

Federation, Green stressed that the federation had been uniquely the work of Gompers, who "firmly believed that it would serve . . . the economic welfare of the workers and in the preservation of peace among the nations of the American continent."[31] There were more than the usual number of delegates in attendance but the spirit of the movement had died with Gompers. A number of conferences during the last years of the 1920s sought to revive the federation, but the interest was insufficient. With the onset of the depression, money to support activity in Latin America could not be easily spared, and efforts to develop a joint labor federation of the Americas were temporarily suspended.

CHAPTER THREE

The End of Isolation

THERE WERE sporadic discussions on the reaffiliation of the AFL with the International Federation of Trade Unions between AFL President William Green and Jan Oudegeest, head of the IFTU, but the AFL was not anxious, during the 1920s, to rejoin. The reasons usually given were the cost of affiliation (which did not seem high even by the standards of the time), and the IFTU's espousal of policies opposed to positions taken by the AFL. It appears that Oudegeest met Green's complaint on this score by stating that each national trade union center was free to accept or reject resolutions enacted at the IFTU conferences.[1] Oudegeest's view was not acceptable. In carrying out the instructions of the 1925 AFL convention, Green acknowledged that the "trade union movements of all countries are agreed upon main objectives and earnestly desire increasing betterment of all mankind."[2]

Reaction to the victory of the Nazis in Germany.
   Hitler's victory in Germany, his appointment as chancellor, and his persecution of Jews, trade unionists, and socialists, deeply affected the attitudes of the AFL leaders. It stirred them into more sympathetic consideration of proposals for cooperating with European labor movements. Hitler's rise to

45

power came, after all, during the depths of an economic depression in both Germany and the United States. The unions of the American Federation of Labor had failed to increase membership in the prosperous years of the 1920s, and the sharp decline in employment in the early 1930s seriously affected enrollment and income of the affiliated organizations as well as of the AFL.

Boycott of German goods.

In its report to the 1933 convention, the executive council denounced the "ruthless treatment of German labor and union organizations," and the destruction of the independent labor movement. The protest was underlined by the declaration of a boycott of German manufactured goods. National and international unions were urged to help in this campaign of economic ostracism until the rights of the German working people were restored and "repressive policies on the Jewish people" were ended.[3] A committee to aid the enforcement of the boycott was appointed since the AFL lacked the resources to carry out an effective boycott against the German economy alone. But AFL leaders aimed primarily to show their loathing of and opposition to the bestial policies of the Hitler government.

The executive council, in its report to the 1934 convention, justified the boycott and again demanded an end to annihilation of the trade unions of Germany and persecution of Jewish people "because they are Jews."[4] According to the executive council, some success had been achieved in the boycott and the 1934 convention voted that the campaign be continued. It also endorsed the Chest for the Liberation of Workers in Europe, and elected five top leaders of the organization — John L. Lewis, David Dubinsky, Matthew Woll, Arthur Wharton, and Charles P. Howard — to serve on the committee. William English Walling, a known writer on social and economic problems and a one-time socialist, was its executive secretary.[5]

Criticism of these activities was made by a number of men who believed that the AFL should tend to its knitting in the United States, but its leaders did not budge from their positions.[6] The Chest for the Liberation of Workers in Europe was a relief and rescue operation: a number of German and Austrian labor leaders were able to elude their persecutors and flee to France, England, the Scandinavian countries, Canada, and the United States as a result of the aid received. Tours to acquaint the American people with conditions in Europe were arranged for Walter Citrine, the secretary of the British Trades Union Congress, for Gerhart Seger, a former member of the German Reichstag, and for Julius Deutsch, the Austrian socialist leader who had headed the resistance to destruction of the Austrian socialist and labor movements by the government of Chancellor Dollfuss. In its first year the Chest collected over $46,000 which was used to support labor victims of fascist terror.[7] Despite its limited success, the 1935 AFL convention voted to continue the boycott and called on American sport organizations to avoid the Olympic Games scheduled for Berlin.[8]

With the intensification of Jewish persecution in Germany, Green appealed to both national and international unions to intensify their boycott of German goods and services. A successful boycott was beyond the powers of the AFL, but it showed the feeling of the leaders and many members and it was, from that point of view, well worth the effort.[9]

While the federation continued its campaign against the fascist countries of Europe, it was opposed to actions by the United States government which might exacerbate the strained relations between Japan and the United States.[10] It rejected a request from Walter Citrine that the AFL ask the American government to join in an embargo of Japanese goods after the Japanese invasion of China. The council told Citrine it was "reluctant to make representations to the United States government."[11]

The War in Europe.

At the outbreak of the war in Europe in 1939, the AFL reaffirmed its non-intervention policy. The convention of that year called upon the United States to "pursue [its] determination to avoid involvement in European conflicts or in European wars."[12] This was the federation's historic position and it represented the view of virtually the whole American nation. After the conquest of Poland and the lull in the fighting (the phony war), the AFL executive council, in February 1940, again called upon the American government to follow a policy of "strict neutrality and peace." At the same time, the council denounced the Soviet attack on Finland as imperialist aggression, condemned the joint Nazi-Soviet dismemberment of Poland, and pleaded for aid to Finland without endangering American neutrality.[13]

The Soviet armies conquered Poland; the Nazi legions rolled over the low countries. The executive council denounced both, but reiterated its "first declaration that the United States should remain out of the war."[14] At the same time, the AFL sought aid for leaders of the German labor movement who had been driven out of their country by the Hitler terror. In an appeal to its members, the council compared German unions to those in the United States, and asked them to assist their German colleagues who were "performing an honorable work. . . ."[15]

The Congress of Industrial Organizations.

By 1939, the AFL was no longer the exclusive spokesman for unionized workers in the United States. A competing labor federation had been founded as a result of the dispute over the adoption of the industrial form of organization in the mass production industries. The Congress of Industrial Organization had fewer dues-paying members than the AFL, but in the late 1930s and early 1940s, its influence among the working population and the country at large was considerable. With the outbreak of war in Europe, CIO president John L. Lewis declared that "organized labor . . . [was] opposed to any involvement in the war,"[16] and the 1939 convention passed a resolution endorsing President Roosevelt's "neutrality policy."[17] The long resolution does not mention the antagonists in the European war by name. It is padded by declarations such as: "we will defend the free institutions of this Republic, the greatest democracy on earth," and other such sentiments. Sympathy for the victims of Hitler's terror, growing by millions weekly as Nazi troops cut across the Polish plains, is studiously avoided.[18] This was no editorial oversight, but partly a result of Lewis' isolationist views and even more a manifestation of the influence of American communists within the unions belonging to the CIO. Remember that ʌhe war started following a pact between the two dicators — Hitler and Stalin: American communists were following the Party line of neutrality. Not until Germany's attack of the Soviet Union were they to speak a word for the Allied cause.

The 1940 CIO convention, the last one presided over by Lewis, reaffirmed its earlier views and warned that "this nation must not enter into any foreign entanglements which may . . . drag us down the path of entering or becoming involved in the war."[19] A number of delegates, Walter Reuther among them, pleaded for a more realistic appraisal. He told the convention that he did not like conscription, but that it was a better alternative to what was going on in Europe. He warned that the United States had a stake in the war, and that Hitler, Stalin, and their junior partner,

Mussolini, were already preparing plans for "carving up the rest of the world."[20] Reuther's speech was unheeded and the convention unanimously adopted a position which discouraged even non-military aid. (Lewis was, at the time, engaged in fronting for a millionaire with close ties to leading Nazis.)

Joining the International Federation of Trade Unions (IFTU).
As noted in Chapter One, the AFL refused to join the IFTU after its revival in 1919. As the situation for European democratic labor movements became more desperate, leaders of the AFL began to consider affiliation as a means of strengthening the IFTU morally and financially. The 1935 AFL convention noted that one of the first acts of the Nazis was to liquidate the labor movement. It added that unless an effective "vehicle for international labor solidarity can be created, the trade union movement may be further weakened in those countries adjoining these dictatorships and over which these dictatorships exercise profound economic power."[21]

The convention endorsed reconsideration of the issue. Walter Schevenels, secretary of the International Federation of Trade Unions, and Walter Citrine, secretary of the British Trades Union Congress and an officer of the IFTU, visited the United States to explain the need for a closer alliance between the labor movements of Europe and the United States. During these discussions, Citrine thanked the AFL for the aid that had been sent by the Chest for the Liberation of the Workers in Europe, "particularly in the last two years."[22]

In 1937 the AFL joined the IFTU and sent Matthew Woll, a vice president for more than 20 years, an internationalist in his thinking, and one of the best informed labor leaders on foreign affairs, to its Warsaw meeting. Woll's right to be recognized was challenged by Léon Johaux of the French Labor Confederation, and Camille Mertens, a delegate from the Belgian labor center. Their challenge was based upon a claim that the AFL was no longer the predominant labor federation in the United States, having been replaced by the Committee for Industrial Organization. After several hours of discussion behind closed doors Woll was seated, and a statement calling for labor unity in the United States was issued.[23]

The IFTU was facing unexpected problems at the time. Woll reported that Schevenels and Jouhaux were on their way to Moscow to sound out Soviet trade unions on affiliation with the IFTU. In prior discussions, Soviet trade union leaders had indicated that their admission would necessitate giving one of their members a top post in the IFTU. No agreement was reached: the AFL executive council was satisfied with the results but was disturbed to learn that the failure was not based upon principle but on a disagreement of terms.[24] Upon learning of the negotiations, the council declared itself "unequivocally against the proposals." Its objection to the acceptance of Soviet labor organizations was that they were "not trade unions in the sense which that term bears in every democratic country and which it has always and everywhere borne until the rise of dictatorships since the world war. They have no more freedom of action than have the official organizations commonly known as 'labor fronts' in Italy, Germany and Austria."[25]

Walter Citrine, secretary of the British Trades Union Congress, told Green the delegation to Moscow had violated its directives, one of which was trade union liberty "as an indispensable condition for an effective representation of the interests of the working class. . . ."[26] He was, however, soon confronted with a similar situation at home. The British Trades Union Congress had within its ranks a number of organizations which favored closer relations with the labor movement of the Soviet Union. With war in Europe on the horizon, sentiment for cooperation with the Soviet organizations increased within the British labor movement. In consonance with this sentiment, the British Trades Union Congress submitted to the 1939 meeting of the IFTU a proposal for the affiliation of the Central Council of Trade Unions of the Soviet Union. Green was informed of the situation.[27] He answered that the affiliation of the Soviet unions would lead to a withdrawal of the AFL from the IFTU. He told Citrine that the AFL could not "consent" to the proposal as much as it sympathized with the "political and military situation confronting the British workers and British people. ..."[28] The British proposal was rejected by the IFTU.[29]

The War and the ending of the IFTU.

As long as the Soviet Union was loosely allied with Hitler's Germany, pressure for bringing Soviet trade unions into the IFTU ceased. With the capitulation of the Petain government, it became necessary to transfer IFTU headquarters to London. A milestone was reached when William Green, vice president of the IFTU, attended the meeting of the executive committee held at the AFL headquarters in Washington, D.C. on January 30 and 31, 1941. Citrine, president of the IFTU, presided. In a desire to be of increased help, the AFL agreed to pay the full affiliation fee to enable the IFTU to expand its activities. In general, the AFL tried to cooperate in the work of the IFTU, and with the onset of the war there was a deepening interest in foreign affairs among members of the executive council and active trade unionists in the United States.

With the entrance of the Soviet Union into the war as a result of Hitler's unprovoked attack, the outlook of English trade unionists underwent a dramatic change: good-will that had been dissipated by the Hitler-Stalin pact of 1939 returned many-fold. The heroic Soviet armies, which were holding the Nazi forces at bay for the first time, were a cause of satisfaction to Soviet labor bodies as well as to British trade unionists. The dormant sentiment for collaborating with Soviet labor bodies rose again, and stronger. British unions had tried to cooperate with the Soviet organizations in the 1920s: an Anglo-Soviet Trade Union Committee had been established, but ran aground as a result of harsh criticism by Soviet trade union leaders over the conduct of officers of the Trades Union Congress during the 1926 general strike. Now, on the initiative of British trade union leaders, a new Anglo-Soviet Trade Union Committee was established. The British suggested the inclusion of representatives from American organized labor, and Walter Citrine was deputized to inform them of events and to invite them to join the new arrangement.[30]

The eight-point program accepted by leaders of labor in both Britain and the Soviet Union empasized mutual assistance in the war against Hitler's Germany, strengthening the industrial efforts so as to enable each country to reach its maximum production of war goods, helping to supply the Soviet armies with needed arms, supporting the people of occupied countries against tyranny, organizing a program of mutual aid and exchange of information for the trade unions of the two countries, and strengthening the contacts between leaders of the British Trades Union Congress and the All-Union Council of Trade Unions.[31] Green suggested that Citrine come to the United States and meet with the AFL executive council on May 13, 1942.[32]

When discussing the affiliation of the AFL with the council, Sir Walter was a bit on the defensive. He called attention to the different positions of England and the United States, but nevertheless proposed that the AFL join the Anglo-Soviet Trade Union Committee. He felt it was almost impossible for him to convey adequately the state of mind of the British public while Russia was being attacked by Germany, and he noted that the United States was a long way from the scene of conflict. He told the council that "the people of Great Britain . . . after a period of intense suspicion . . . gradually transformed themselves into a high state of almost unreasoning admiration."[33] Such admiration for the Soviet armies permeated all ranks in the population. It led to the proliferation of Anglo-Soviet committees, many of which "contained the potentialities of communist subsidiary bodies with which we are familiar."[34]

The question, as Citrine saw it, was: what was the British labor movement to do in this situation? Resolutions were pouring in from trade unions and the political labor movement congratulating the Soviet government and promising assistance. Citrine felt that it was better for the British Trades Union Congress to take the lead than to allow other organizations to do so. Moreover, in view of the joint committee with the French, Citrine could find no reason for not setting up the same arrangement with the Russians now that they were in the war. Citrine said that he could have put forward reasons based upon ideological or political considerations for refusing to cooperate. However, he was convinced that they would have been rejected as valid grounds for non-cooperation.

Since Citrine believed that it was imperative that the Trades Union Congress handle the matter, he himself drafted the memorandum and, after its approval by the General Council, inquired of the highest officials in the government whether it would cut across government policy. The government not only declared that it would not, but expressed cordial interest in the proposal. Citrine emphasized that the Russians had agreed that neither country would interfere in the internal affairs of the other. He stressed that the committee was consultative and advisory, and he suggested its enlargement into the Anglo-Soviet-American Trade Union Advisory Committee, or another acceptable name. He also stressed that the recommendations would have to be ratified by the respective appointing bodies before they became operative.

The functions of the committee would be to unify the efforts of the respective trade union movements, to consult on common problems, and possibly to interchange information and collaborate in the postwar period, though this need not be included.[35] It was to be understood that no interference on questions of internal matters was permissible, and that each body had exclusive responsibility in its respective sphere. Each country would finance its own delegation of five representatives.

The following day, at the opening of the meeting of the AFL executive council, President Green spoke of the differences in prevailing conditions in the two countries, and said that if he were English he would look at the situation "in about the same way as Brother Citrine outlines it." He then reemphasized that conditions were different in the United States, and stated that he favored the creation of a committee, jointly with the Trades Union Congress, for closer cooperation on matters affecting the war.[36]

In a public statement, the executive council stressed its duty to "secure for all time freedom everywhere," and called for "fuller cooperation among the labor movements of the different countries." It therefore welcomed the visit of Citrine as "evidence of the strong and mutually helpful fraternal relationships that have long existed between the American Federation of Labor and the British Trades Union Congress." Nevertheless, the AFL rejected the invitation and, as a face-saving gesture, an Anglo-American Trade Union

Committee, made up equally of members from each organization, was established. This committee was to keep Soviet trade unions informed of matters in the United States which would be of special interest to them.[37] Its results were of no significance.

As noted above, the AFL had ceased to be the exclusive representative of organized workers of the United States with the formation of the Congress of Industrial Organizations in 1938 (the CIO had recruited several million members, many of whom were employed in heavy and mass production industries). Under the rules of the IFTU, only one national federation from a member country — the predominant one — could affiliate. However, the issue with which the joint committee was concerned at the time was not affiliation, but rather the war effort. Philip Murray, who had been elected president of the CIO to succeed John L. Lewis, protested to Citrine about his failure to invite the CIO to the conference with the AFL.[38] At the same time, heads of the railroad unions (who had not been affiliated with either labor federation in the United States) also asked for recognition.[39]

Green, after learning of the request from the railroad brotherhoods, showed annoyance. He reminded A. F. Whitney, president of the Brotherhood of Railroad Trainmen, that not one of the railroad unions had ever before shown the slightest interest in the relationship between the AFL and the British Trades Union Congress.[40]

This latest difficulty arose out of a long-standing AFL position. The split in the labor movement was, by the end of 1941, five years old. Those who had fought on either side of the battle of industrialism in the mass production industries were, with the exception of Lewis, still at the helm. Moreover, the leaders of the AFL thought in terms of dual unions and secession and did not fully believe that the CIO would survive. On the other hand, the CIO was convinced that it deserved recognition on an international level and that to have been locked out of the Anglo-American committee was unfair and in stubborn disregard of its importance. Upon learning of the proposed joint committee, limited to the AFL as the only American representative, Philip Murray described it as "unacceptable." In retrospect, the AFL's view can be seen as narrow, and the exclusion of the CIO as a cause of mischief which was ended only due to the much greater problem of conflicting objectives between the free and the communist controlled trade union movements. This sentiment was reiterated by the 1942 CIO convention.[41]

One of the main arguments of the AFL against allowing the CIO a place on the joint committee was that the CIO had opposed aiding the allies before the attack upon the Soviet Union by the Nazis, in June, 1941. This was true, but Green himself conceded that Murray was "different," and that Murray had never participated in this opposition. As head of the CIO, he had broken with Lewis on the issues of Roosevelt's defense policies and aid to England. Nevertheless, those who had attacked the defense policy by indirection, and had failed to say an encouraging word for the allies at three conventions, now proclaimed: "Hitler and the Nazi government, in their drive for world conquest, directly menace the security of the United States."[42] This was a true assessment of the existing situation, but it was a belated one, induced by the attack upon the Soviet Union. Many delegates discussed the resolution, but Murray's speech is important because he stated a position which was at variance with that of his predecessor, who had been a delegate to the 1941 CIO convention but had remained silent.

After alluding to the fact that there was "no labor organization more deeply rooted in defense production than our CIO organizations," he painted a picture of the meaning of Nazi aggression:

I have watched . . . the steady march of those forces of
aggression, those forces of brutality in Europe, and I have
ever been conscious of the one outstanding fact that in
each of the countries overrun by the Nazi forces the
labor movement was the first to feel the impact of the
terrifying blows of the German army. The leaders of
every labor organization in every country taken over by
Germany, including the unoccupied portions of certain
countries in Europe, have either been killed, murdered
or put in concentration camps, and the organizations in
each instance have been completely obliterated. There
are no labor organizations any more in any of the
countries overrun by Hitler. There are no conventions of
labor being held in these countries today. There are no
open forums. There are no democratic privileges.[43]

Murray's speech was a repudiation of the position held by
Lewis, who never forgave him for his independence. In
fairness to Lewis, his views were long held and were unin-
fluenced by the leaders of communist dominated unions in
the CIO. He had his own reasons for avoiding entangling
alliances, although we now know that he was not above aiding
a Nazi sympathizer. Murray's break with Lewis was a difficult
decision. Obviously, Roosevelt was grateful, and the administration sought to have the AFL agree to the admission of the
CIO to the Anglo-American Trade Union Committee. In
addition, important elements in the Trades Union Congress
favored admitting the CIO to any joint committee upon
which Americans were represented. Because of that sentiment, Citrine cabled, on August 12, 1942, an urgent plea that
the CIO and the railroad brotherhoods be allowed to affiliate
with the Anglo-American labor committee. The CIO itself
was determined to be accepted as an equal.

In his subsequent comment upon the situation, Citrine
said:

Then the Government took a hand. I can say at this table what I would not like to be said publicly, that the Prime Minister was the first person to intervene in this. He put to me that they had had advices from Washington and he said if we went on with the committee meetings we would very greatly jeopardize Anglo-American relations.

On the basis of the pressure exerted by both the Prime Minister and Eden (in response to a telegram from Lord Halifax, the British Ambassador in Washington), the meeting planned for late September, 1942, was postponed.[44]

Hutcheson attributed the refusal to grant admission to the CIO to the fact that it was regarded as a dual federation, and expressed hope that the two federations would again become united. Citrine again took the floor and explained the difficulty this refusal raised for the British Trades Union Congress.[45]

Green answered that the CIO had denounced Britain "for conducting an imperialistic war and demanding the United States withdraw any support. . . ." He charged that the same group was still in control, but he absolved Murray from the charge. "He," said Green, "was a miner the same as John L. Lewis."[46] He was not impressed with the reasons given for the cancelling of the September meeting of the Anglo-American Trade Union Committee. He said he was:

satisfied . . . the CIO got to the British Embassy and to the White House and there exercised their influence to prevent that meeting, because the White House called me in. The White House called me in . . . to agree to postpone that meeting until a later date, that it would best serve the war effort, that it might interfere to some extent at least if we held it then. Of course, I felt as a good soldier it was my duty to respond to the request of the Commander-in-Chief, but Sir Walter had communicated with me before I communicated with him because they had got to him in London a little before they got to me. They got to the British Embassy and pointed out it was going to create turmoil and strife and injure the war effort and hurt production in the factories so that the matter had been disposed of even before I communicated with Sir Walter.[47]

The AFL finally refused to join with the CIO and the railway brotherhoods in the Anglo-American Trade Union Committee.[48] Following the rejection, the British delegation met with Murray and several other leaders of the CIO. Murray showed anger when some of Green's statements were repeated; he found the statements offensive, and insisted [rightly] that he had supported lend-lease, and that his support of England was one of the causes of his break with John L. Lewis.[49] It was a trying conference for the British delegates — and for Murray.

The exclusion of the CIO had serious and unexpected consequences which might have been avoided had the AFL been less intransigent in its opposition to the CIO's participation in foreign affairs. The AFL was compelled to share places with the CIO on the War Labor Board and on commissions in other war agencies.

Because the CIO was not allowed to participate, Philip Murray requested that the Trades Union Congress initiate steps toward the formation of a new world labor movement: "This step was taken to assure the CIO its rightful place in the affairs of the world." His request was made because he was convinced that the opposition of the AFL made the CIO's affiliation with the IFTU impossible. "It, therefore, became necessary for the Congress of Industrial Organizations to seek the creation of a new world labor movement; one which would give rightful representation to all bona fide labor organizations in the United States."[50]

Responding to pressure from the CIO, the TUC Southport Congress, in September 1943, decided to convene a World Trade Union Conference "to which . . . all the trade unions of the world regardless of their political, national or religious differences" would be invited.[51] The proposal had been discussed by the secretaries of the IFTU and the TUC who concluded that an understanding in the ranks of labor was imperative.[52] It was believed that only an international conference would be able to smooth out the differences within the labor movement, and that the TUC was the appropriate organization to issue the invitations.[53] Invitations were issued on November 3, 1943; in their reply in February of 1944, the Soviet unions asked that the conference be called by the British and Soviet unions, and the CIO. When the British refused to accept these changes, the original plans were followed. Citrine informed Green that the TUC general council believed that the trade unions must find it possible to work together, to discuss their common problems, and to "find a constructive policy to rebuild our great international movement. . . ."[54]

Green was unconvinced of the appropriateness of the procedure followed. He claimed that the IFTU, of which the AFL and the TUC were members, was the agency to call international conferences of world labor. He also asked why the affiliates were not consulted before the TUC issued the invitations.[55]

Walter Schevenels, secretary of the IFTU, tried to soften Green's and the AFL's opposition to the membership of Soviet unions in an international labor confederation. He recognized the validity of the AFL's objections to meeting Soviet delegates claiming to represent their fellow workers. However, for Schevenels, "The problem of whether and how far trade unions are or are not under the control of government is no doubt of fundamental importance for the future, but it should be discussed at a later stage." Schevenels then presented the novel view that although Soviet delegates were not "free agents" they would express the policy "that will actually be upheld by and on behalf of 39 million industrial workers of Soviet Russia."[56] Schevenels' argument meant that labor organizations were obligated to accept representatives chosen by their governments, as their policies would ultimately be those which workers of the countries represented would have to accept.

The CIO readily accepted the invitation and Murray appointed a delegation.[57] The AFL executive council issued a statement critical of the manner in which the labor conference had been organized, and questioning both the TUC's authority to convene such a conference and the absence of the IFTU in planning the enterprise. While the AFL was technically correct in its criticism, it was clearly apparent that Schevenels and other members of the IFTU executive council had acquiesced. Of greater validity was the charge that it was improper to call a special conference without consulting all affiliates since the "delegations of some nations invited to attend cannot truly represent free and democratic labor because no free and democratic labor movement exists in those countries."[58] Furthermore, the statement noted that many representatives at the conference came from countries that were still under occupation and could not speak authoritatively for their workers. Representatives from neutral countries, under the influence of the axis countries, had also been invited, and the AFL doubted that they had democratic solutions available for postwar problems. The executive council favored the calling of a conference "under proper auspices" and at an "appropriate time" so as to unite the ranks of labor in support of the war and the United Nations, and which would aid in devising solutions for postwar problems. The proposed London conference did not meet these tests, and the invitation to attend was rejected by the AFL.[59]

The AFL's unwillingness to join in promoting a new labor international had no effect upon those planning the enterprise. Nevertheless, there was some hesitancy and doubt among some of the prospective members. One of the leading international trade secretariats, the International Transport Federation, rejected membership because the constitution drafted by the administrative committee required "integration of the existing international federations by trade or industry, which have always been independent and autonomous. . . ."[60]

The meeting for setting up a new world labor federation took place in Paris, on February 3, 1945; it reaffirmed the declarations of the London conference and accepted the constitution. The aims and purposes of the newly formed World Federation of Trade Unions (WFTU) were overwhelmingly adopted. The only large national trade union center that would not immediately affiliate was the American Federation of Labor. But while a surface unity existed, unexpressed misgivings lurked among a number of those present at the launching. Citrine warned the Paris conference that the job was to build a trade union international capable of carrying on day-to-day work and to secure practical results for individual members. He told the assembly that the WFTU should not serve as a vehicle for spreading the doctrines of socialism, and said: "If once we get into the maze of politics, as surely as I am standing at this rostrum, this international will perish."[61] He informed the delegates that the acceptance of the WFTU constitution by the British Trades Union Congress (TUC) depended upon satisfactory negotiations with the international secretariats, made up of unions of the same trade or industry of different countries.

It is unlikely that the leaders of the TUC were unaware of

the purposes of those in control. They were too sophisticated, too well informed and experienced to be taken in by the maneuvers of the promoters of the new international. However, refusal to go along at this stage might have precipitated a serious conflict within the TUC which the leaders wished to avoid at a time when the first majority Labor government was in office. The proponents of the new departure controlled several of the large unions and were influential minorities in others, and the leaders might have assumed that within a relatively short time "this too will pass."

Louis Saillant, a leading French communist, was chosen secretary, the official who controls the administration. In accordance with the plans, the IFTU was liquidated at an executive committee meeting on October 26, with the AFL protesting.[62] While accepting the dissolution of the IFTU, the British were wary of their newly found associates. At a meeting of the general council of the WFTU in Paris, on October 5, 1945, Citrine said that the new federation was in a "formative period" and until it was known what it meant "in organizations, individuals, directions and in policy, the TUC completely reserved its right as to whether it continued membership of the Federation."[63] The unwillingness of the TUC to break its long-time relation to the AFL was also a straw in the wind. Citrine cabled Green, on October, 1945, that the general council of the TUC had provisionally agreed to form a joint committee with the CIO, and invited the AFL to join. The AFL rejected the offer, and asked for the continuation of "our long-standing relationship with the British Trades Union Congress." This view was accepted by the TUC with "regret."[64]

The attitude of the TUC was not the result of bad faith but of reservations with respect to the ability, or even willingness, of a federation dominated by a communist bloc to work together successfully with other labor centers for the limited goals the British and other non-communist federations favored. Irving Brown, the representative of the AFL in Europe, sensed the British disenchantment and their suspicions of the operations of the WFTU, and reported that they:

> continue to hope for improvement emphasizing that the Russians are "on trial" and they, the British, must show their own people and the world how much time and opportunity have been given to build a world labor organization with the Russians. There seemed to be an undertone of complete disillusionment but openly there can be no break until and unless the relationships between the four powers change basically.[65]

The split was to come (sooner than Brown had expected) as a result of differences over the Marshall Plan. The launching of this program of European reconstruction by the United States could not have been anticipated, but Brown's view that a break among the four powers was an essential step for severing the connections of the trade unions of democratic countries with the World Federation of Trade Unions was soon to be borne out.

CHAPTER FOUR

Germany

PHILIP MURRAY'S ELEVATION to the presidency of the Congress of Industrial Organizations marked a substantial change in attitude toward the allied cause. In contrast to his predecessor, John L. Lewis, Murray recognized the dangers inherent in the Nazi movement, and his view was shared by the heads of a number of CIO unions. In addition, substantial minorities in some of the other organizations were opposed to following the communist line in foreign affairs. Walter Reuther spoke out against the isolationist resolution, sponsored by a number of delegates from organizations then under communist domination, at the 1940 convention. Murray as well as William Green, president of the American Federation of Labor (AFL), appeared before the Senate Foreign Relations Committee on behalf of the lend-lease legislation, and both independently called for the protection of labor conditions and laws in the administration of that policy.[1] American labor also aided French and German labor officials who were fleeing from the Nazi tentacles after the collapse of organized resistance. They were helpful in intervening with the State Department over passports for fleeing labor activists, and provided relief funds.[2]

Increasing interest in and concern with foreign affairs was

an inevitable result of the economic and political changes taking place within and without the borders of the United States. The setting up of a special convention committee, in 1913, to consider issues that affected governments, workers, and peoples living outside the United States was one small step. Thirty years later, in 1943, the convention authorized the appointment of a standing committee on international relations. Matthew Woll, an AFL vice president widely informed in this area, favored a more active role, but William Green, the AFL president, was at first doubtful of the advisability of embarking upon this difficult enterprise. However, Green did not actively oppose the proposal when it went before the convention of 1943.[3] A department of international relations was established in 1946, the same year that the CIO set up a similar unit.

Woll was appointed chairman of the standing committee. In addition, Secretary-Treasurer George Meany, William McSorley of the Lathers' Union, Edward J. Brown of the International Brotherhood of Electrical Workers, Elmer J. Millman of the Brotherhood of Maintenance of Way Employees, and Robert Watt, AFL representative at the ILO and at the IFTU, were appointed. Woll played a significant role in influencing international labor relations from the 1940s until his death, and the free world owes him a great debt. A man with great energy and a sharp mind, devoted to free trade unions and a free world, Woll worked tirelessly in behalf of fair treatment for unions of the occupied countries and for a foreign policy that would serve the democratic world.

The Free Trade Union Committee.

This committee was established by the 1944 AFL convention with Matthew Woll as president, William Green as honorary president, George Meany as honorary secretary, and

David Dubinsky as vice president. In the resolution setting up the committee, the convention noted the approaching end of the war, and said that victory over Germany and Japan:

offers no automatic assurance that freedom and democracy will be restored or that the workers of such countries will regain or be secure in their rights as free men and free workers.

The resolution, moreover, recognized that

free, democratic trade union movements in all lands . . . demonstrated that they are the firmest pillars of peace and democracy and the most uncompromising foes of all forms of tyranny and aggression. . . .

The resolution therefore called for the prompt "reestablishment of powerful free and democratic trade unions," for assuring the worker a rising standard of living, and for eliminating exploitation throughout the world. The emphasis upon the great importance of free trade unions was essentially an American view, initially developed by the ideas and work of Samuel Gompers, and the resolution was based upon the assumption that the ending of the war in Europe and Asia would not eliminate tyranny and oppression, and that the greatest defense against these evils was the free trade union.

The convention called upon its affiliates to help raise $1,000,000 "in order to assure prompt practical assistance to the workers of liberated countries in Europe and Asia as well as the workers of Central and South America to organize free democratic trade unions." The fund was to be administered under the supervision of a special committee (appointed by the president of the American Federation of Labor) which would issue "public reports on all receipts and expenditures of the Fund."[4]

Jay Lovestone was appointed executive secretary of this committee. Lovestone had been a founder of the Communist

Party of the United States, and was its secretary in 1929 when he left over a doctrinal dispute. He was the leader of the Communist Opposition for a few years, and then served on the staff of the International Ladies Garment Workers Union. He is a man with an encyclopedic knowledge of world affairs, especially as they impinge upon the labor movement. Tireless and industrious, his work in the last thirty-five years has been in behalf of the free world, and he has contributed as much as any single person to the weakening influence of the international communist trade union apparatus. Lovestone arouses strong feelings, stemming partly from past and even forgotten controversies, but mainly from his uncompromising opposition to totalitarianism. In 1949, Woll explained:

> The Free Trade Union Committee deals exclusively with international labor relations and our country's foreign policy.... We have maintained a representative in Germany; a European representative; publish magazines in Italian, English, French and German; publish a considerable number of pamphlets every year; send representatives to various international trade union conferences; support the Free Trade Union Center in Exile; provide Care food parcels for many thousands of needy trade unionists abroad; answer at least 3,000 pieces of mail from all over the world every month; prepare basic policy material for the AFL and help reeducate top government officials as to the role of labor in the worldwide struggle for human liberty and decency.[5]

The Free Trade Union committee was always headed by a high officer of the AFL who was responsible to the international relations committee. In turn, the latter reported to the executive council, who guided overall activities. The work of the committee was financed by the AFL and the affiliated unions, with the task eventually devolving on the AFL. The accounts of the committee were regularly audited, in the same manner and by the same firm as those of other departments.

The main initial task was to help restore the shattered trade unions of the European continent and to make them capable of resisting communist infiltration, which was especially serious at the end of the war. In addition, the committee was given the assignment of aiding the formation of trade unions in the underdeveloped countries, and the rebuilding of a free trade union international federation.

In carrying out its duties, the committee found that the occupation authorities could not always distinguish between a communist and a trade unionist or social democrat. It was the job of the representatives of the committee to make these distinctions clear so that viable democratic organizations could be built. In the areas where the communists were in full control, the committee sought to establish effective minority groups.

Financing the Free Trade Union Committee.
From February 1945 through August 1947, the unions donated $163,818.27 for the work of the committee: in 1948, $94,217.60 was contributed. Most of the money came from the treasuries of the organizations; a small amount from individual members. In 1945-1947, contributions were made by 97 organizations, and a number of unlisted individuals donated slightly more than $1,500.

Unions Donating More than $1,000 in 1945-1947 (rounded to closest $100).

Bakery and Confectionary Workers .	$ 2,100
Boilermakers	7,000
Bookbinders	1,500
Building Service Employees	1,000

Railway Carmen	1,700
Carpenters	6,200
Central Labor Unions (unidentified)	3,200
International Brotherhood of Electrical Workers	2,500
Operating Engineers	1,500
Photo Engravers	1,400
Federal Labor Unions (not identified)	3,000
Firemen and Oilers	1,000
Ladies Garment Workers	22,000
Hatters	8,000
Hotel and Restaurant	3,600
Machinists	15,000
Maintenance of Way Employees	1,700
Meat Cutters	1,300
Miners, Progressive	1,200
Musicians	1,300
Painters	4,800
Paper Makers	2,100
Plumbers	3,500
Pulp and Sulphite	13,000
Seafarers	3,300
Street Car	6,000
Teamsters	10,200
Mine Workers, United	10,000

In 1948, the American Federation of Labor contributed $25,000 for the support of the work of the Free Trade Union Committee. In addition, 18 international unions donated $1,000 or more apiece. Contributions were sent by the following organizations:

American Federation of Labor	$25,000
Boilermakers	5,000
Carpenters	5,000
Cement, Lyme and Gypsum	1,000

Glass, Flint	2,500
Hatters	1,000
Hotel and Restaurant	5,000
Ladies Garment Workers	15,000
Locomotive Firemen and Engineers .	1,000
Maintenance of Way Employees . . .	1,000
Molders	1,000
Musicians	1,000
Painters	3,500
Plasterers	1,000
Railway Clerks	1,000
Street and Electric	2,000
Seafarers	5,000
Sheet Metal	1,000
Teamsters	10,000

Subsequently, the AFL became the exclusive contributor aside from the International Ladies Garment Workers Union, which provided free office facilities.

European representatives.

By the end of World War II national European labor movements, with the exception of those in Sweden and Switzerland, had ceased to exist. Their funds and property had been seized, and their leaders silenced, exiled, or killed. The IFTU had been liquidated, and the communist dominated World Federation of Trade Unions (WFTU) erected in its place. Only the AFL, in the years immediately after the war, had the will, the resources, and the influence to challenge the trend. It recognized the danger to the workers and peoples of Europe, as well as to the United States, from allowing communists to fill the vacuum created by the destruction of European labor movements. In addition, it was aware that the American government and its representatives abroad must be encouraged to follow policies that would support democratic institutions and prevent the revival of reactionary militarism or communist totalitarianism.

Irving Brown was appointed to the general European post, while Henry Rutz was given the job of covering Germany and Austria. Brown had been active in the labor and socialist movements since the early 1930s. He was acquainted with European labor in all its forms. Rutz was a member of the International Typographical Union in Milwaukee. Active in workers' education, he had studied at the University of Wisconsin, and had served as a major in the United States Army.

The AFL opened an office in Paris, but faced minor difficulties in Stuttgart, where formal opening of an office was opposed by General Lucius Clay, Commander of the American forces in Germany. He feared it might stimulate a request by the WFTU for similar treatment, and therefore suggested that Rutz work nominally out of Geneva or Brussels on a two month renewable permit. The arrival of the American representative ended the situation whereby the WFTU sponsored meetings of trade union leaders in the four occupation zones, with the WFTU supplying a chairman. Speaking as head of the Free Trade Union Committee, Matthew Woll demanded that the AFL be granted equal recognition in all four zones, similar to that accorded the WFTU. This action was precipitated by information from Irving Brown to the effect that the American military government was allowing the WFTU to influence labor policy. In his demand, Woll said that the AFL was concerned that Germany be allowed to develop free trade unions. He emphasized that the concern was not of recent origin, for even in the "darkest hour" the "AFL was true to the solidarity of international labor battalions of German workers after Germany was defeated."[6]

It was the first challenge to the hegemony of the WFTU

over European labor, and it seemed an unequal contest since the AFL had no open allies in the labor movements of Europe; all the major national federations were affiliates of the WFTU. The AFL's influence was on the North American continent, and its non-collectivist philosophy would not have much appeal for the masses of European trade unionists and their leaders who had been schooled in several brands of socialism. It was not, however, a weak David confronting a powerful Goliath, for many of the European labor movements, it appears, were only captives of the moment of anxiety and fear, and were destined to break the weak ties that bound them to the WFTU. Yet the WFTU was feverishly active in its drive to win control over labor movements on the Continent, especially those of Germany. Its leaders understood better than many in the West the advantage of controlling the mighty hosts of the burgeoning unions, and it may be said, paraphrasing Lenin, that he who controlled the unions of Germany controlled Germany, and he who controlled Germany controlled Europe.

The CIO, which had participated in the launching of the WFTU, appointed Sidney Hillman, whose prestige and influence in the organization were second only to Murray's, a member of the WFTU executive bureau. Adolph Germer, a former national secretary of the Socialist Party, a member of the United Mine Workers of America, and a leader in organizing CIO unions, was made assistant secretary of the WFTU.

A WFTU commission investigated conditions in Germany and recommended that Germany be kept as an agricultural nation and allowed to develop "peaceful domestic industries."[7]

The WFTU sent committees into Greece, Iran, and Poland to aid in the revival of unions, and planned to send others to Japan, Korea, China, Indochina, and Indonesia. The CIO was active in the work of the WFTU, and Sidney Hillman played an important role on the world labor scene. In 1945, as a sign of its heightened interest, the CIO appointed Michael Ross as liaison between the State Department and the overseas trade union centers.[8] There was therefore no other organization to counter the widespread activity of the WFTU except the AFL.

There was much to be done. Toward the end of 1947, Irving Brown reported that those who were fighting in behalf of free trade unionism, and who were opposed to the dominance over trade unions by the communist apparatus, were gravitating toward the AFL. As a result the federation had become the main target of daily and weekly attacks by communist functionaries.[9] Brown established relationships with trade unions in countries where unions were controlled by Socialists and Christian Democrats, and concluded that even though most of them were affiliated with the WFTU, their views paralleled closely those of the AFL. In France and Italy, where communists dominated the trade unions, he advised the encouragement of minorities built around socialist and syndicalist groups. Brown noted that trade union opposition to the communists was weak in Italy, but that it should be supported nevertheless. He also claimed that the AFL had helped to prevent a communist takeover of the trade unions in Greece.

Brown suggested concentrating on the international secretariats (organizations made up of unions in a single industry and dealing largely with economic problems) as centers of opposition to the WFTU, the rallying of European labor around an economic program with democratic objectives, as well as financial support to efforts in opposition of the communists.[10]

Tasks in Germany.

In January 1946, the AFL executive council stressed the need to restore Germany to the "family of civilized nations" by aid and encouragement. This aim could be achieved only through the rehabilitation of free democratic trade unions, the revival of a free press, and by genuine democratic political parties and local and national self-government based on universal elections. The council outlined a program which would make these aims possible. It urged that the occupation should allow for speedy restoration of German labor unions as voluntary democratic organizations, and that facilities should be made available so that trade unions could carry on their activities.

Trade unions should be allowed the right to extend their activities into adjoining areas and to federate on a local and national basis. Buildings, meeting places, office space, and equipment should be given so as to make possible day-to-day administrative tasks. The works council legislation of the pre-Nazi period should be reestablished. Collective bargaining should be allowed and machinery for encouraging dispute settlements developed. Encouragement should be given and facilities provided for the speedy return to Germany of approved refugees formerly associated with the labor movement so that they might, if they chose, resume their activities. The AFL executive council also called for utilization of the services "of persons known to be proven foes of Nazism and proven associates and friends of free labor." The services of anti-Nazi and pro-labor forces should be used not only in administrative offices but also "in establishing advisory councils to work with the occupation and civil authorities."[11]

The statement further declared that the most effective safeguard against a revival of German militarism and totalitarianism did not rest "in the Potsdam Agreement or the

Morgenthau Plan but in the lifting of restrictions on organizations of labor and encouragement of free and unfettered unions."[12] The council statement insisted that no plan or representations advanced by the World Federation of Trade Unions on behalf of labor in the United States should be given recognition by the United States military government. "After all, the American Federation of Labor is the unquestioned dominant labor organization in the United States and as such should be so recognized and consulted in all matters relating to foreign labor and labor relations in preference to all others."[13]

First demands of the AFL.

At the end of the war, statewide unions along industrial lines rose up in all parts of Germany. A committee appointed by the WFTU announced that the unions had not been organized "from the bottom up" by the membership, and consequently had to be disbanded. Shortly after the visit of the WFTU committee, the unions in the American zone extending beyond the local area were ordered dissolved. Hereafter, it was decreed, only unions on the plant level would be tolerated.

Upon the arrival in Germany of the AFL representative, this order limiting German unions was protested. The claim that it was undemocratic to organize a labor union beyond the local plant was manifestly absurd, and the purpose of such an order did not escape AFL observers. It was apparent to Louis Saillant, secretary of the WFTU, that the Socialists and Christian Democrats had outmaneuvered the German communists by taking over the leadership of the movement to establish trade unions in the western zones. The error could be retrieved only if these organizations functioned on a plant basis, as it was reasonably certain that under such circumstances they could never develop a leadership capable of meeting the challenge of the communist mass movement that Saillant and his close associates hoped to stimulate.

The AFL's protests led to the withdrawal of the restrictions; industrial unions were allowed on a statewide basis, then grew successively into zonal-wide unions, and inter-zonal federations. Finally, in 1949, the German Federation of Labor (Deutscher Gewerkschaftsbund) was founded. Throughout its early years, the American labor movement nurtured and protected this movement because of its conviction that a free democratic trade union movement was vital for the protection of the German worker. In addition, the AFL was convinced, it would serve as a bulwark against the revival of any totalitarian impluse that might have survived the Nazi tragedy.

Infiltration.
The Free Trade Union Committee was concerned with another immediate problem, the infiltration of American communists and fellow travelers into the occupation apparatus. Most persuasive and influential in this group was George Shaw Wheeler, who was born and raised in Oregon, and became a fellow traveler while employed by the federal government in the 1930s. He subsequently defected to Czechoslovakia and, between rounds of teaching at Charles University, may have enjoyed watching the Soviet troops marching through Prague. Wheeler was chief of the Allocations Branch of the Manpower Division, to which a number of other fellow travelers were attached. In these positions, they could exercise influence on the formation of trade unions, and on the kinds of privileges they would be granted by the occupation authorities.

For example, a group working with Wheeler devised a rule that the American Military Government (AMG) could not recognize a union for two years: this would have enabled others to take over the solutions to labor problems. An American officer ordered the Hesse Union Federation disbanded, and was only overruled at the insistence of the AFL representative. The same person ordered a trade union committee enlarged by adding 12 known communists. An American in charge of the Manpower Division in Württemberg-Baden, a well known journalist and author active in the farmer-labor movement, was threatened with court martial for irregularities: this was only prevented by the protests of the American representative, who at the time of the incident was on the staff of General McSherry. It was the intervention of Henry Rutz, at the risk of punishment for violating military orders, and the efforts of Colonel Dawson, military governor of Württemberg, which induced the authorities to dismiss the charges.[14] Woll brought the danger to the attention of Secretary of State Marshall and warned against being bluffed by subversives posing as democrats.[15]

Forced repatriation.
     The AFL sought to modify the policy of forced repatriation of refugees from Eastern European countries. Some of those sent back were guilty of war crimes or desertion from the armies of their native lands. Others were, however, opponents of Soviet power who had left their countries before the beginning of the war. An AFL committee found Secretary of State George Marshall sympathetic to the plea that the United States government not cooperate in this kind of enterprise. He endorsed "the principle that no coercion of any kind should be exercised on . . . people, and that we should follow our traditional policy with other countries in providing an asylum for people who, because of religious, racial and political purposes refuse to return to their state of origin." He promised to discuss the matter with the President, and the committee believed that

"something would be done about the . . . coercion that has been exercised by officials in some of our government agencies."[16]

Care packages for trade unionists.

Reports that many trade union officers could not carry on their activities, because of low food allowances, were responsible for the initiation of the Care package program in the fall of 1946. The first shipment of $60,000 in goods was made in November 1946, and was financed by the AFL and its affiliate, the International Ladies Garment Workers Union. Independently, the Congress of Industrial Organizations (CIO) also carried on such a program, financed by funds collected through donations.

In its appeal, the AFL noted that the Labor League for Human Rights had been one of the 26 organizations which founded Care (Cooperative for American Remitances to Europe). Through this aid thousands of trade unionists were able to keep going and carry on their work under adverse circumstances inevitable in a country defeated and devasted in war. In 1947, the AFL sent several thousand packages monthly to Germany and to Austria. They were sent to help feed the new union leadership, who were generally worse off than their brothers employed in the plants: the latter usually received a supplementary meal at the plant canteen. In contrast, trade union officials had to depend upon a ration of 1,000 to 1,500 calories a day. Beginning in 1947, the AFL Care program was reaching 1,000 trade union leaders with a care package every two months. This program was supported by funds raised from local and international unions, and also by direct contributions of members. The program was carried on for six years.

In appealing for support, Matthew Woll urged the international unions to appeal to their locals to aid in the program.[17] While CIO relief activity was less formally organized, in 1948 its Community Service Committee provided food and clothing amounting to over $100,000, with affiliated unions contributing additional funds.[18]

Furnishing printing material.

The free trade unions of Germany had been destroyed by the Hitler government in its first years of power, and its leaders driven into concentration camps, exile, or death. Sentiment for trade union organization survived the Nazi disaster but the emerging trade unions found themselves without the necessary printing materials by which they could communicate with their members and appeal to the unorganized to join their ranks. AFL President Green wrote to Secretary of State James F. Byrnes describing the need of the German unions. He told Byrnes that a trade union's existence depended upon the contacts that its officers could establish with each other and with their memberships: "Without this interchange of information, ideas and personal contact, union activity cannot exist. I ask that you do everything in your power to make certain that sufficient equipment is made available to the German trade unions as promptly as possible. In this situation, I would like to suggest that within the Department of State the Office of Foreign Liquidation Commissioner is in a special position to assist this project."[19]

Green also noted that the War Assets Administration had about $2.5 billion of surplus property at its disposal overseas. "Certainly," said Green, "this includes in Europe and particularly Germany much of the equipment for which the German trade unions have such desperate need."[20] Replying for the State Department a month later, Dean Acheson assured Green that the Department had "consistently subscribed to, and actively supported the policy of encouraging the formation of democratic trade unions in Germany." He told Green that their operations would be facilitated by providing them with the needed materials, and that he found the "suggestion as to the possibility of making available to German trade unions some of the surplus property still held by the United States . . . a helpful one."[21]

General Lucius Clay, the United States Military Governor in Germany, assured Green that his staff members were in constant touch with the German trade union leadership which enjoyed freedom of expression. He also told Green that the Office of Military Government had licensed a weekly trade union publication.[22]

The problem for the American authorities was a difficult one. Shortages of virtually all goods existed and paper was no exception. It was extremely difficult for the trade unions to supply their members with literature to acquaint new recruits with their program. The situation remained critical, and Woll, in letters to Secretary of State Marshall and to Secretary of Defense James Forrestal, sought to alert them to the danger of the policy being followed. He charged that the military government had failed to provide the trade unions with a minimum supply of paper: "We feel that if the Russian dictatorship can find sufficient supplies of paper for its totalitarian propaganda in Germany, our democratic government should be able to find the necessary paper for pleading the cause of democracy." Woll believed the task of supplying paper was an urgent one because "the most effective way of counteracting Russian propaganda in Germany is not through our own military authorities but by the genuine democratic organizations themselves."[23]

Significance of the trade unions.

One of the major tasks undertaken by AFL representatives was to convince military authorities of the importance of the role of the trade unions. Woll pointed to the errors made by the American military government in reorganizing the German economy. To some who dealt with economic problems, the trade unions might have appeared as a destructive (or obstructive) force. It is easier to make unchallenged decisions, and an effective trade union is a doubtful blessing to a military bureaucrat, whether he is a professional military man or on temporary leave from an executive post in business.

The German trade unions had no direct means of influencing the American military government's decisions, but Woll urged that they be allowed to play a "constructive and responsible role" in the restoration of the German economy. He believed that the policy of discouraging the democratic trade unions played into the hands of the Soviet Union "and its tireless and well financed agents" who boasted of the importance given to unions in the Soviet zone. Woll recognized "that the Russian unions are a fraud. But the American military government's mistake of omission is seized upon by the Soviet ... lackeys to arouse German labor against America. It is essential that this error be corrected promptly."[24]

The military government promised to mend its ways, but no reforms were introduced. The American military government was called upon to explain whether Woll's charges were correct. After justifying the allocations that had been made, the American military governors said that they were seeking means "to increase German paper production sufficiently to give 100 tons of newsprint to the American zone trade unions.[25] Secretary of the Army Kenneth Royall answered Woll's complaint on the shortage of newsprint for German trade unions. He claimed the amount of newsprint requested was three times the amount which the bi-zonal German economy could produce.[26] He also denied that the American military authorities in Germany were hostile to trade unionism, and that they were unacquainted with their functions.

Woll objected to Secretary Royall's lumping the trade unions with other democratic institutions as far as their importance to reconstruction was concerned. He told Royall that the trade unions in Germany "have by far the largest membership and occupy the pivotal position in the reconstruction of the country." If the trade unions were to fall into the hands of the enemies of democracy, Woll warned, "then the country will fall into the hands of the enemies of democracy."[27]

More paper was made available. In addition, the AFL sent from the United States a monthly supply of thin paper suitable for pamphlets to be distributed in the Soviet zone. An important role in the fight against Soviet propaganda on the trade union level was carried on by the Free Trade Union Committee's monthly, *International Free Trade Union News*. It was distributed among 15,000 trade union activists, and its articles were occasionally reprinted in the labor and political press. The committee also published two pamphlets which were in great demand: *The Slave Labor Camp Map of the Soviet Union,* and *Who Is the Imperialist?* The pamphlet on slave labor was posted in offices and meeting halls throughout Western Germany, and the original printing of 700,000 was exhausted. Special printings were made for the Soviet zone.

Return of Trade Union property.

When the Nazi government came to power it suppressed the trade unions, seized their property and turned it over to the government controlled Labor Front. Under Directive 50 of the American military government, the trade unions could reclaim property which could be identified as theirs. This rule meant that buildings and other real estate which had been seized by the Nazis and sold to favorites could not be reclaimed, since they were not classed as Nazi property and therefore were not subject to confiscation. The AFL regarded Directive 50 as unfair and harsh. Woll wrote to Secretary of Defense Forrestal that the AFL international relations department and the Free Trade Union Committee were distressed by the legal provisions for the distribution of the assets of the Nazi Labor Front. He believed that the trade unions should be given the assets and property "stolen from them . . . when Hitler grabbed power . . . also the assets accumulated by this Nazi outfit through enforced collection of dues from the workers."[28]

Woll tried to impress upon Secretary Forrestal the importance of free trade unions for the "development of virile democracy in the heart of Europe" because no other type of organization compared with the trade unions in economic importance and in ability to educate the masses against the infiltration of totalitarian doctrines. Under-Secretary of War William H. Draper rejected Woll's view. Draper did not believe that the military authorities were not returning physical property formerly belonging to the unions.[29] The military authorities, in his opinion, were doing everything possible. Jay Lovestone, writing on behalf of Woll, suggested that the question be taken out of the hands of the zone commander, and the assets of the Labor Front be declared the property of the trade unions.[30]

Devaluation of the currency and trade union funds.

During the discussion on the return of property, a devaluation of the currency, and its adverse effect upon the savings of the trade unions, became a concern of the AFL international relations committee. Both Woll and Lovestone conferred with General Eberle and a number of aides from the State Department on providing some softening of the effects of this program.[31] Woll had addressed letters to Secretaries Marshall and Forrestal noting that financial reform was inevitable in Germany and had asked for special consideration for trade union funds. He recalled the confiscation of union treasuries and their restoration by the "reviving unions of Germany through hard work." Woll suggested that trade union funds should be compensated for any loss in value as a result of the reform of the currency.[32] It was hoped that the French and English would raise no objections to such a program.[33]

The American authorities were not inclined to accept the views of the AFL on restoration of property. Secretary Marshall had failed to reply to Woll's letter and Woll again raised the issue. He complained against the behavior of the officials of the State Department on several occasions. Those in the AFL were "amazed and distressed," said Woll, to learn that the United States embassy in Rome had placed a car at the disposal of James B. Carey, an officer of the ILO and head of one of its unions, to attend a meeting on May Day staged by the communist controlled Italian Confederation of Labor which was dedicated to attacking the United States.

Woll also protested the behavior of the American Ambassador in Prague who congratulated Clement Gottwald, head of the Czechoslovakian Communist Party, upon his elevation to the presidency of his country.[34] Woll suggested that the American Ambassador could have pleaded illness: "Perhaps," said Woll, " 'diplomatic illness' was invented for just such occasions. It would have been more fitting to let some satellite like Albania and not a free country like America, congratulate Gottwald, leader of the crew which murdered democracy in Czechoslovakia."[35]

Woll was disturbed by such behavior because it was utilized by the communist apparatus to undermine opposition to its rule and was dispiriting to those who opposed the communists on their home grounds.

The complaints were not given much attention, but General Clay objected to a criticism made of the military government by the 1948 AFL convention. He denied that there had been "a willful lack of appreciation of the role of labor. . . ." He defended the policy of not returning property taken from the trade unions by the Nazis. The problem for the military government was not an easy one: properties of the trade unions, and other properties as well, had been amalgamated into large corporations, and the separation of property belonging to the trade unions from other property was a complicated task. It had to be solved by "arbitrary measures." All identifiable property had already been returned. Additional property was to be returned only if the unions could establish legal title to it in the courts.[36] A restitution law was adopted and German tribunals set up to which union claims could be submitted.

Woll tried to placate General Clay by expressing appreciation for his "outstanding service" in organizing the Berlin airlift. But he emphasized the historic fact that "the free labor movement has always been the strongest and only consistently democratic force in Germany."[37] Because of its reliability as a bastion of freedom and democracy, Woll believed it was imperative that the properties of the Labor Front should be turned over to them. Woll argued that the dues that had been collected during the Nazi period by the Labor Front should also be given to the trade unions created since the end of the war.

One of the complicating factors was that there was no necessary connection between the unions existing before and after the Nazi period. Prior to 1933, three central labor federations functioned in Germany: the free trade unions, the *Allgemeiner Deutsche Gewerkschaftsbund* (ADBG); the

Christian labor organizations, the *Gesamt-Verband der Christlichen Gewerkschaften;* and the liberal Hirsch-Duncker associations, the *Verband der Gewerk-Vereine.* The free trade unions were the largest federation and were moderately socialistic in outlook. All three had been destroyed in the first days of the Hitler regime. The postwar unions did not divide on the basis of religious conviction or ideology as did the pre-Hitler labor organizations. Moreover, they were structurally different from their predecessors in that they were industrial in form. Woll argued that the differences did not warrant penalizing the unions by withholding from them property rightfully theirs. He claimed that the program of the AMG would encourage litigation and "sap the treasuries of the unions." Woll also complained of the numerous instances in which Nazi activists had been able to retain properties that had been awarded to them for faithful Party service. Despite the efforts of the AFL and the promises that had been made to Vice Presidents David Dubinsky and George Harrison, the AFL failed in its efforts to reverse the AMG's policy on the restitution of trade union property.[38] The only concession it gained was the promise that the AMG would provide legal assistance to unions in preparing claims to contested properties.[39]

Works councils.

The AFL became involved in a dispute with the American occupation authorities over the right of the Republic of Hesse to allow for the setting up of works councils, bodies chosen by the direct vote of those employed in the plant or office. Business groups opposed this provision on the theory that it would be an instrument of the radical rank and file. After consulting with a number of labor leaders, the AFL took a different position. It urged General Clay not to interfere, since that would break a promise by the AMG that

German parliaments could legislate on economic and social issues.[40] When Under-Secretary of War Draper said that the Hesse law would be suspended but not vetoed pending the preparation of a new constitution for the Republic, Woll branded the decision as "most unfortunate,"[41] and one which played into the hands of the communists. In a letter, Woll pleaded with Draper "to heed our viewpoint and to alter our government's present unfortunate policy in regard to the Hesse Works Council Law."[42]

The CIO begins to change its views.

As noted above, the CIO was one of the principal organizations that actively helped to establish the World Federation of Trade Unions. As long as the war lasted and the Soviet Union was an ally of the United States, the communists presented no serious problems to the head of the organization, Philip Murray, nor to the unions in which they were a minority. As long as the war lasted and the United States and the Soviet Union were allies, the unions dominated by the communists followed an ultra-patriotic line. They were willing to give up conditions and make sacrifices which other labor leaders did not regard as necessary. But a change in the policy of the Soviets regarding their relations with western nations took place soon after the ending of the war, and many of the American leaders followed the example. The antagonistic attitude of the communist dominated unions to the policy of reconstruction in Western Europe posed a problem for the leadership of the CIO, whose hostility to the communist position was already evident at the 1947 convention.[42]

General George Marshall was a speaker at the convention; introduced by President Murray as "one of the world's greatest champions of peace."[43] The resolution on foreign policy and the world emergency, however, did not mention the Marshall Plan whose author addressed the convention. But a number of delegates, including Van A. Bittner, George Baldanzi of the CIO Textile Workers' Union, and Walter Reuther, pointedly attacked the communist delegates by indirection. The most important criticism was made by Van Bittner. Both he and Murray had started their union careers in the United Mine Workers of America, and had broken with its leader, John L. Lewis, over support for the allies at the outbreak of the war in Europe in 1939. Bittner's jeering remarks at the communist delegates was a signal that they were almost at the end of the road.[44]

Reuther and Baldanzi had been supporters of the anti-Nazi cause, and had been critical of deviations of the communist delegates. Reuther rebuked the communist delegates by calling attention to their behavior at the 1940 CIO convention at which they called Roosevelt a "war monger"; the same people were now applying that epithet to President Harry Truman.[45] The communist delegates and their followers remained silent in the face of attack. One delegate from the International Fur and Leather Workers, at the time a faithful follower of the Party line, pleaded for tolerance. The changes in policy which led to the eventual expulsion of the communist dominated unions from the CIO was extremely important at a time when the United States was preparing its program of aid to European reconstruction. It meant that the communists could not use the CIO as a forum from which to attack American foreign policy, and also that the CIO would not long remain a member of the communist controlled World Federation of Trade Unions (WFTU).

The 1947 AFL convention was interesting because it showed views on a number of foreign policy questions which became of increasing importance with the years. A statement on foreign policy warned against the making of promises that were not accompanied by performance. A "truly democratic and constructive . . . foreign policy must not bear even the slightest earmarks of either appeasment or aggression."[46] The AFL called for the abolition of conscription in peacetime by agreement among the governments of the world, release of war prisoners with the right to return to their homelands, and extension and acceleration through the UN of "self-government and national freedom for colonial and subject people."[47] It reiterated that the fate of democracy in Germany was tied to the existence of free trade unions. It warned that "if the German trade unions will be captured by the Communists and their stooges, they will be coordinated as part of a giant war machine run by the Russian dictatorship in its drive for world conquest and war."[48]

Dismantling of Germany industry.

Germany had attacked her neighbors and had inflicted immense damage upon their economies. The nations which had suffered from the thrust of the Nazi war machine, especially the Soviet Union, were seeking reparations in both goods and machinery. The transfer was only vaguely, if at all, related to the Morganthau Plan (sponsored by Secretary of the Treasury Henry Morganthau). This plan envisaged reducing Germany to a nineteenth-century agricultural nation, and did not survive the first criticism made of it. Nevertheless, agreement was reached at the Potsdam conference that 918 German plants would be dismantled and used for reparations for the countries which had suffered severe industrial damage.

The AFL was, from the outset, suspicious of the dismantling program. It believed that all countries would benefit from only a limited program of dismantling, for that would allow the German economy to produce effectively, with all countries drawing reparations from the increased output.

An AFL labor mission conducted a two month investigation at the invitation of the AMG. It criticized the "wisdom" of vast deindustrialization.[49] The report also criticized the division of the country into zones, creating a series of economic barriers resulting in diminished economic activity. Unification of Germany was recommended as the means for facilitating the flow of food stuffs and raw materials through the country.[50]

Resistance to dismantling on the scale contemplated in the Potsdam Agreement began to appear among German workers. On July 19, 1947, delegates representing the Federation of Bavarian Trade Unions appealed to the AFL to prevent the dismantling of the Schweinfurt ball bearing plant by having the problem reexamined by the AMG. The unions based their request upon the importance of this plant for the continuation of industrial production. As a result of the lack of sufficient ball bearings, bottlenecks already existed in the manufacture of mining machines, and of agricultural, railroad, and electrical equipment. Even if the two plants in Schweinfurt were to remain in full operation, Germany would be lacking 10 million units. Absence of dollar credits made it impossible to substitute imports. Thousands of present and former workers would lose their pension and disability benefits invested in the plant's inventory. Half the plant had been moved to the Soviet Union in 1946, and the remaining parts had to be kept together or they would be of no use.[51]

In a letter to President Harry Truman, William Green asked for a "reconsideration of the United States economic policy for Germany." Green said that while everyone favored preventing Germany from producing war materials, no one had envisaged interference with production for civilian purposes. He noted that the directives of the Joint Chiefs of Staff, in April 1945, had set the levels of production in accordance with the Potsdam Agreement which was the basis of the Allied Council's decision, in the spring of 1946, for the production facilities to be dismantled and shipped as reparations. However, the severe restrictions on steel and chemical production had prevented the revival of industry which was necessary for Germany and other countries.

Green suggested that reparation payments could be more effectively met by allowing the use of German labor in German plants to produce goods which could be shipped to countries entitled to reparation payments: "If the production plants and machinery remain where they are, with skilled workers available, they can provide the goods needed for the revival of production in Continental Europe and enable all the nations to become self-supporting."[52] Green regarded the moving of productive facilities as wasteful and was convinced that "countries to which reparations are due would gain more through reparation out of the proceeds of production."[53] In response to complaints, Congress provided, in the Foreign Assistance Act of 1948, that the Secretary of State was to obtain agreement from the countries concerned that "such capital equipment as is scheduled for removal as reparations from the three western zones of Germany be retained in Germany if such retention will most effectively serve the purpose of the European recovery program."[54]

Pursuant to this section, Paul Hoffman, administrator of the Economic Cooperation Administration (ECA), appointed a committee headed by George Humphrey, to examine the removal of plants as reparations from the three western zones. This committee reviewed the status of 381 plants listed for removal, and basing their suggestions on the reports of two separate engineering firms, recommended to the Secretary of State that 174 plants should be utilized for reparations. The recommendations were attacked by the leaders of the AFL and the CIO on the grounds that the policy recommended would seriously increase unemployment in Germany. At the same time, European industry would be deprived of thousands of tons of raw materials and machinery and would thus impede the economic recovery of Europe. Moreover, the decision of the foreign ministers of Britain and France, and the Secretary of State, in the summer of 1948, went beyond the recommendations of the Humphrey committee, and American labor regarded the decision as a throwback to the Morgenthau Plan.

Green again called on Secretary of State Acheson to halt the dismantling. He told him:

> German industries and German trade unions are appealing for protection against dismantling plans which deny workers jobs and interfere with expeditious progress in economic recovery for Europe and implementation of Atlantic pact ... Dismemberment of Hamburg Thyssen low cost production plant indefensible in view of world steel shortage. The key to democratic Europe is a busy, courageous Germany. Urge end of dismantling as constructive policy necessary for rehabilitating European economy and in establishing understanding cooperation worthy of democracy in this world crisis.[55]

Dean Acheson replied that the dismantling program had been reviewed by a committee of American industrialists, and their recommendations taken up with the foreign ministers of France and England. As a result of the agreement negotiated, 159 plants were removed from reparation lists on the grounds that their retention in Germany would serve the interests of European recovery. He added:

> Recent agreement on reparations part of Washington agreement on Germany which lay the basis for establishing democratic German Government and full participation Germany in organization for European

Economic Cooperation and represent coordinated policy Western European powers on policy toward Germany. We have given Germany full and important place
in European recovery and taken into account factors
mentioned in your telegram. I seriously question
desirability renewed efforts to revise Reparation Program.[56]

Woll continued to attack the dismantling of German
plants, and called upon the British Trades Union Congress,
and the French CGT *Force Ouvrière* to demand a reversal of
this policy. Speaking for the AFL International Labor
Relations Committee, Woll warned that persistence in this
policy was dangerous, tending to create antagonism between
the western powers and the democratic forces in Germany.
He scoffed at the fear of German rearmament, and expressed
the AFL's "complete solidarity with the German trade
unions against the policy of dismantling."[57]

Walter Reuther also protested "the senseless destruction of
industrial capacity in Germany," in a letter to President
Truman.[58] Reuther wrote specifically about six steel and
three chemical plants found to be necessary for European
recovery. While Paul Hoffman had recommended that the
plants be retained for Germany because of their importance
to European recovery, the three-power agreement "ear-
marked those plants for reparations."[59] Reuther told the
President that the destruction of the above plants by
dismantlement conflicted with any hope of enlarging steel
production capacity. Reuther recommended that the plants
be retained in Germany, "and nations entitled to reparations
be assigned the output of these plants up to the value they
would have received through dismantlement."[60]

In a statement made on June 20, 1949, Woll pointed to
the danger that dismantling carried, its enforcement requiring
mobilization of troops in the British zone. He charged,

moreover, that the agreement of April 13 ignored the recommendations of the Humphrey Committee. He attacked the planned dismantling of the August-Tyssenhütte in Hamburg, employing 13,000 workers, as a threat to the revival of German industry as well as of the European continent, and ridiculed the claims of a British commander that this plant could only be used for the manufacture of war goods. Finally, the "AFL expressed its complete solidarity in the protest of the German trade unions against dismantling," and demanded that German labor "be given an opportunity to earn a livelihood under conditions of peace and freedom."[61]

The 1949 CIO convention criticized the dismantling of German industry, eliciting some heated debate, and directed its delegation to the international trade union conference to explore the problem with the leaders of Western European labor movements.[62] The AFL on a number of occasions intervened with the British authorities, and in 1950 stopped the total destruction of the steel mills at Wattensteck-Salzgitter.[63]

A twelve-point program.

In the spring of 1948, the Free Trade Union Committee issued a statement on the state of the world and a program for its improvement. It called for positive steps to establish "a bona fide democratic German Republic . . . endowed with all the attributes of sovereignty and full authority and an economy which shall have the capacity and opportunity to provide for its people and to do its appropriate share for the reconstruction of the continent."[64] To carry out these objectives, the statement called for the establishment of a national German government with a constituent assembly given full powers to determine economic and legal relationships. A bill of rights should be included. Opposition to dismantlement of German factories and their mobilization for economic reconstruction should be carried out. A number of proposals dealt with the abolition of the "wage stop," working out an equitable tax system, and the return of property to the trade unions. Finally the Free Trade Union Committee advised Europe to devise a joint defense system to oppose aggression and the extension of Soviet influence.

Codetermination (Mitbestimmung).

Codetermination became an issue after the issuance of Law No. 75 by the military government directing the organization of the coal, iron, and steel industries. In the original plan, the trade unions were not given representation on the boards of trustees. As these industries had been among the major supporters of the Nazi regime, the leaders of the German trade union movement demanded that the workers be allowed to choose several trustees for the boards of directors. These trustees, it was claimed, would be alert to any resurgence of Nazism or militarism and be able to warn the community of the impending danger. Labor representation was first permitted in the coal and steel industries, and a general codetermination statute, not altogether satisfactory to labor, was enacted in 1952.

Before its adoption, the labor unions mounted a campaign in behalf of the proposal, and the employers challenged this measure by furious resistance to what they believed was the first step on the road to socialization. The AFL rallied to the side of the trade unions despite the fact that it did not favor such a program in the United States. This attitude was in keeping with the AFL tradition that the workers of each country should decide upon the policies suitable to their needs, as understood by them. Woll, in a letter to General Clay, said that the AFL's view of private enterprise was favorable: it had

time and again declared that our country does not and

must not seek to impose any type of economy or economic policies on any country. ... Therefore, we must avoid creating the impression that we want to compel other peoples – in one way or another – to adopt one or another form of Americanization. Directly or indirectly, such attempts would be only prejudicial to the healthy democratic development of other countries. ... We should be careful, even timid, about trying to impose our ideas on Europe.[65]

Later, President George Meany informed the German Federation of Labor that the AFL had "never declared itself against codetermination," and called attention to the fact that the AFL had "helped formulate" the resolution at the second world congress of the International Confederation of Free Trade Unions (ICFTU) in 1951, approving the demand of workers to participate in the "management of enterprises and industry on all social and economic matters."[66]

Meany noted that American workers were not interested in codetermination as they believed they could protect their interests through collective bargaining. However, the AFL had supported the demands of the German unions. In a letter to General Clay, on January 5, 1949, Woll said:

If we have to choose between reliable democratic trade unionists who do not choose for Germany free enterprise, as we know it in the United States, and employers who were pro-Nazi and who seek to win back their influence by trying to impress themselves upon American authorities as defenders of the United States brand of free enterprise, we should not hesitate to choose democracy and human freedom and should reject outright and unmistakably all fellow travelers of Nazism.

On June 20, 1949, the AFL International Labor Relations Committee declared that the effective way to prevent the return to power of reactionary industrialists is to "encourage the growth of free trade unionism in Germany and to guarantee the bona fide democratic labor organizations a full voice in the economic affairs of their country."[67]

In another letter, on July 25, 1949, Woll proposed that "there be constituted for the coal industry in the Ruhr a Board of Trustees like the one which has been constituted for the German steel industry. We further propose that the bona fide free trade unions be given representation in this Board for the coal industry just as they have been accorded representation in the Board of Trustees named for the steel industry."[68] Woll argued that it was necessary to give German workers a voice in the industry, and that such representation would "inspire them to make valuable suggestions for its continued improvement." He was certain it would make for stability and for a more responsible interest in production as well.

On November 26, 1951, Woll told the State Department: "The elementary principles of democracy require that the German people themselves determine the form or forms of ownership of the steel plants of their country."[69]

Cooperation between AFL and CIO.

By 1948, the AFL and CIO were beginning their cooperation in developing common policies and attitudes towards international labor relations. In the spring of 1948, a mission was set up consisting of Irving Brown, Henry Rutz, Michael Ross—the CIO's director of international affairs, and Arnold Steinbach of the office of international labor affairs in the United States Department of Labor. The committee spent a month interviewing a large number of officials of the military government, trade unionists, and employers association officials; it found that the 4,500,000 union members needed to be educated in democratic unionism, but that the leadership was informed, politically sophisticated, and courageous. German trade union leaders had charged that "scores of former Nazis and extreme nationalists have returned to leading positions in the governmental hierarchy. . . ."[70]

The report advocated a careful watch by labor-management boards over changes in the economy, the encouragement of trade union membership, increased allocation of newsprint, more direct contact with the military government, extension of collective bargaining as far as possible under the occupation, training of young trade unionists, and investigation by a committee, upon which the trade unions should be represented, of the increase in the influence of former Nazis.

Appointment of Nazis and former Nazis.

The 1948 AFL convention demanded that "no industrial or financial magnates who have been friends and supporters of German militarism and Nazism . . . should be given any position of authority in the rebuilding of Germany."[71] The resolution was directed against the appointments of Heinrich Dinkelbach and Heinrich Kost to high posts in the administration of the economy after they were de-Nazified. Dinkelbach and Kost had been cleared under the existing regulations; Woll defended the action of the convention in a letter to General Clay. The AFL, he said, did not seek

a reversal of judicial verdicts by administrative decision; but we do hold that a fellow traveler (Mitläufer) of Nazism is not particularly qualified to play a leading role in the public life of Germany, merely because he has not been sentenced to suffer some penalty for a provable crime. Certainly, this should not entitle him to any Military Government support of his attempt to win a position of high influence.[72]

Refusal to AFL representative of entry into the French zone.
The hostility of the Soviet occupation authorities to the activities of the AFL is easily understood. Less comprehensible is the action of the French authorities who took umbrage at the circulation of the *International Free Trade Union News* because it was critical of the already noticeable communist-line proclivities of the French *Confédération Générale du Travail* (CGT), and denied an entry permit to the AFL representative, Henry Rutz.[73] On behalf of the AFL, Woll protested to Prime Minister Paul Ramadier, the socialist heading a coalition government which at the time included representatives of the Communist Party. "We have not denied CGT," Woll told the Prime Minister, "the right to criticize us and its Communist official [Benoit] Frachon has even threatened life of AFL representative Irving Brown if he establishes office in Paris. Despite these slanders and threats against American labor . . . AFL has never sought to prevent them from touring American zone."[74]

For a unified movement.
The AFL always favored a single federation and believed that division along denominational lines was undesirable as it led to internecine conflicts among workers and dissipation of resources. It may be recalled that Gompers would not, during the Paris peace conference in 1919, aid the Christian trade union federation to gain admission to the International Federation of Trade Unions.[75] Whatever influence the AFL possessed after World War II was exercised on behalf of a unitary movement within each country. However, it ran into the European tradition of denominational unions which was very powerful in some sections of labor. The German trade union leaders were, nevertheless, able to avoid fragmentation of the labor movement and succeeded in maintaining a unified federation.

Pressure for division existed and received sustenance from both political and religious sources. The DGB was not formally a socialist group although many of its early leaders were social democrats. In the interest of unity they avoided putting their socialist foot too far forward. At the first convention at Munich, in 1949, Hans Böeckler, head of the British Zone Federation, was elected president of the DGB, and held this office until his death in February 1951. At a special convention in Essen, Christian Fette, head of the Graphic Trades Union, was elected president. The Metal Workers Union unsuccessfully supported Walter Freitag, one of their own, although he was not formally a candidate. The Berlin convention, in 1952, showed a noticeable change in the composition of trade union membership, with an increase in younger workers among the delegates. The convention called for the extension of codetermination to industries other than steel and coal, and came out for national ownership of a number of basic industries. These votes aroused a reaction in conservative employer circles and some charged that the trade unions had embraced "cold socialism." The answer made was that codetermination had as its major aim the exercise of public control over ownership, and the raising of those who labor to the same status as those who own. Representation upon boards of directors of corporations, it was argued, would be demanded in a nationalized as well as a private industry. The purpose was to allow a voice in management and not to change the form of ownership.

This demand became a burning issue within the trade union movement, and criticism was directed at the president of the DBG, Christian Fette, and his executive board because they had not been sufficiently aggressive in demanding a general codetermination law. The dissatisfaction manifested itself at the 1952 convention in a move to replace Christian Fette as president by Walter Freitag. Efforts were made to prevent serious division, and in the end, Freitag, head of the powerful Metal Workers Union, was chosen to serve for the next three years.

A split by the adherents of an independent Christian trade union movement had always been feared, and their drive for independence became more formidable after the defeat of Fette. The DGB's neutrality was questioned, and the separatists had support in political circles and industry. They also found support from Dutch and Belgian Christian union leaders and the *Katholische Arbeiterbewegung* (KAB), the Catholic Workers Movement, which encouraged discussion of a separate denominational labor movement. A demand was made for greater representation on the boards and committees of the DGB. Implied in this "ultimatum" from a number of important Christian trade unionists was that failure to meet the demands might lead to a split. As an independent trade union movement on denominational lines became the subject of increasing debate, the West German bishops called for a neutral world outlook and "genuine tolerance." Their statement praised the KAB for seeking to infuse the social order with a Christian spirit. It also thanked union members for their efforts to preserve a neutral trade union movement.

George Meany entered the lists. A practicing Catholic, his forthright criticism of Chancellor Adenauer for threatening the German labor movement, and his declaration that the "German labor movement must remain free", had a great influence in halting the movement for separatism. He asked the German people not to let their government "take that first step which will lead Germany down the path to war and ruin,"[76] and the statement received widespread notice in the German and European press.

Meany was expressing a long-held view of the American labor movement against denominational labor organizations. During Gompers' presidency such organizations had been officially criticized by the AFL's executive council, which had several Catholics among its members.[77] The AFL had opposed the setting up of denominational unions in European countries and sought to persuade the active trade unionists against this policy — unsuccessfully in a number of countries.

The DGB rejected the ultimatum that the "Christian" membership on the DGB executive board, state federations of labor councils, editorial boards of union publications, and other trade union bodies be increased. A Catholic youth conference, in November 1953, came out against division, and there were reports that the Papal Nuncio for Germany was unhappy about the demand. The separatist movement also failed to gain support from leading Catholic trade unionists including Jakob Kaiser and Karl Arnold, members of the Adenauer government. The KAB tried to keep separatism alive, but the issue lost momentum. It would have weakened the trade unions, and for that reason it had some employer support.

Solutions for the German problem.

In a long letter to the Secretary of State, Woll wrote: "No reform of Allied-German relations will be sound unless it enables Germany to participate constructively in the common efforts of the democratic world for peace and social progress."[78] He urged the United States to take the initiative and discard old slogans and prejudices. He feared the alienation of the democratic forces in Germany who had shown the greatest attachment to the West and had opposed all forms of totalitarianism. "It is in this spirit," said Woll, "that the activities of the German Trade Union Federation (DGB) and the Social Democratic Party, which is generally considered the principal expression of the labor movement, have been conducted."

Woll urged drawing Germany rapidly into full partnership with the West so that the suspicion that there was a desire to reduce her to semi-colonial status might be erased. He added; "No effective military or economic contribution by the Federal Republic of Germany is possible without the unstinting moral and material support of the German people."[79] He called for regard for trade union interests and full sovereignty for Germany, and warned against demanding from the German people that which could be fairly and justly made only by a nation already "enjoying the full opportunity to assume these obligations freely and independently."[80] Release from foreign rule, Woll said, "is an absolute necessity for the development of any healthy democratic nation. This applies to Germany as well as other countries." The failure to recognize this simple truth has become "a costly obstacle to closer cooperation between the people of Western Germany and the democratic world." He felt that as long as Germany was denied full equality, her participation in defense and in decisions on her political and economic future must be clouded in uncertainty.[81]

Woll's letter was answered by Geoffrey W. Lewis, Acting Director of the Bureau of German Affairs in the State Department, who found it "ranging over nearly the entire gamut of German problems ... [and] a highly useful contribution to the discussion of one of the major concerns of American foreign policy."[82] He agreed with many of Woll's opinions and hoped that the negotiations then going on would lead to a relationship between the three western democracies and Germany of "substantial equality."[83] He told Woll that "if the discussion of American foreign policy can be maintained on this level of intelligence, there is hope for ultimate agreement on a formulation of those objectives which all men of good will basically desire."[84]

Woll answered Lewis' letter, telling him that the "substantial equality" envisaged by the State Department was not full equality. Cooperation between the democratic world and Germany could not be attained, according to Woll, by "granting to the German people an equality conceived in the Orwellian sense − that is a relationship wherein some parties are 'more equal' than others." Woll also opposed requiring advance commitments to a European army from the Germans because the labor movement in that country held to be imperative that an "army be subject to strict parliamentary control."[85]

Woll was sharply critical of the designation by the Allied High Commission of new owners of the reorganized steel companies because such designation constituted prejudging the question of future ownership.

The elementary principles of democracy require that the German people themselves determine the form or forms of ownership of the steel plants of their country. The tender consideration shown by the Allied High Commission to the Ruhr industrialists is a flagrant violation of the solemn pledge made in the Preamble to Law No. 27 and in plain contempt of the wishes of German democratic labor. No wonder it has aroused bitter resentment among German democratic workers and other democratic forces who have not forgotten that these Ruhr industrial magnates were the ones who made it possible for Hitler to come to power.[86]

Kurt Schumacher, head of the Social Democratic Party of Germany (*Sozialdemokratische Partei Deutschlands*), expressed gratitude at the 1947 AFL convention, since the help which the AFL has given us, through the visit of its special delegation to Germany and by sending food parcels and publications, constitutes an extremely important contribution to the strengthening of the German democratic labor movement. However, the

onslaught of the Communist machine with its enormous
financial resources and horde of agents and functionaries must be resisted with much stronger forces than
ever before.[87]

Schumacher discussed the needs of Germany, and urged
continued cooperation of the workers' movement of the
United States in strengthening the democratic forces within
his country. In a letter to President Green, in which
Schumacher thanked him for his "friendly invitation" to
address the convention, he said: "We wish the best success to
the positive European policy of the AFL."[88]

In 1953, the German government conferred upon Matthew
Woll the well deserved honor of the Grand Order of Merit.
No one was more devoted to the establishment of a
democratic labor movement within a free Germany. He gave
his time and energies without stint, only asking his
countrymen to recognize the realities of the danger facing
free men and democracy. The award directly recognized the
contributions of the AFL to German freedom and to the
growth of a free and democratic labor movement.

Personnel activity of the AFL.

The American military government employed thousands of
German workers and it was at first assumed that they would
enjoy the same rights, wages, hours, and working conditions
as those in private industry. Over a time, the role of the
United States forces changed from "utilizer" of labor to
direct employer. This change meant that the United States
performed the usual personnel functions of placement,
classification, and processing of payrolls. Another result was
that no collective bargaining was carried on between the
military government and the trade unions, in line with the
policy of that time. As a result, the American representative
acted as an intermediary between the German trade unions

and the American authorities. Downgrading of jobs, improper classifications, failure to pay the proper rates, and dozens of other complaints were filed on behalf of the German trade unions. In 1953, it was agreed that the head of the DGB would handle complaints and would take the matter up with the German official in contact with the Allied military forces. Should a satisfactory arrangement not be reached, the AFL would be notified and its representative would then take up the matter with the American government authorities in Germany.[89]

When the United States Army dismissed forty employees of the Bavarian Motor Works on two hours notice, the AFL sought to have the order canceled. Only one of the discharged was reemployed, but General W. M. Hodge assured the AFL that "directives have been strengthened so as to preclude any possibility of a future dismissal prior to a thorough review of the facts in the case. During this review the employee may be denied access to an installation if deemed necessary in the interests of national security, but will continue to be carried in full pay status."[90]

This was a relatively small matter when viewed in the context of the total German situation. However, the AFL also played a role in High Commissioner John J. McCloy's lifting the suspension of the Wurtenberg-Baden codetermination law, and in vetoing the civil service law favorable to former Nazi officials and the tax program regarded as inequitable by the unions. In a declaration, "The Crisis in Europe," the AFL executive council commended "highly the initiative of United States High Commissioner John J. McCloy . . ." for his actions. Despite the fact that the AFL had favored the appointment of Charles LaFollette as German High Commissioner, it found McCloy reasonable and understanding, and willing to help in the development of a democratic Germany."[91]

Austria.

For years prior to the 1930s, Austria had a thriving labor movement active on both the political and economic planes. The trade unions were, however, divided, with the largest federation closely tied to the Social Democratic Party; Christian, German nationalist, and after 1927, Heimwehr (Home Guard) federations were also active. In 1934, the free trade unions were suppressed, and Chancellor Dollfuss replaced them with the United Trade Union, imitative of the Italian fascist labor organizations. Compared to what was to follow, the Dollfuss regime was a mild one, with some of the old trade union leaders continuing to exercise underground influence. This situation changed with the taking over of Austria in the spring of 1938 by the Hitler legions. With the integration of Austria into the Nazi empire – the *Anschluss* – the United Trade Union was suppressed, and its property taken over by the German Labor Front (DAF). With brutal efficiency and speed a most severe regime was introduced, and many trade unionists went into hiding, fled abroad, or were sent to concentration camps. In a real sense, Austria was the first victim of Nazi aggression.

Immediately after the liberation of Vienna in 1945, trade unions were revived. A national Federation of Trade Unions was organized and allowed to operate. Its officers came largely from former trade unions. In contrast to the prewar situation, only one trade union federation was established. It affiliated with the World Federation of Trade Unions in 1945. Many of the problems that beset postwar Germany were absent in Austria. It was generally recognized that Austria had been a minor and unwilling partner of Nazi Germany and had herself been a victim of aggression. Moreover, Austria, to a much lesser degree, possessed resources which could be exported, although the Soviet government, on the theory that certain enterprises were

German, took possession of and exploited a variety of industrial facilities.

The occupation by the western powers was relatively mild. Austria's lack of responsibility for the tragedy of war was informally recognized. Austrian trade unionists, from the beginning, shared in the Care program of the AFL. One of the first acts on behalf of the Austrian trade unions was the appeal of the AFL to the State Department for permission for a relief consignment of food and medicines collected by the Swedish Help Committee for Austrian trade unionists to pass through the American Zone.[92] Permission was granted.

In 1948, the Austrian unions negotiated an arrangement with the American military government whereby indigenous employees of the Army would receive the same terms, including dismissal compensation, as the Austrian government's employees. However, due to objections from the Comptroller General, the payment of dismissal allowances to about 250 laid-off employees was not made. The Austrian unions protested this denial to the AFL, and Matthew Woll, speaking on behalf of the Federation, said "this is not a matter merely of finance;" that there were "severe political repercussions in this situation." From the point of view of total expenditure in Austria by the occupation authorities the sum was not large. However, the AFL believed that the "Army in Austria ... which is technically an army of liberation rather than an army of occupation should avoid acting in such a manner."[93] The Army answered that "the arguments presented by you were given full consideration ... in reaching a final determination by the Secretary of the Army on this matter."[94] The Secretary determined administratively that dismissal compensation could be paid from the funds of the United States military establishment. The decision was in accordance with Austrian law which the Army followed in this instance.

The above difference was solved by the Secretary, recognizing that the consequences of allowing dissatisfaction were not worth the cost. Not many complaints were raised against the American authorities during the period when Lieutenant General Keyes served as Commanding General of the American military forces and also as High Commissioner. Personnel policies were devised in the Labor Division in conformity with Army regulations and military need. Although the Austrian trade unions believed that full recognition of Austrian labor law, participation in collective agreements, and the use of the labor court system were preferable, they were reasonably satisfied with the procedures worked out during General Keyes' tenure.

In October 1950, military functions were separated from those of the High Commissioner. As the labor division remained with the office of the High Commissioner, relationships remained satisfactory in that area, and the right of employees to be represented was recognized. Differences were discussed and worked out. However, no labor division was established by the Army in Austria, changes in working conditions were made without consultation with the trade unions, and requested changes were long delayed or made in a manner which aroused protest. Woll demanded the establishment of adequate channels of discussion between the Army and the labor organizations. Ambassador Donnelly, who also served as High Commissioner, sought to have the Army change its policy and failed. "But an Ambassador," said Woll, "can only make suggestions – the Army will react only when ordered to from superiors in the Pentagon."[95]

Woll pleaded with the Secretary of Defense for a reexamination of labor policy and the establishment of regular contact with the Austrian Trade Union Federation.

We of the American Federation of Labor, Mr. Secretary, would appreciate prompt and favorable action by you in this vital matter. The Austrian trade unions have been in the forefront of the fight against every attempt of Communist infiltrators and subversives. They are the very backbone of the democratic and anti-totalitarian forces. It is most timely and important that our government's policies in Austria, particularly in relation to organized labor, should demonstrate in deed and reality the democratic way of life and also reveal to the working people of Austria our appreciation of their loyalty to the democratic cause and of our readiness and determination to treat them on the basis of equality in every way possible.[96]

The Secretary of the Army answered Woll's letter and denied that there was an absence of communication between the Army and the trade unions on personnel matters. He said that the United States Forces Civilian Personnel Office had continued "the structure existing prior to October 1950."[97] Woll challenged the accuracy of this statement and indicated that a staff officer was the cause of the difficu'ty. He told Secretary Pace that relationships had deteriorated, and that this "will not be denied if the Commanding General . . . would by-pass his Chief of Staff and meet with these Austrian trade union leaders personally to discuss this problem."[98] Woll cited a list of specific grievances which had not been resolved, and warned of the possibility of a strike of Army employees.

Secretary Pace suggested a meeting with the commanding general, but it was slow in coming. Finally, Lt. General George P. Hays was informed that in view of the seriousness of the situation the AFL was being asked to demand an investigation "as to the complaints made by one of America's best European friends — the Austrian Trade Union Federation — against the U.S. Army. I believe such an investigation will find that anti-labor officers . . . do not fit in the United

States plan of selling modern democracy to Europe."[99] While General Hays challenged the view that a serious conflict had developed, steps were taken to remedy the situation.[100] Some of the problems reappeared when the Mutual Security Administration (MSA) began to operate. The Austrian trade unionists believed that working people were being excluded from their share of benefits from the increased productivity which the MSA was stimulating. After a protest by the AFL, the Deputy Director of the MSA, W. J. Kennedy, assured the AFL that steps to "alleviate the bad feeling between the MSA and the Austrian trade unions would be undertaken."[101]

Although the problem of the Austrian trade unions might not have seemed important, the AFL recognized that the good will and loyalty of the members to the West should not be impaired. In addition, the AFL believed that its task of defending the rights of the Austrian workers was justified as it was the only route by which grievances could be presented to the occupation authorities and their equitable resolution made possible. Neither the Army nor the High Commissioner's office could be compelled by the Austrian trade unions to rectify inequities. The AFL was willing and able to go over the heads of the Austrian "viceroys" to heads of the departments in Washington, and to the President and Congress if this appeared necessary and warranted by the issue. In this fashion, the AFL not only promoted fair labor relations but prevented the dissipation of good will among Austrian workers and the leaders of the trade unions.

The Austrian Treaty and Article 16.

The American Federation of Labor opposed the forcible repatriation of refugees from iron curtain countries, and denounced Article 16 of the proposed peace treaty with Austria as a threat to Austrian sovereignty. Article 16 had been tentatively accepted by the 1954 Berlin conference of the "Big Four" foreign ministers. Under this proposal Austria would "render full assistance to the allied and associated powers concerned in regard to the voluntary repatriation of their nationals. . . ." Accredited representatives of allied countries would be allowed to visit the camps and centers of displaced persons for the purpose of conferring with their nationals. Committees and centers opposing repatriation were to be immediately dissolved, and not allowed to distribute propaganda.[102]

It was feared that the adoption of Article 16 would be a signal for the forcible repatriation of an estimated 38,000 to 50,000 refugees. At a meeting of AFL and CIO representatives in Washington, at a time when the Austrian treaty was being discussed by the foreign ministers, the AFL came out strongly for opposition to repatriation. The CIO supported the view of the Austrian Federation of Labor which was willing to concede repatriation and risk sacrificing thousands of defenseless refugees for a peace treaty. The AFL executive council denounced Article 16 on May 4, 1955, and declared that its acceptance would allow the Soviet government to

> plant on Austrian soil teams of Soviet political police serving as Austrian citizens friendly to refugees and displaced persons. Through their notorious secret police methods, the swarm of Soviet agents would seek to drive them back into Iron Curtain countries where they would be subjected to torture, slave labor and the firing squad.[103]

Article 16 was also denounced by *The New York Times* which drew "attention to one problem which imposes a moral responsibility on the West. This problem concerns some 30,000 refugees from behind the Iron Curtain who are now living in Austria, and whom the Soviets seek to recapture and punish as a warning to others who might wish to escape to freedom."[104] The Soviet Union finally agreed to withdraw its demand for the incorporation of Article 16 in the Austrian treaty. It was the insistence of American public opinion, of which the AFL formed the only labor component, which prevented the betrayal of thousands of hapless . refugees in search of freedom, to exile, prison, or the hangman's noose.

CHAPTER FIVE

The Marshall Plan

THE REGARD FOR DIFFERENCES which is the basis of cooperation among independent labor groups, was never considered an important operating principle by General Secretary Louis Saillant of The World Federation of Trade Unions, a long-time French communist. Slightly less than two years after the founding of the federation in 1945, Frank Rosenbloom, a vice president of the Amalgamated Clothing Workers, and Adolph Germer, the American assistant secretary of the WFTU, complained that the AFL's refusal to affiliate placed the burden of opposing the communists and the Russians upon their shoulders.[1] Even more significant was the view of Jan Oldenbroek, a leading Dutch trade unionist active in international labor affairs, who predicted in December 1946 that the WFTU could not hold European labor together and urged the AFL not to surrender the field.

The key to the future lay with the British Trades Union Congress, the oldest and most respected labor federation. A substantial minority believed that unity of all labor, irrespective of political ideologies, was imperative if another world cataclysm were to be avoided. In addition, there was always present at annual congresses a small but influential communist contingent whose power to create difficulties for the leaders had to be taken into account. Irving Brown was nevertheless convinced, by 1948, that the break would soon come.[2]

The British may have had reservations about the viability of the WFTU from the beginning. First they regarded the organization "as an industrial, as distinct from a political, body;"[3] the kind of distinction that is not recognized in communist theory or practice. The TUC also made the working out of an agreement between the WFTU and the international trade secretariats – a union of organizations in different countries in the same industry or calling – a condition of affiliation. As soon as the administrative arrangements had been completed, the British criticized them, believing that no account had been taken of their experience in the international labor movement. Nevertheless, they avoided open recriminations and made constant efforts to find a basis of accommodation. They were, however, forced to recognize "the basic cleavage which presents itself." The British found that political questions almost always intruded in discussions of trade union policy, and matters put forward by some of the national centers almost always became subjects for propaganda. Nor were the objections of WFTU leaders stated in gentle terms: "The stream of vilification and abuse," said the statement,

> which has been poured on the British TUC, American labour and the leaders of those national centers who are not prepared to become subservient to Communist doctrine and dictation is not restrained by any desire to overcome inherent difficulties. Any realization that international trade union unity depends on the good will and good relations between trade union movements of the participating countries is completely absent in the tactics we have encountered.[4]

Until Murray and his supporters threw down the challenge

to the communist bloc within the CIO, the position of the communists had been restrained. Murray made decisions on crucial issues, and those who disagreed were free to challenge him, though with little chance of success. Murray had shown, by his invitation to Secretary of State George Marshall to address the 1947 CIO convention, that he would not tolerate any opposition to the European Recovery Program from the communist minority. As already indicated, Walter Reuther and George Baldanzi sharply attacked the communist bloc at the 1947 convention. Because the Marshall Plan was not mentioned by name, the vote for European recovery was unanimous. Murray took a further step: he endorsed the Marshall Plan publicly, submitted a memorandum to President Truman on a number of its aspects, and testified before Congress in its support.

The challenge was more open and direct at the 1948 convention at which there was a great deal of bitter feeling between the CIO administration and the communists. The latter had supported Henry Wallace as a third party candidate for president in the hope of defeating President Truman's bid for reelection, and had failed. Murray was in no mood for compromise, and the resolution endorsing the European Recovery Program (ERP) said:

> Free, democratic labor and other organizations in Europe have welcomed the ERP and have cooperated with their own governments and the American labor movement in the work of the Economic Cooperation Administration (ECA). We endorse and commend the work of CIO officials and members in cooperation with and functioning within, the ECA.[5]

The resolution also condemned "the organized opposition to ERP by the Soviet Union and its satellites and the way by which the economic misery of Europe is used for political advantage and to promote chaos and confusion."[6]

The AFL leadership was in favor of the Marshall Plan from the beginning. The 1947 convention directed that a conference of the labor movements from the sixteen Marshall Plan countries should be called, to devise a plan for the participation of the labor movements of the different countries in the administration of the relief and reconstruction program, and to make certain that the rights of labor would be protected and collective bargaining enhanced.[7]

Green, Meany, Woll, and George Harrison, all members of the AFL executive council, conferred with President Truman in December 1947, and assured him of AFL support for the Marshall Plan. In a subsequent statement, the federation declared that it favored

> aid to all countries prepared to cooperate earnestly, energetically and sincerely in the mutual undertaking to secure European reconstruction on a continental basis. Any nation which has not accepted the Marshall Plan shall be considered eligible for aid as soon as it honestly breaks with all moves and schemes calculated to interfere with the execution of the European Recovery Program and agrees to cooperate wholeheartedly with other nations on a collective basis. In this spirit, the AFL endorses the Marshall Plan and calls upon Congress to lose no time in approving the emergency aid program of $597,000,000 for France, Italy and Austria.[8]

In this comprehensive statement, the AFL said that "primary emphasis must be placed on the protection and promotion of human rights." It called for recognition of collective bargaining in carrying out the program, and said that there "must be no forced labor — in any form whatsoever — in the carrying out of the European Recovery Program." This was a direct reference to a suggestion by a WFTU committee that German workers be forced into the coal mines to help overcome the coal shortage. The statement

also suggested mobilizing the resources of the colonial areas
and at the same time

> improving the economic conditions of the dependent
> peoples. The utilization of these resources of Africa and
> other areas should be conducted on an international
> democratic basis — free from all imperialist practices
> and privileges and geared to the promotion of human
> rights and liberties of these dependent peoples.[9]

It repeated a demand for directing German industrial
potential into peaceful uses for the benefit of all Europe, for
an end to the dismantling of German industrial plants, and
for the unification of the three Western zones under a
government whose form should be decided by the German
people.

On self-determination, the AFL said:

> The AFL proposes that our government forcefully
> reiterate and firmly adhere to the policy that all nations
> we aid have the inviolable right to decide democratically
> their own political and economic relations. Our govern-
> ment cannot emphasize too strongly that it is not the
> purpose of American economic assistance to impose on
> any nation any particular political pattern or econ-
> omy. It is not the purpose of American assistance as
> envisaged in the Marshall Plan to infringe in the least on
> national sovereignty or independence of any people.[10]

With this statement went a proviso that the United States
should not encourage totalitarian movements of either the
right or left, and should place the greatest reliance upon the
democratic forces within a nation, including the free trade
unions.

Opposition from the communist bloc and the Soviet Union.
When the Marshall Plan was announced, the executive
bodies of the WFTU were in session in Prague. Neither the

top officers nor the delegates from Eastern Europe offered any criticism. For several months, their official publications were silent and did not even discuss the Marshall Plan. Finally, in November 1947, the Cominform, the international arm of world communism, flashed the signal. According to it, the Marshall Plan was an adroit attempt at "imperialist penetration" by the United States to reduce the nations of Europe to a colonial status which the Soviet bloc and its supporters were obliged to prevent. The opposition of the Soviet Union was based upon the assumption of the communist strategists that the United States would soon be bogged down in a serious postwar depression, a "crisis of capitalism." This would offer an opportunity to the communist bloc to advance its influence and even seize power in a number of countries.

Communist strategy was upset by the Marshall Plan. Unionists in the democratic countries enthusiastically rallied to the Plan, for they saw in it a method of recreating viable economies in which democratic institutions could exist and prosper, or at least of speeding the process. Obviously, the communist dominated trade union bodies in democratic countries were compelled to follow the same line of attack against the Marshall Plan. It should be clear that the willingness to change policies is never regarded in terms of consistency or ethics among communist strategists. One has only to recall the shift from opposition to fascism and Nazism in the late 1930s to the alliance with Hitler; the ultra-patriotic stance after the attack upon the Soviet Union, and the postwar return to the bludgeoning of the Western democracies. Whatever "justification" such a policy may have had for those in Eastern Europe, it could certainly not be argued in terms of the interests of the people of Western Europe or the United States. Nevertheless, communist groups within trade unions in the West joined in the assault upon the

Marshall Plan in language as injudicious as it was inexact. As an affiliate of the WFTU, the CIO sent delegates to a session of WFTU executives in November 1947. Its delegates tried to present a review of the Marshall Plan in the hope that it would be discussed by the conference. At first the request for presentation was denied, and after the Marshall Plan had finally been presented, opponents of the program refused to comment. The report in the WFTU *Information Bulletin* was described in a CIO publication as "inaccurate and dishonest."[11]

Dissatisfaction with the activities of the WFTU was widespread among affiliated trade union centers of the free countries. The use of the organization as a propaganda weapon finally became intolerable. In a statement issued jointly by the BTUC, the CIO, and the Confederation of Free Trade Unions of the Netherlands, criticisms of the CIO were repeated. The statement noted that the

calumnies systematically poured out against the non-communist trade union leaders can no longer be counted. "Trud," the official organ of the Central Council of Soviet Trade Unions, in its issue of November, 1947, went so far as cynically and brutally to demand that the WFTU rid itself of its "reformist" leaders.[12]

The reformist leaders whose removal was demanded were representatives of non-communist trade union federations who stood in the way of the political propaganda which the communist apparatus believed was the primary purpose of the WFTU.

The statement declared that, in various missions appointed by the WFTU,

the Communist delegates in every instance tried to introduce one-sided political objectives. . . . What most interested the Communist delegates were shortcomings in denazification procedure in the British, American and French zones. Shortcomings there undeniably were in these three zones, and the representatives of the German workers, availing themselves of the liberty which they enjoyed in these zones, did not fail to report them to the delegation of the WFTU. And the British, American and French representatives on such delegations made themselves responsible for following up complaints relating to their country's zones.[13]

The report contrasted the situation with that in the Soviet zone, and noted:

By contrast, in the Soviet zone, the trade union organization had been so well prepared by the Soviets and their German communist agents that no workers' delegate would have risked revealing the abuses committed by the Soviet military authorities. . . . Moreover, in Germany, as in many other countries, the communists had greatly simplified denazification. Indeed, the adhesion of a Nazi to the Communist Party was sufficient reason for exonerating him entirely in the eyes of the Soviet authorities. Nevertheless, it is a matter of record that Nazis were found in the Soviet zone by WFTU delegations. It is also a matter of fact that Soviet representatives on such delegations bitterly resented any questions on the part of other members implying criticism of Soviet administration. There were tense struggles within the delegation to Germany to prevent the communist delegates from turning the reports into a propaganda instrument directed against the Western democratic nations and approving, if not complimenting, the Soviet administration.[14]

The statement sums up the purpose of the WFTU in these early and crucial years. Adverse reports on the activities of the occupation authorities in the Western zones could be used as an effective propaganda weapon in the campaign to undermine reconstruction of Europe, and the Soviet unions and their followers in other countries recognized their importance and the stakes involved. International trade union unity was a secondary concern, and could be sacrificed to the major political purpose. A serious blow to the WFTU was the refusal of the international secretariats to affiliate. These organizations were mainly concerned with economic problems affecting their memberships, and the WFTU's desire for control over their functioning was the major reason for this refusal. At a Paris meeting in September 1948, the international secretariats decided that their interests could "best be served by continuing their independence until such time as the negotiations can be resumed with a Trade Union International that may bring the Trade Secretariats together on a basis of autonomy acceptable to them."[15] The labor federations in the democratic countries might have continued their WFTU affiliations and tried to work matters out, but they could not tolerate the program of sabotaging the Marshall Plan, one of the great humanitarian and political endeavors in history. The 1948 CIO convention directed that, in consultation with the democratic trade union centers, CIO officers were authorized to take any action on continued membership in the WFTU that they believed was warranted. Withdrawal was approved in 1949.

Writing in the summer of 1947, Matthew Woll said that the Marshall Plan should, in its central purpose and substance, be welcomed by all democratic minded people and all other lovers of liberty. There is neither shame nor crime to be attached to American policy if it seeks to continue American prosperity and prevent an economic depression at home by promoting reconstruction and popular welfare abroad. This is not imperialism. It simply marks a realization that our country cannot long stay prosperous if Europe and the rest of the world are bankrupt and in a state of economic collapse. It is not imperialism, but good and true internationalism for America to base its own prosperity and progress not on the poverty and misery of other peoples but on their own prosperity and progress.[16]

AFL President William Green submitted a series of recommendations regarding "the reconstruction of the economy of Europe and the administration of the Marshall Plan," as requested by President Truman. His first point was: "Emergency relief should be extended as a separate policy for the sole purpose of providing food and fuel to maintain life."[17] The second proposal requested that "the reconstruction program should provide for investments in capital equipment in order to revive and facilitate production."[18]

Green explained that it was necessary to realize that the communist parties of all countries had been directed by the heads of their international organization to sabotage the Marshall Plan. He urged that the trade union organizations should be encouraged so that workers might have an alternative to communism as a means of protecting the interests of those who worked, and added:

> To freely and voluntarily choose communism is one thing but to have a minority force it upon people, results in lowering of individual dignity and national respect.[18]

Green recommended that a new operating agency should administer the Marshall Plan, and not the existing government agencies. Included in the directors of the corporation should be "representatives of primary economic functional groups, such as industry, agriculture, and labor, in order to assure and establish that degree of confidence which generates cooperation." He asked that nations accepting the

Marshall Plan seek to maintain financial stability, and that no forced labor should be used "for economic rehabilitation." He believed that "under either public or private ownership, free, competitive enterprise should be the permanent objective sought." He opposed restrictive policies, cartels, and any other form which relied on "special privileges." Finally, he asked that the "extension of both emergency and permanent relief to the people of the democratic nations of Europe, should be based upon the fact that in conformity with democratic processes the people of each nation may establish their own form of government, free from outside interference, control or domination."

First steps to a meeting of free trade union centers.

The opposition of the Soviet Union and the organizations which followed its lead placed the unions of the free world in a serious dilemma. If they retained their affiliations with the WFTU, they would tacitly be endorsing attacks on the European Recovery Program. But mere withdrawal was not enough: a positive policy of support of the Marshall Plan and a simultaneous defense of worker interests so that all the economic gains would not be diverted to economic growth and capital improvement had to be evolved. The need to break away from the dominance of the WFTU and at the same time create another organization to join the separate national centers was widely recognized.

The AFL was, in the meantime, sounding out sentiment in Europe. From his visits to a half dozen countries, Irving Brown advised:

> We should avoid too much boasting or "told you so" attitude towards British. . . . It would be wise to be modest and magnanimous at this time vis-à-vis the British, but firm on principles.[19]

Brown's advice was excellent and did not fail to impress

those members of the AFL executive council who were active in foreign affairs. A conference of free trade unions was imperative, but some leaders of the free trade union centers might have resented an AFL initiative. Louis Major, national secretary of the Belgian Federation of Labor (*Fédération Générale du Travail de Belgique*), notified William Green and J. H. Oldenbroek that the AFL had better abstain from inviting representatives of the trade unions to a conference, for such an invitation might backfire.[20]

Oldenbroek suggested that the heads of the labor movement in the Benelux countries and the British Trades Union Congress issue the invitations. Sponsorship by the latter was important because the TUC was still a member of the WFTU.[21] The AFL's concern for credit was not great, and it willingly surrendered a position it might have claimed through its leadership in the fight against communist domination. It could also have claimed a leading part since the Marshall Plan had originated in the United States. The AFL executive council accepted the invitation to attend, and did not object when it was announced that the CIO would be a participating federation. In fact, William Green explained that as a supporter of the Marshall Plan, the CIO would automatically be invited to the conference.[22] It sent James Carey, Elmer Cope, and Michael Ross to the meeting. Recognition was also given to the Railway Labor Executives Association, which delegated Bert M. Jewell to represent it.

The three Benelux countries — the Netherlands Federation of Labor, The Belgian Federation of Labor, and the Luxembourg Federation of Labor — and the TUC issued the invitations. The AFL was anxious to send a delegation from heads of the organization but could not do so because of a "tremendously important conference of AFL political arm. . . ."[23] The cablegram breathes an air of disappointment mixed with elation that at long last the trade unions of the free world were going to meet.

Oldenbroek, in a confidential letter to David Dubinsky, one of the leading supporters of the AFL's expanded activity in foreign affairs, explained the necessity for speed in holding the meeting. Even more interesting is Oldenbroek's comment on the role of the AFL:

> Now let me first of all say that I think the AFL have handled this Marshall Plan business in a masterly way. Though you had taken the initiative for a calling of a conference, you did not insist when it became clear that there were forces at work in Europe which pursued the same purpose. The AFL have thereby still more endeared themselves to those trade unionists who are in the WFTU without really belonging to it. . . . The Belgians decided to go all out for the Marshall Plan and to call a conference with the idea of inviting the AFL. The Dutch and Luxembourgers supported them and if the TUC had not come round in time they would have joined forces with the AFL.[24]

Oldenbroek pleaded for haste, necessary because of certain political maneuvers being carried on by different groups. He told Dubinsky:

> An international trade union conference on the Marshall Plan with American participation would have a stimulating effect upon the workers particularly if it is pointed out by our American friends that Moscow is afraid of the recovery of Western Europe, because it would lead to an improvement in the standards of living, which are already very much higher than in Russia and in the satellite countries. . . .[25]

He discussed the maneuvering between the British and the WFTU, and urged the AFL to send delegates to the March meeting.

The problem was a difficult one for the AFL. It was satisfied with the turn of events, and regarded the approaching conference of free world unions as primarily the fruition of its own long efforts. Its leaders believed that the conference was important, and that several members of the executive council should be in attendance. There was, however, a serious conflict over timing, for the first meeting of Labor's League for Political Education was to hold its meeting on the same date, and the AFL leaders had to be present. The League had been established as a full time political arm of the AFL in reaction to the passage of the Taft-Hartley Act. It was tested in the Presidential election of 1948, and contributed to the surprise victory of Harry Truman. Three members of the executive council, David Dubinsky, George Meany, and George Harrison, who were active in international affairs, were also among the top AFL strategists in the domestic political area. The AFL was anxious to secure European labor support for its participation in the administration of the Marshall Plan, and it had made an earnest and sincere effort "since last July to see a Marshall Plan Trades Union Conference which could lay the basis for joint cooperation by European and American labor in this program of joint reconstruction."[26]

Irving Brown and Frank Fenton, director of organization, represented the AFL, with Henry Rutz as secretary. As scheduled, the conference on the Recovery Program met on March 9, 1948. Twenty-eight organizations from thirteen countries which had accepted the Marshall Plan were represented. The Italian Confederation of Labor (CGIL) refused to attend and Italian unionism was represented by minority groups. The French General Confederation of Labor (CGT) also followed the communist line and rejected its invitation. In its place the newly organized CGT *Force Ouvrière* sent delegates.

The principle of exclusive jurisdiction or representation as practiced by the former International Federation of Trade

Unions was not applied. This was important to the United States, for it made it easier for AFL leaders to accept the parity of the CIO at international meetings. Not all rivalry and suspicion of the CIO had evaporated, but the necessity for cooperation was apparent. In addition, the CIO leadership had friendly connections with European labor leaders. Nevertheless, rivalry over appointments to both committees and offices was to persist until the merger. Another factor in this rivalry was the feeling of the AFL's leaders that they had carried a solitary burden, that they had been correct in their appraisal of events, and that they, despite some feelings of hostility, had saved certain European leaders from their own folly.

Nevertheless, there was a large measure of cooperation between the three American labor delegations, with all speakers from the United States striking a generous note. James Carey, speaking for the CIO, forecast the disappointment of the opponents of the Marshall Plan if they relied upon division in the ranks of American labor to interfere with carrying out the recovery program.[27]

Frank Fenton, who spoke for the AFL and the Railway Labor Executives Association, reflected the spirit of the American labor organizations when he told the European delegates that all American labor was united behind the recovery program, and that different groups within American labor had worked together to assure Europe sufficient aid to overcome existing obstacles to economic progress. He assured the conference that aid would be given "with no strings attached." Fenton expressed the fear that a continuance of economic demoralization would threaten "not only the institutions of Democracy . . . in Europe but the common heritage of Americans and Europeans."[28]

In outlining the basic principles which would govern the plan, Fenton said that

Economic needs were to be determined by Europeans themselves, aid should be provided on a unified basis, as long as democratic methods are used no political conditions should be attached, and administration should rest primarily with European countries through their respective governments.[29]

American labor, he said, was

united in our desire and willingness to assist you in this huge undertaking. We are not here to demand or dictate. You are right up against the gun here in Europe. It is our intention to work with you and to engage in this common task which is vital to our common trade union existence.[30]

Almost every speaker expressed appreciation of the American program, and the conference placed on record "its high appreciation of the initiative taken by the American labour movement, in complete unity of spirit, in the formulation of the European Recovery Programme."[31] The European Recovery Program Trade Union Advisory Committee was established to handle business between conferences, collect and analyze and circulate information, promote cooperation among affiliated groups, develop representation of trade unions in all countries involved in the administration of the ERP program, and to work closely with the Committee on Economic Cooperation. The American delegation was satisfied with this first conference, and the AFL had the added satisfaction that the conference welcomed, at its insistence, German delegates from the three Western zones "into the top councils of international labor." It was largely through the efforts of the AFL delegates that the Germans were seated. They were also instrumental in having the minority from the Italian Federation of Labor accepted after that federation refused to be represented at the conference.[32]

While the AFL and CIO cooperated at the conference of the European Recovery Program unions, differences over the appointment of labor representatives soon appeared. The AFL insisted that its candidate be appointed to the ERP Washington office, which Woll regarded as more important than the one being established in Paris. At the time that this issue arose, the CIO had not yet disaffiliated from the WFTU and Matthew Woll believed that the AFL was entitled to this top job. He believed that the AFL through the top labor office, could exercise an influence on the Marshall Plan, and felt that, "in every avenue of contribution in behalf of the Marshall Plan, on the foreign field, as well as domestic, the AFL has been ahead of the CIO."[33]

Green took up the matter with President Truman and the State Department, and urged that the top labor post should not be assigned to the CIO, in view of its association with the WFTU. In fact, the AFL executive council informed Administrator Paul Hoffman that it would not serve unless the top labor post was given to one of its own appointees.[34] This view was supported by the executive council.

At this time, members of the CIO staff were active in Europe, and had begun to break their ties with the WFTU. But the AFL's position was also influenced by pride of place. Matthew Woll, and others active in the foreign field, believed that the AFL had fought the battle alone, and that it had not only been subjected to attack from the WFTU (which was expected), but also from such journals as *The Economist* in London and *Foreign Affairs* in the United States because it would not join the WFTU. Its membership was also higher than the CIO's. The CIO was a competitor for attention and prestige, and the AFL felt constrained to assert its rights, even while it showed great understanding and generosity toward the views and feelings of European labor leaders.

The London Meeting.

Irving Brown was a *de facto* member of the ERP Trade Union Advisory Committee, and it was he, at the Paris meeting on June 29, 1948, who suggested that the Trade Union Advisory Committee become the official and formal advisory committee to the ERP, and "that we request the appointment of European trade unionists to the ERP machinery."[35] Brown strongly urged that Green and other members of the AFL executive council attend the second trade union conference in London in July since American labor organizations were anxious to stimulate active interest and participation of the European trade unions in the administration of the Marshall Plan.

The American delegation was anxious to have two issues placed on the agenda: (1) The role of America in the reconstruction of Europe; and (2) a labor code for the European reconstruction program. They asked for a meeting with the members of the TUC, prior to the opening of the conference on July 29, to discuss these proposals.[36] Vice Presidents David Dubinsky and George Harrison, with Jay Lovestone as secretary, represented the AFL, and Victor Reuther, Michael Ross, John Grogan, and David McDonald were sent by the CIO. The two delegations had met before and reached agreement on a common approach.

The conference met on July 29-30, 1948, and was attended by forty-five delegates from twenty-five organizations in sixteen countries. Its main problem, as seen by the American delegates, was the inertia of the TUC, and it was decided "to do everything to push the TUC forward."[37] In the event that the TUC remained adamant, the American delegates decided that they would take the initiative. The Americans also wanted the press to be allowed to cover the sessions.[38] Lovestone was directed by the united delegation to prepare "a statement of united American labor policy to be presented to the TUC at the preliminary session." At the prefatory meeting, the British strongly opposed admission of the press to the conference. Moreover, the American delegates found the agenda "rather vague . . . our proposals . . . could be included under certain sections of the items suggested by the TUC." The Americans believed the British "resented our active intervention to make the conference fruitful."[39]

The differences in approach of the Americans and the British were to manifest themselves in future situations. The latter favored a passive policy while the American delegates urged a more activist one. It

> was evident that there were sharp differences of viewpoint. . . . Brothers Harrison and Dubinsky, supported by the CIO, stressed the importance which American labor attaches to the International ERP Conference and to the need for rallying world labor to the energetic support of reconstruction.[40]

There were no differences between the views of the AFL and CIO delegates. Each favored a more aggressive policy and more active participation of the trade unions of Europe in the administrative machinery of the Marshall Plan. Lovestone's report contained several friendly references to the activities of the CIO delegation at the conference. The American delegates were hopeful that the TUC would assume more active leadership on the continent, and encourage resistance to the communist thrust in a number of countries in which that ideology dominated the trade unions.

The difficulty, as seen by some observers, was that American trade union leaders were pressing the British to develop closer economic cooperation with the Western countries on the continent. Such cooperation went beyond the plans of the Labour government then in power, and it was unlikely that the TUC would embark upon a program that would embarrass it. On the other hand, the TUC did not want to see leadership of the European trade union movement shift to the United States. The TUC was, however largely inactive in shoring up the democratic forces within French and Italian trade union movements. In France the AFL supported the CGT *Force Ouvrière* as a rival to the communist dominated CGT, and encouraged a rival to the Italian Confederation of Labor.

Conference with General Clay.

After the London conference, AFL vice presidents Harrison and Dubinsky, and Jay Lovestone, were invited to Berlin by General Clay. Once there, they conferred with eighteen leaders of the Independent Trade Union Organization of Berlin (UGO), and heard complaints against the occupation authorities. These eighteen men had served a total of more than 130 years in Hitler's concentration camps. They expressed gratitude for direct aid in Care food parcels and for interest in the revived trade union movement. The list of grievances was presented to General Clay, who agreed to several requests made by the AFL delegation. Assurances were given that Berlin labor leaders would be given a voice in the determination of ERP policies, that employer-association suggestions on the allocation of raw materials and other supplies would be cleared with the trade unions, and that wages would be unfrozen as prices had already been. General Clay also agreed to accept applications for the return of seized property to the trade unions. Harrison and Dubinsky promised to seek more paper and office supplies so that the unions could carry on their work.

The AFL delegation was satisfied with the outcome of its trip, and reported that the conferences with General Clay would "enhance the solidarity of the bona fide free trade unionists of Germany with the American Federation of

Labor and will strengthen their faith in the American people as a force for democracy and social justice."[41]

At the meeting in Switzerland, which took place in Berne on January 22, 1949, the only issue which aroused a dispute was the candidacy of Walter Schevenels for general secretary of the ERP Trade Union Advisory Committee, which had been put forward by a committee made up of Vincent Tewson, Léon Jouhaux, and Evert Kupers of the Netherlands Confederation of Free Trade Unions. Irving Brown attacked the candidacy as "not acceptable to the AFL." Schevenels was secretary of the WFTU, as he had been of the IFTU before it. While Carey, of the CIO, went along with Schevenels' candidacy on the theory that this appointment was a European matter and did not concern organizations in the United States, Brown refused to approve. In Brown's opinion, "the British intend to consolidate their hold on the European organization. . . . This is why they insist on Schevenels who is their choice and agent."[42] The AFL supported Brown's position and refused to cooperate with Schevenels — as long as he remained in office, the AFL would not meet its contributions.[43] A compromise was worked out.

Toward a Free Trade Union International.

One of the advantages of the ERP meetings was that they gave the Western trade unions an opportunity to meet and discuss the problems facing their countries. Inevitably, the issue of a permanent international came under discussion. After the Berne meeting, a "private conference" on a new international was held. A liaison committee made up of representatives from the British, Italians, French, Dutch, the CIO and the AFL was established. Arthur Deakin, head of the British Transport and General Workers Union and one of the more powerful leaders in the TUC, was to discuss the possibilities during a forthcoming trip to the United States.[44]

The AFL executive council applauded the severance of the free trade unions from the WFTU. It declared that it had "opposed the WFTU as a communist dominated agency dedicated to the task of serving Soviet totalitarianism and its imperialistic aggression."[45] It called for the joining of organizations in the Western democracies in an international, and maintained that it was

> sheerest folly to combine into one international federation the free trade unions with the state controlled company unions like those in Russia and her satellite lands. The AFL has repeatedly warned and the record of the WFTU has amply confirmed the soundness of our warning that such a combination only prevents the trade unions in the democratic countries from playing their rightful role in world affairs.[46]

American Labor and the Recovery Program.

Both the AFL and the CIO actively supported the European Recovery Program. In the CIO, endorsement of the program became one of the major causes of a split within its ranks. In mid-1950, the CIO began to demand that emphasis be placed on raising the standard of living of workers in the nations receiving aid, stating that economic rehabilitation was not enough. "Direct improvement in real wages of European workers and their families, and to strengthen the democratic alternative to the propaganda promises of the communist movement" were major demands by the CIO. Its detailed suggestions for improving foreign aid programs so that they would reach workers and farmers were presented.[47]

The AFL found the recovery achieved by the ERP in Western Europe "amazing." Yet the 1950 report of the executive council sounded a note of disappointment. It found signs of "leveling-off" in productivity gains, and decided that European integration, which the AFL strongly urged, was being "frustrated by the political and social obstacles as well as the maze of traditional trade barriers which form a restrictive web across Europe."[48] The AFL noted, however, that a number of favorable developments which might in the future lead to closer economic cooperation had taken place.

In succeeding conventions, the views of the AFL and CIO followed the same pattern. There was little difference even in emphasis, although there sometimes were disputes over patronage. As the two federations moved toward unification in 1955, their views on foreign relations showed virtually no difference: criticism of communism and the Soviet Union was as sharp in the CIO as in the AFL. They both supported rises in the standards of living of European workers and the Point Four program, which sought to aid underdeveloped nations economically. The CIO was

in full support of the expanded campaign of the Economic Cooperation Administration to raise the standards of living of European workers by increasing productivity under conditions which will assure an equitable distribution of the benefits. In view of the past record of most European employers we believe that the only way to ensure that workers get an equitable share of improvements lies through the activity of strong democratic trade unions.[49]

The AFL emphasized the same view and noted that

the defense of the democratic way of life cannot be secured by armaments alone. The efforts of the Marshall Plan to improve the standards of living in European nations so that the benefits of economic and political democracy can be enjoyed by all those who are called upon to defend it must be re-emphasized.[50]

Point Four.

The 1949 convention of the CIO welcomed President Truman's program of providing technical assistance and declared that it should be accompanied by "assistance to the workers so that mechanical modernization of industry will be matched by the modernization of workers' rights."[51] The AFL laid down a nine-point program to be followed in giving aid to underdeveloped areas, calling for demonstration by words and deeds that the desire to aid was not motivated by a desire to oppress or to seize special privileges. Aided or recipient countries were to be encouraged to develop suitable projects: "There should be no interference in each other's domestic affairs or political life and no infringement or violation of their respective sovereignities." The other suggestions urged that democratic forces within the recipient countries should be strengthened, and that "the dominant control and principal ownership of important projects should be placed in the hands of the country aided in accord with the economic forms its own people democratically determined, so as to avoid the evils of absentee-ownership."[52]

After the communist victory on the mainland of China, the AFL executive council underscored the "great urgency of speeding up the application of 'Point Four' policies in the non-communist areas and countries of Asia." It asked for aid for India in overcoming its immediate food difficulties, and for an American "initiative in the World Bank for a loan to speed the development of an agricultural expansion service in India."[53] Both the CIO and the AFL stressed the necessity for labor representation on the administrative units managing these programs. They believed that by developing democratically led and administered trade unions, a source of ability and strength would be developed. In this regard the two federations spoke as one, as they did about many other matters.

Mutual Security: The Atlantic Pact.

In a statement to European workers, William Green, president of the AFL, endorsed on behalf of the AFL the North Atlantic Pact "and its implementation through the Military Defense Assistance Program. American labor is united in the desire to see the free nations of Western Europe recover prosperity, stability and strength."[54] The CIO supported

the Atlantic Pact as a necessary defense measure for Western Europe against Soviet threats of aggression. We reaffirm our devotion to peace and reject as absurd the charge of war-mongering against our country. We believe that democracies must take the necessary defense measures against the dangers which threaten them.[55]

In its report to the 1950 convention, the AFL executive council noted that the foreign ministers of twelve countries had signed a defensive pact as a result of a "common peril." It described briefly the aim and functioning of this agreement as a necessary defense for democratic nations.[56] In reviewing the defense posture of the United States in the following year, the AFL executive council declared: "Reliance on pacts with Franco, Perón and similar dictators must be rejected as weakening the unity of the democratic world. . . ."[57] In a statement to the United States Senate in March 1949, Matthew Woll, speaking for the AFL International Labor Relations Committee, had urged "prompt and favorable Senate action in the interest of world democracy, recovery and peace."

America and the rest of mankind [said Woll] are not facing or fighting an obnoxious theory. We are facing an over-awing condition and cruel challenge. . . . The AFL believes that the only time to prevent war is before it breaks out. The AFL believes that it is far better to prevent a war than even to win it most decisively.

History has taught us that the best way to defeat aggression is to deter it. Only the active and permanent cooperation of free peoples — armed with unshakeable determination and unbeatable power to maintain freedom and peace — can be strong enough to deter aggression, to prevent war, to preserve human dignity and liberty and to assure peace.[58]

Slave labor.

Reports of an extensive network of slave labor camps reached the Western countries in the 1930s. The reports were denied by the Soviet government and denounced by its Western supporters as slander. But these systems did exist, and spread to the satellite countries after World War II. Based upon the testimony of refugees and former inmates of the forced labor camps, the AFL in March 1947 denounced "this expanding system of slave labor" as "a dire threat to the free workers of all countries."[59]

Through Matthew Woll and David Dubinsky, AFL consultants to the United Nations, the AFL had submitted, on November 24, 1947, a request to the Economic and Social Council of the United Nations that it "make a survey of the extent of forced labor in all member nations of the United Nations."[60] Not until March 1949 were preliminary steps taken for an inquiry. The debate was opened by Willard Thorpe, U.S. representative to the Economic and Social Council, who said that "slavery represents an intolerable form of human degradation . . . completely at variance with the objectives and standards of human rights so clearly defined in the United Nations Charter."[61]

Miss Toni Sender, assistant to the AFL consultants, said:

The American Federation of Labor has received testimony from persons who have succeeded in escaping from the hell of slave labor camps; testimony which contains accusations of such a nature that no one can read these statements without the deepest feeling of horror and pity. . . . The reliability of these statements mentioned is demonstrated in the fact that all these persons, although unknown to each other, describe the cruel circumstances in similar terms. In great detail they describe the use of political opponents, of stateless persons, and of prisoners of war for forced labor. These people are kept in concentration camps after having been torn from their families and deported, undergoing the most harsh, often cruel, treatment. . . .[62]

The AFL presented affidavits from former inmates of Soviet concentration camps, and demonstrated that the system had spread beyond the borders of the Soviet Union. On March 7, 1949, two years after the issuance of the AFL manifesto attacking this monstrous system, the U.N. Economic and Social Council decided — despite the efforts of the Soviet representatives, assisted by members of other iron curtain countries — "to transmit the memorandum of the American Federation of Labor and the records of the Council's discussions on the subject to the Commission on Human Rights for consideration in connection with the drafting of the Covenant on Human Rights."[63]

It required two more years before the Economic and Social Council, acting with the International Labor Office, approved the United States resolution despite the bitter opposition of the Soviet delegate, who stated that the inquiry by a "small committee composed of so-called independent individuals," would be "an instrument of propaganda and slander against the USSR." The committee examined evidence and documents, and requested statements from governments.

The Soviet Union was on the defensive. The AFL representative said that "one of the essential features of the

forced labor system in the USSR was that forced labor was
inflicted on so-called class-hostile elements as well as on the
so-called unstable elements among workers because they
disagreed with the regime in power." The federation was in
possession of

> "a strictly secret document" showing the categories of
> persons deported from the Baltic countries and sent to
> concentration camps: The categories included "persons
> who had occupied prominent positions in the civil or
> communal services ... prominent members of the
> anti-communist parties, social democrats, liberals, small
> farmers, active members of Jewish organizations ...
> mystics, such as freemasons and theosophists, industrial-
> ists, wholesale merchants, owners of large houses, ship
> owners, owners of hotels and restaurants, persons who
> have been in the diplomatic service, permanent repre-
> sentatives of foreign commercial firms, [and] relatives of
> persons who have escaped abroad." Thus it was a crime
> to belong to certain professions or to be related to a
> person who had been successful in escaping to a free
> country.[64]

At one of the sessions, the representative of the United
States said that the American government had come into
possession of an official economic plan, "which had been
confidential," and which

> gave a clear picture of the part played by forced labor in
> the economic life of the Soviet Union in 1941. He cited
> data from the Plan showing that the NKVD — the
> People's Commissariat of Internal Affairs, which had
> administered the prison labor — had been assigned more
> than 14 percent of capital construction during that year,
> mainly in the fields of mining, logging camps and
> military and railroad construction. There were indica-
> tions that in addition the NKVD had farmed out some

of its forced labor for projects financed by other commissariats, so that the actual percentage of capital construction by means of forced labor was even higher.[65]

The AFL gave details on the use of forced labor in the Soviet Union. Based upon confidential information, its representative claimed:

In all the plans, the share of the NKVD in industrial production was greatly underestimated in terms of rubles. The NKVD probably supplied the cheapest labor because it paid only very low salaries and provided no social services. Forced labor projects under NKVD control supplied one-eighth of the total timber production, 10 percent of all furniture and kitchenware production and 40 percent of the total chrome production of the USSR since 1938; 75 percent of the gold production had been the result of forced labor. The Komi Republic was almost entirely in the hands of the MVD.[66]

These charges were supported by the International Confederation of Free Trade Unions. The AFL representative submitted a photostatic copy of the regulations of one of the forced labor camps, and said it "could thus be seen that subnormal diet for the laborers was at a starvation level."[67] Representatives of the International Confederation of Free Trade Unions charged:

Heavy work, systematic starvation, disease and insufficient medical care, lack of protection against work accidents and harsh climate brought in their wake an extremely high death rate in the Soviet concentration camps ... However, it is not only slow death which menaces the inmates of Soviet concentration camps. On several occasions Soviet prisoner camps have been the scene of mass assassination of the defenseless victims of the Soviet regime. In 1937-1938, about 1,300 political prisioners . . . were executed in the brick plant of the Vorkuta Camp on orders of an NKVD troika. . . .[68]

The Soviet Union and its satellites, and representatives of the World Federation of Trade Unions replied to the allegations. According to their representatives,

it was a gross libel to insinuate that forced labor existed in the Soviet Union. The slanderous campaign waged by the United Kingdom and the United States of America at the instance of the American Federation of Labor was devoid of all foundation. The documents submitted to the Council as evidence by those who made the allegations were inadequate, defamatory, tendentious and inaccurate.[69]

The Soviet Union used its customary tactics of answering charges by claiming that they were false and the products of fascists and the American and English intelligence services. "The evidence supplied by the American Federation of Labor could be dismissed at once as tainted," was the Soviet answer.

It was not a successful maneuver, for it failed to placate Western public opinion. In fact, the Economic and Social Council of the United Nations voted for another inquiry into slave labor in the Eastern socialist countries. Although these conditions were widely known among Western liberals, among others, it was only the perseverance of the AFL which brought such a monstrous institution to the attention of the world.

CHAPTER SIX

The International Confederation of Free Trade Unions

Beginning.

The AFL waged a relentless struggle against the World Federation of Trade Unions (WFTU), and it eventually achieved, or at least greatly contributed to, the departure of free trade union centers from its ranks. However, if the vacuum created by the dissolution of the International Federation of Trade Unions (IFTU) was to be filled, and the democratic labor organizations were to be unified and able to defend themselves on the international plane, a new organization embracing democratic trade union federations had to be constructed.[1] Veteran trade unionists recognized the need for such an organization, and the British Foreign Minister, Ernest Bevin, in a letter to David Dubinsky, expressed the hope that the "democratic trade unions of all countries would pool their resources and join their forces in the protection and promotion of their welfare and liberties."[2]

The AFL executive council took note of the situation and, in a statement in February 1949, endorsed the discussions then being conducted for the formation of a new international. Arthur Deakin, head of the British Transport and General Workers Union, and Victor Tewson, secretary of the

British Trades Union Congress, visited the United States in March in connection with the proposed joint Anglo-American productivity committees, and discussed the forming of an international trades union center with both the AFL and the CIO. It was agreed that the CIO would participate in the founding of the new international as a full and equal member. In accordance with this agreement, the British Trades Union Congress convened the preparatory conference in Geneva on June 25, 1949. The CIO sent Secretary-Treasurer James Carey, John Brophy, Elmer Cope, and Michael Ross; the AFL delegates were George Meany, Irving Brown, and George P. Delaney.[3]

The Geneva conference.

The conference elected Arthur Deakin chairman and rapporteur. The delegates recognized the need for collaboration of the free unions of the world, and appointed a preparatory committee to draft a constitution and program for the international trade union organization which they hoped would emerge from their labors.[4] They expected that the new international would embrace all the free trade unions of the world and establish close ties with the international trade union secretariats.

The preparatory committee was directed to convene, as early as possible, a world trade union conference for establishing a new international federation to handle the needs of newly established unions in underdeveloped areas, and to devise a plan for their assistance. The international was also to aid trade unions in the war-devastated areas so that they might participate in the rebuilding of the war-ravaged economies and at the same time promote policies which aimed at full employment and the protection of workers' rights.[5]

Small differences.

Inevitably, the proposed constitution and bylaws aroused debate. AFL President Green suggested thirty changes, mostly in language and emphasis. More serious disagreement arose over regional organizations. The Trades Union Congress (TUC) believed that these entities should be under the jurisdiction of the planned international, and the AFL favored allowing the national centers to promote regional federations. These differences were not unduly serious, however, and the conference opened as scheduled in London, on November 29, 1949. It remained in session until December 6. Billed as the "Free Labor Conference," an apt and accurate name, it ended as the first session of the International Confederation of Free Trade Unions. Its sessions were attended by representatives from 59 trade union centers in 53 countries with a membership of over 48 million. In addition to the AFL and the CIO, the United Mine Workers of America, which had seceded from the AFL in 1947, was represented.

The AFL sent William Green, George Meany, Matthew Woll, George Harrison, David Dubinsky, and several others. These men were the most knowledgeable and active in foreign affairs. CIO delegates were Walter Reuther and David J. McDonald, heads of the CIO's two largest unions, along with Allan Haywood, the executive vice president of the CIO.

The launching of the new international.

In opening the trade union conference, Arthur Deakin emphasized the differences between a free trade union and one controlled by a private employer or a government. He described the latter as "a State 'stooge' Association," and he saw no reason why the genuine free trade unions should seek the cooperation of such organizations. He argued that the state unions were not free agents; they could not defy the decisions of their governments, and were therefore powerless to compel the acceptance by their government employer of policies which it opposed. "Therefore," he said, "in the sheer logic of the matter, we must restrict our association to bona fide trade union bodies."[6]

In obvious anticipation of criticism, Deakin noted that the modern trade union might deal with a variety of employers — individuals, private associations, or governments. However, the basic requirement was that the trade union be free and autonomous, irrespective of the parties with which it dealt or to which it was related. It must manage its own affairs, choose its officers, and set its own rules. Free trade unions must carry on, and be "responsible for," their own negotiations and not depend upon instructions from employers or a political party for their programs. Free trade unions were not dependent upon governments for the right to carry on their activities, nor did government decide the area or the manner in which they would function. The test of a *bona fide* union was its freedom from interference of employers or government. Such freedom extended to the right of the union to criticize the government, and even to seek to change or abolish it by legal and constitutional means.[7]

First reactions.

Both the AFL and the CIO enthusiastically welcomed the formation of the new international. The AFL hailed it as of "inestimable significance in the history of world labor."[8] It saw in the ICFTU an institution which could assist the working people of the world in their striving for economic security and a better life. It was especially pleased by the high degree of unity which had been achieved by delegates from widely diverse social and economic backgrounds. For the CIO, the new international labor federation was an effective instrument for spreading the gospel and the practice of free trade unionism throughout the world.[9] Committees to devise methods of financing the organization, and to deal with staff problems, met in Brussels on January 17 and 18, 1950; the discussions were amicable. Both Irving Brown of the AFL and Elmer Cope of the CIO served on the interim finance committee.[10]

The next meeting of the committee, on March 16-18, 1950, was described as an "emergency meeting." Most of the discussions were routine — on finance and appointments. The meeting reached no decision on regional organization. The Greek trade union situation came under discussion, and Irving Brown's report, written after his visit there with Elmer Cope, was considered. The meeting agreed to send a representative to Greece immediately to aid the Greek Confederation of Labor.[11] Some friction developed over the appointment to the office in Singapore. Matthew Woll requested that an American delegate be invited to attend the meeting for the purpose of forming an Asian regional conference, basing his request upon the fact that Victor Tewson, secretary of the TUC, had been invited to attend a meeting in Mexico City to set up a regional organization of workers. While such differences in treatment were not always important, they showed a tendency to slight the Americans.[12] The Americans were also inclined to follow an anti-colonial line which occasionally brought them into conflict with delegates from home countries. For example, the Americans "insisted upon supporting those elements in Algeria and Morocco who are fighting for the right of free trade union association. (This is the point of conflict with our French friends.)"[13]

Consultants to the United Nations.

A more serious source of difficulty was the mixup concerning consultants to the UN. Although the issue was settled amicably, President Green and Vice Presidents Dubinsky and Woll threatened to resign as consultants for the ICFTU. It was President Green, who had been ignored in the making of appointments, who pleaded with Woll and Dubinsky to "see if we may find a way by which . . . the situation which you reported in your letter can be adjusted." Green asked that the resignations of the consultants be held in abeyance while efforts to solve the differences were made.[14]

Despite these minor conflicts, the American labor movement was pleased by the results of the ICFTU Milan Congress, held in the summer of 1951, and believed that significant progress had been made. The membership gain of several millions and the acceptance of George Meany's views on totalitarianism were favorably regarded. The AFL believed that the ICFTU was moving in the right direction.[15] In their report to the 1951 convention, the CIO officers commended the ICFTU for its "forthright opposition to all forms of oppression, for its unqualified stand against Soviet-Communist aggression and against resurgence of reactionary pro-fascist forces."[16]

There was, however, growing discord. The AFL had agreed not to accept the posts of chairman or reporter of committees, while the CIO had not. There was also a division within the American delegation over the election of Vincent Tewson as president, a post controlled by the executive committee. The AFL was against large power domination and believed that Tewson's election would not help the ICFTU in colonial areas, but the CIO believed the decision of the executive committee should not be overruled.[17] The self-denying attitude of the AFL can be regarded as a sentimental carryover, for such a policy inevitably places administrative control in the hands of small-power representatives. There is no evidence that such people are wiser or more devoted than nationals of the big powers, and subsequent events showed the danger of this self-denying view triggered by fear of British domination.

Financial Support. Another problem was the attempt to raise $700,000 in the next three years to finance ICFTU regional activities. The AFL executive council declined to contribute, and this decision received widespread coverage in the London press. By the time of the Milan Congress the British had already donated $300,000 to that fund. The report to the AFL suggested that the internationals might be of "some assistance to the ICFTU in this campaign to raise funds for our world-wide regional activities."[18] It appeared that a studied campaign had been launched to compel the AFL to discontinue its independent activities on the international level. Brown believed that the AFL should consider merging its activities with the ICFTU or, as he put it, "develop our international activities more and more within the framework of the ICFTU."[19] The CIO donated $100,000 for the organization of workers in undeveloped areas.

Division also developed on the admission of the *Unione Italiana del Lavoro* (UIL) to the ICFTU, with the AFL in opposition. The AFL's position was based on the feeling that the UIL should merge with the *Confederazione Italiana Sindacata Lavoratori* (CISL), thus creating a strong opposition to the dominance of the trade union movement by the communists. The UIL was accepted by a vote of 9 to 3. Another source of dispute arose over the refusal of the ICFTU to accept the affiliation of the Australian Workers Union, a militant anti-communist trade union center. The position on Yugoslavia was a third source of difference.

George Meany favored conditional support of Yugoslavia.[20] Economic aid, the AFL believed, should be provided, but Tito should be asked to give up his claim to Trieste, cease assisting guerrillas in Greece, and cancel his plans for a Balkan federation. The AFL was not enamored of Tito's brand of communism, but believed that Yugoslavia's geography and resources made it a minor menace to freedom as compared to the Soviet leviathan.

At the meetings of the AFL executive council in May and August 1951, donation to the ICFTU was considered, and opposition was expressed because of low per capita income.

Seeking an understanding.

These differences caused serious concern to both the AFL and the CIO. In an effort to eliminate friction, Vincent Tewson and J. H. Oldenbroek conferred with the International Labor Relations Committee of the AFL. John Owen and Secretary-Treasurer Thomas Kennedy, of the United Mine Workers of America, were also in attendance. Victor Tewson recalled three-and-a-half years of visits leading to "common understanding" following the breakup of the WFTU. "Today," said Tewson, "we are both in one International and should attempt to overcome differences. This is the feeling of the TUC International Committee."[21]

The meeting was an outspoken one. Staff people were silent; only principals spoke. Green asked that differences be discussed openly, without recriminations. Meany presented the complaints of the American Federation of Labor. He recalled Arthur Deakin's insistence that the AFL give up its opposition to the inclusion of the CIO, and that the AFL agree "despite strenuous objections of President Green. We made all concessions and efforts to have a real International."[22] Meany objected to the domination of the ICFTU by the TUC (which the TUC denied) and raised a question on the handling of a number of reports by Walter Schevenels, an assistant secretary of the ICFTU. His final complaint was: "We don't want to be in a situation in which no matter what we bring up it is defeated under TUC leadership. We want to be partners. Britain is not just one member but is running the show. We want to be consulted."[23] Meany said that the AFL would remain in the ICFTU, but would not cooperate as long as the attitude towards the Americans remained the same. He also noted that the CIO and the United Mine Workers of America wanted to be consulted. Meany complained vehemently of the treatment of the Cypriot delegation — a "little matter for Europeans, but to us a basic question" — charging that "Europeans don't have our concept of underdog and fair play."[24]

Thomas Kennedy explained that the United Mine Workers of America had stayed out of the WFTU because it was dominated by communists, and that his organization agreed with the AFL on the ICFTU. At a recess, the AFL members agreed that they must work in the ICFTU, and Meany said: "No danger of withdrawing, we are fighting inside ICFTU."[25] At the reconvening of the conference, Harrison reviewed the views and activities of the AFL in foreign relations, and noted:

> You realize that we feel we have been appendages and not partners; that British have consciously or unconsciously dominated. Scandinavians and Europeans in general follow British . . . British are leaders and others look to you.[26]

Meany expressed the same views. He said: "We begin with premise ICFTU run by British. We want to be partners. We want to be in the picture." Harrison added: "It's psychological. We want to be consulted. Meany feels AFL has been left out. TUC makes up its mind and all the chickens get into the coop. This is our picture of the ICFTU today." Tewson said: "Purpose of my visit here is that there should be cooperation. We want full partnership with AFL." Meany added: "Hopeful differences will be cleared in near future and we can take our place in ICFTU."[27]

Some of the differences, such as the affiliation of the *Unione Italiana del Lavoro* were transitory; others, if not permanent, tended to reappear. Some might be regarded as inevitable, reflecting the outlook and experience and even the geography of national centers. Despite the internationalism of many Europeans, they were more tolerant of colonial activities. Organized labor in the United States was raised in an anticolonial tradition and favored freedom for all nations. Europeans were also more friendly to Tito and his brand of communism than was the AFL. Yet the AFL was anxious to stay in the ICFTU and cooperate. In its report to the 1952 convention, the AFL executive council said:

> We shall continue to be a most active affiliate and shall seek to meet and clear up any differences, which may arise, within the ranks and through the ICFTU organization channels. . . . The AFL is determined to continue its policy of doing everything within its power to build the ICFTU into an even stronger, better and more effective world organization of free labor. . . .[28]

In contrast to the AFL, the CIO was more than satisfied with the work of the ICFTU. Its delegates participated in the Berlin meeting of the ICFTU general council, to which the AFL had not sent representatives. It concluded that "the ICFTU General Council meeting adhered to the spirit and hopes of the organization for promoting trade union strength, without particular political bias."[29] The CIO's fourteenth convention stressed the view that the ICFTU was "going ahead with its tasks," and, in an obvious slap at the AFL, called attention to the ICFTU's work in underdeveloped areas, stating that the "American trade union movement had a special responsibility to participate in this work and last year the CIO acknowledged this responsibility by a substantial contribution."[30]

In 1953 the CIO and AFL both showed satisfaction with the work of the ICFTU. There was only one difference between the two American federations. At the resignation of Paul Finet as president of the ICFTU, the executive committee appointed Victor Tewson of the TUC in his place. In accordance with its views that the representative of a big-power nation should not head the ICFTU, the AFL refused to approve and abstained from voting. The CIO agreed with the principle that the large national federations should not over-use their power, but disapproved of vetoing the action of the executive committee.[31] As noted earlier, there was no basis in logic or experience for the AFL's attitude. Experience fails to show that representatives of small countries are more farsighted or magnanimous. Publically, the AFL was friendly and cooperative, but privately there was some criticism of inactivity in Eastern Europe and in the underdeveloped areas.[32]

The AFL and CIO merger.

At the time of the merger, in 1955, the attitudes and policies of the two federations did not differ greatly. At most, the differences were in emphasis and over minor issues. Their resolution on the ICFTU, in 1955, was an endorsement of its purposes and efforts. The organization was called upon to extend and to strengthen its work in promoting economic interests "as well as the larger aspirations of labor."[33] The convention urged a program to prevent successful communist efforts at infiltration and subversion of free trade unions, and hoped that the ICFTU would play an effective role in aiding the working people of underdeveloped countries to establish strong free labor organizations.[34] 3

New sources of differences.

While relationships between the AFL-CIO and the ICFTU remained friendly, new differences between the organizations emerged. In 1965, reviewing the prospects of the ICFTU, President George Meany was highly laudatory of its past performance, but not completely satisfied with current activities or with the tendency among some of the affiliates to exchange visits with unions in the iron curtain countries. Meany gave high praise to the ICFTU's efforts to thwart the communists' campaign to dominate the labor movements of Western Europe during the cold war. "The Communists," said Meany, had "lost the battle for Western Europe."[35]

Their defeat, he belived, was in large measure the result of the free trade unions' refusal to have any dealings with the pseudo labor organizations behind the iron curtain. Meany also praised the ICFTU campaign, originally initiated by the AFL, against slave labor. Eventually the campaign led to the adoption of an ILO convention against forced labor, and the abandonment of its use on a mass scale.

Another plus cited by Meany was the moral and financial assistance provided by the ICFTU to unions in the colonial areas. He, nevertheless, noted that the ICFTU had not adapted itself to challenges in the newly established countries. Greater organizational support and educational and training programs were needed. The new unions were short of officers and administrators, and Meany urged that the ICFTU should develop programs to help supply them. Staffs for consumer and producer cooperatives and credit unions should also be trained.

Fraternization with the labor organizations of iron curtain countries.

The AFL-CIO believed that the ICFTU had not shown sufficient vigor in discouraging exchanges between unions in the free world and those in the Soviet Union and its satellite countries. Even more serious was the admittance of communist unions to the international secretariats. From 1955 to the present, the executive board and subcommittee of the ICFTU have issued decisions against "affiliated organizations . . . having relations with trade union organizations in communist ruled countries and communist controlled organizations in other countries."[36] Despite admonitions, some affiliates had ignored these suggestions and exchanged visits with delegations from the Soviet countries without protest from the ICFTU.

American labor's attitude toward dealing with communist trade unions.

The attitude of the AFL-CIO toward dealing with unions in the iron curtain countries was not new. It was not a policy devised by George Meany or suggested by Jay Lovestone. Nor was it based upon the views assumed by a leading American scholar of international labor.[37]

The old AFL believed that the labor movement of each country should decide its own philosophy and tactics. As long as labor organizations were free from controls of government or the private employer, collaboration between organizations of different countries for common purposes was desirable. There was, however, no point in collaborating with organizations which did not have the power to decide their own policies, and which were in fact organs of the state. Basing itself upon these principles, the AFL had informed Walter Citrine, the head of the IFTU, in 1938, that admission of the Soviet trade unions to membership would lead to the AFL's withdrawal. In 1942, the British sought to persuade the AFL to join the wartime Anglo-Soviet Trade Union Committee, and despite pressure from the Roosevelt administration, the AFL refused.

History can establish the age of a policy but may not be an unerring guide to its continuance. The question is then whether the status and role of trade unions in the iron curtain countries have changed sufficiently to warrant a different approach by the AFL-CIO. George Meany does not believe that the unions of the free world can learn anything about trade unions from the Soviet organizations, and that permitting communist unions to join the international secretariats is opening labor organizations and countries of the free world to manipulation and subversion.

It is a fact of life that unions in the Soviet Union and its satellite countries do not deal with the major problems that concern unions in the West. They do not conduct strikes or boycotts; neither do they negotiate wages, working conditions, or fringe benefits. They cannot defy the government employer or demonstrate against the rules. They cannot, as the English have on occasion, resort to slowdowns. Nor can they engage in the several thousand annual stoppages called by workers in the United States. They are not independent and cannot devise policies for their members without the approval of their governments. They are in fact controlled by the government, which can instantaneously change their programs and officers. On January 15, 1970, Ignacy Loga-Sowinski was replaced as Poland's union chief, with other union officials suffering a similar fate.[38] The unions in iron curtain countries perform a number of functions, but so did the company unions of the United States in the pre-Wagner Law days. They are active in administering social security and factory canteens, but these are not the important activities of unions in the West.

Unions in communist countries can make no commitments to seek changes by pressuring their governments. Whether these changes would affect domestic or international problems, unions of the iron curtain countries still cannot take any independent position. The AFL-CIO, British Trades Union Congress, or German Labor Federation all can agree to a policy irrespective of the view of the home government. In fact, they frequently attack the conduct of their governments at home and abroad. No such option exists for a union in Poland, Czechoslovakia, the Soviet Union, or the other communist countries. Cooperation with them only allows intrusion into the affairs of labor organizations and countries of the West on behalf of communist policies. The experience with the Anglo-Russian Trade Union Committee in the 1920s, and the WFTU after World War II, should have demonstrated that collaboration between free and controlled unions was not possible, but such problems are never fully solved; new men and old illusions.

Withdrawal from the ICFTU.
Differences are inevitable in a federation in which the affiliates come from diverse national backgrounds and are subject to varying pressures from their memberships and from public opinion. These facts were recognized by the AFL-CIO, which fought for its own views but accepted decisions of the majority. Its withdrawal from the ICFTU was over a different issue, one which involved interference by the ICFTU in an internal dispute.

In the spring of 1968, the United Automobile Workers of America (UAW), following a lengthy dispute between it and the AFL-CIO, stopped paying its per capita tax and was automatically suspended at the end of three months. On July 1, 1968, the UAW informed the AFL-CIO that it had withdrawn from the federation.[39] Even before the UAW had formally separated, the general secretary of the ICFTU solicited an application for affiliation of the UAW with the ICFTU. The AFL-CIO, which had a direct interest in this matter, was not informed. Subsequently, President Meany was told of the contemplated application of the UAW, and was requested not to oppose it.

The AFL-CIO executive council regarded this as interference in the internal affairs of an affiliate. It was not inclined to engage in a quarrel, but strongly believed that the action of the general secretary made affiliation insupportable.[40] The federation paid its dues up through February, 1969. It requested that the UAW's application be rejected, but the ICFTU tabled the application until early in 1969, when it was refused.

Separation from the international free trade union movement was regrettable. While the AFL-CIO might have been demanding, it had sought to make the ICFTU an effective organization on the international level. Separatism is undesirable from the AFL-CIO point of view as well as from that of the rest of world labor.[41] With the rise of isolationism and trade restrictions, the chances for antagonism are increased and the longer the division persists, the more difficult reunion becomes.

There have always been forces in the American labor movement which favored isolationism. Such sentiment is on the rise again, and the American labor movement will not remain unaffected for long. In contrast to the withdrawal from direct affiliation with European labor in the 1920s, the provocation this time was very great. No self-respecting labor movement can allow itself to be humiliated and undermined by a federation which it, in fact, started. The arrogance of Europeans, as well as their rigidity in international matters, will not be vindicated by past experience. They might recall that the AFL warned against the WFTU, an association the free unions soon regretted. Irrespective of where the blame for the AFL-CIO withdrawal may lie, reunification of the international free labor movement is essential to the democratic world and to the advancement of trade unionism in underdeveloped areas.

CHAPTER SEVEN

France, Italy, Greece and Spain

WITH THE ENDING of the war in Europe, the American labor movement was called upon to morally and materially help the labor movements (or minorities within them) in a number of European countries. Irving Brown, who had visited several of these countries, expressed the view that the trade union federations of France and Italy were under communist control, but that support should be given to minorities, who might be able to carve out a place for themselves in both of those countries. He advised that the labor movement in Greece was led by non-communists who should be supported since a strong communist bloc was determined to seize her trade unions as instruments in the struggle for power. The communist putsch had been repelled but free trade unions were struggling against serious obstacles, and their plight warranted the assistance of the AFL. Spain was in a somewhat different position. No free trade unions functioned in that country, having been destroyed by the Franco dictatorship, with many of their leaders driven into exile. In this country, American labor could only join in occasional protests against the conduct of the regime and offer aid to the exiles who still hoped to challenge the dictator.

France.

The French trade union movement had a long and colorful history. From the beginning there was a struggle between two factions — one which favored political action, and one which placed major emphasis on gaining economic concessions. Leaders and writers supported the second group; they espoused a body of doctrine codified at the Congress of Amiens in 1906. Revolutionary syndicalism attracted a group of intellectuals who were certain that, armed with the simplest syndicalist philosophy, workers could lead bourgeois society out of its decadence, exploitation, and injustice. This heroic phase was not long-lived; by 1914 the movement was spent.

Divisions within labor's ranks following World War I led to a formal split, with the communists establishing a rival federation. The organizations operated simultaneously until the Popular Front in 1934; their merger was designed to strengthen anti-facist forces in the face of enveloping totalitarianism from the Right. This revived federation, after the war, came under complete control of the communists.

The wisdom of supporting a democratic opposition to the control exercised by communists over the trade union movement of France was clearly visible when the Confederation of Labor led a series of crippling political strikes in October and November of 1947. Intended as a blow to the French economy, they failed to attain their objective and stimulated the formation of a competing trade union center, the *CGT Force Ouvrière*. The new organization came into the world with few resources and many needs and responsibilities. The AFL was asked for financial assistance to help defray some of the costs of establishing the non-communist labor confederation and also for its going expenses. Green asked Vice Presidents George Harrison and David Dubinsky to meet with Léon Jouhaux, the old militant syndicalist of

Gompers' time, whose organization had been taken over by the communists, and ascertain its needs. Jouhaux asked for a loan of $35,000, an amount sufficient to carry the organization for the next four months.

Heavy initial costs had been incurred in resisting the furious attacks of the *Force Ouvrière's* communist rival. Funds were also needed to finance its field activities, the publishing of its journal, and the issuance of other propaganda materials. Harrison doubted whether the funds would be repaid, but he believed the federation had sufficient interest in a free European trade union movement to provide the funds even if the possibility of repayment did not exist.[1] Harrison supported the loan at the meeting of the executive council,[2] and Green was of the opinion that "even though we may never be repaid . . . nevertheless, we will render a great international service by supplying the amount of money requested."[3] The AFL gave $25,000[4] and, at Dubinsky's suggestion, the International Ladies Garment Workers Union advanced $5,000, an amount also contributed by the Free Trade Union Committee.[5]

The battle for the ports.

If intervention through assistance could ever be justified, the battle for the ports of France demonstrated that the AFL's actions in the support of a democratic trade union movement were both wise and imperative. For even though the *Force Ouvrière* never became the predominant labor federation in France — it shared minority status with the Christian Labor Federation — its role in the battle for the ports, in 1948-49, would more than justify the support given to it by American labor. Since the fall of 1947, the communist dominated CGT had sought to enlist the French longshoremen and seamen in a campaign of disorganization of the French economy, to undermine the Marshall Plan and prevent the preliminary stages of the Atlantic Pact. The communists hoped, through their control of officers of local unions in both the port and maritime industries, to block shipments of food and arms from the United States in any way possible.

However, not a single vessel was held up, even though dockers who followed the orders of their communist unions left their jobs. Attention concentrated on France's main ports, with Marseille a prime target. The communists failed not only in Marseille but everywhere else, including Cherbourg, the port chosen by the French government for unloading of the first arms shipment from the United States. Neither the longshoremen nor the seamen followed the communist directives. A later attempt, in the spring of 1950, to paralyze the ports also failed. Although the *Force Ouvrière* was not able to wrest majority status from the communist dominated French Labor Confederation, its influence in the postwar period was critical in frustrating a communist assault on the Marshall Plan.[6]

The refusal of the miners' union in England to support the "sabotage" walkouts of the French became an internal source of controversy. A special committee investigating the dispute noted: "The communist leaders of the French took advantage of the admittedly unsatisfactory conditions in the French coal mining industry to sabotage the European Recovery Program."[7] The report quoted the statement of A. A. Zdanov, Politboro member of the Communist Party of the Soviet Union, that it was the duty of communists to lead the "resistance to the American plan. . . ."[8] In slightly veiled language, Stalin's lieutenant suggested that the Marshall Plan should be undermined by making delivery of American aid difficult.

French workers were not unacquainted with communist

tactics, and many of them could interpret their signals accurately. Nevertheless, the AFL's moral and material contributions at this stage should not be minimized. In a letter to Green, the head of a department union (the equivalent of a state federation of labor in the United States), celebrating the first year of his organization's existence, thanked the AFL for the "precious aid which the American Federation has given us."[9]

Italy.

One of the differences between Italy and France was the length of time in which free trade unions had been absent from the economic scene. In France, unions had functioned until Hitler's legions raced across her in 1940. The period of suppression was a relatively short one. In Italy, more than twenty years had passed since free labor organizations had been driven out of existence by Mussolini's blackshirts and replaced by organizations which became part of the "corporate state." While the memory of free organizations was non-existent among many workers, they nevertheless divided on traditional lines after the collapse of the fascist government. Socialists, Communists, and Christian Democrats established trade unions, and all gained adherents. Simultaneously, a movement toward unifying the divergent organizations began, and on June 3, 1944, the Pact of Rome, which laid down the conditions of merger, was signed. Under the terms negotiated, the separate groups were to be disbanded and absorbed into the Italian Labor Federation *(Confederazione Generale Italiana del Lavoro*-CGIL).

The three major political parties – Communist, Socialist, and Christian Democrats – were given representation on governing boards. The CGIL was to be nonpolitical in principle, even though a communist activist, Giuseppe Di Vittorio, was selected to head it. This action soon put a severe strain on the non-partisanship proclaimed by the promoters of unity.[10]

A Challenge and Split.

The communists, in part because they represented the largest number of members and also because of their superior organization, soon dominated the CGIL. Following the general line of international communism, the CGIL refused to participate in the trade union conference on the Marshall Plan. Giulio Pastore, leader of a Christian trade union group within the labor federation, demanded that the federation send representatives so that it might decide its attitude to the Marshall Plan on the basis of its possible effect upon Italian reconstruction. He attended the London conference as a minority representative of members of the federation, and was joined there by Giovanni Canini and Enrico Parri, who represented socialist and republican moderates. This was the first challenge to the communist leadership, but more important ones were soon to follow. On July 14, 1948, Palmiro Togliatti, leader of the Italian Communist Party, was shot, and the federation responded by calling a general strike as a protest against the attempted political assassination. In a number of places the protest took on the appearance of an attempt to seize power. The Pact of Rome, imposing political neutrality, had been breached beyond repair and the movement of non-communist trade unionists out of the CGIL began

The first move was made by a group which formed the General Confederation of Labor *(Libera Confederazione Generale del Lavoro)*. This group was largely made up of Christian Democrats and had, at the beginning of 1949, 600,000 members.[11]

The socialists, with a democratic orientation, and the republicans found their position within the CGIL too difficult and withdrew, establishing the Federation of Italian Workers, *Federazione Italiana del Lavoro* (FIL). A movement to bring the two organizations together began, and in a meeting attended by Irving Brown, European representative of the AFL, Pastore, and Giovanni Canini, the two groups were urged to merge. In May 1950, unity was achieved and so began the Italian Confederation of Labor Unions (*Confederazione Italiana Sindacata Lavoratori* — CISL). However, a group of socialists, alleging that CISL was unduly church dominated, established the Italian Labor Union (*Unione Italiana del Lavoro* — UIL). The basis of UIL opposition was that CISL was a labor organization with a Christian Democratic majority.[12]

The UIL was essentially an offspring of the Republican and Unitarian Parties, both anti-communist and anti-clerical. Pastore's position was that he was seeking a trade union federation divorced from the dominance of any political party or religious body.

Pastore denied that the CISL was a Demo-Christian organization, and argued that the only alternative in Italy to free unionism was one based on ideology or religion. CISL was independent on both counts, he claimed. Green was brought into the debate, receiving a letter from several members of the *Unione Italiana del Lavoro* (UIL) which charged that Pastore's organization could never win the confidence of Italian workers. It told Green that the AFL was supporting "corrupt leaders," and called upon Green to have the AFL renounce its Italian policies.[13] The heads of CISL denied the charges and claimed that American labor had helped in the initial unification of the Italian labor movement.[14]

During this controversy, the AFL was charged with favoring the Catholic or Christian unions and these charges created some concern. George Meany stated that the AFL favored non-political and non-religious unions in Europe. He believed, however, that the problem was not a simple one: there had existed denominational unions in Europe for almost 100 years. He maintained that the basis of socialist opposition to CISL was a belief that it was Catholic dominated. He regretted the division because he believed the charges were unfair and untrue. He believed that if the Italian trade union movement divided permanently on religious and ideological lines, it would serve as a bad example to Germany, where the AFL had done "everything possible to help the trade union movement since the end of the war in bringing about the creation of a non-religious trade union movement. . . ."[15]

Thus, the debate over the structure of the Italian labor movement became entangled with the issue of sectarian trade unionism. The United States had no such problem. It may be recalled that when the AFL and Gompers were attacked by the Catholic clergy over their attitude on the Mexican revolution, Frank Duffy, a member of the executive council and a practicing Catholic, said that the "AFL had no religion." The AFL was critical of the Catholic labor organizations active in Canada, and American labor leaders, irrespective of their religious views, did not favor religion as a basis of trade union organization.

The American labor movement, both AFL and CIO, came to the conclusion in the early 1950s that, in some European countries, the existence of trade unions based on religious belief had to be accepted as a fact of life. Anxious to set up national and international labor organizations that would be able to meet the powerful thrust of international communism for gaining control over world labor, the AFL and the CIO appealed to the Christian trade unions to join the newly created International Confederation of Free Trade Unions. The invitation said: "So long as they are free, non-communist unions, whether neutral, or 'Christian' (Catholic, Protestant or non-sectarian) in their institutional character, they are eligible for membership and are welcome. In affiliating with the International Confederation of Free Trade Unions (ICFTU), they will retain their autonomy. . . . It draws no religious lines."[16]

The Christian trade unions rejected the invitation. Matthew Woll regarded this refusal as an error.[17] On the other hand, August Cool, a leader of Christian trade unions in Belgium, believed that joining a purely secular trade union international such as the ICFTU would mean that the Christian trade unions would lose their "specific individuality."[18] Woll, a practicing Catholic, rejected this argument on the grounds that it was "necessary to have the closest possible unity of free labor, if the latter is to accomplish its task of defending and promoting freedom and social justice in the teeth of the Communist menace."[19] Woll went on to note that trade union organizations were no longer restricted to Europe and North America, but were spread through much of the world. In his view, "one of the principal tasks of free labor is to foster free trade unionism in the underdeveloped areas of the world so as to enable the workers of these countries to raise their living standards." Finally, he called attention to the fact that the Christian trade union international had been limited to a few countries. His argument had no effect on the unwillingness of the Christian trade unions to become part of a unified free labor movement.

Woll persevered in his effort to prevent division of European labor movements on denominational grounds, and he

> spoke to the Holy Father, the Pope, about this matter and urged that he consider the importance and advisability of finding occasion or an opportunity at some time to advise the workers not to divide on

religious and political lines but to federate on the basis of unitedly combating Communism in any of its forms or any ideologies designed to undermine or destroy the freedoms which have proved of such great blessings to the people where permitted to grow to full fruition.[20]

For Woll, who was raised in the AFL tradition that dual or competing unions were a menace to labor's welfare, the existence of unions with a religious base could not be justified on any principle. In that regard he was speaking for all American organized workers irrespective of religious belief.

In Italy, the socialist oriented *Unione Italiana Lavoro* (UIL) turned out to be the reluctant partner in a merger with the *Confederazione Italiana Sindacata Lavoratori* (CISL), which was finally ready to unite with its socialist rival. The AFL and the CIO, at times joined by the ICFTU, had pleaded for unity, but their pleas were regularly rejected by the UIL. After considerable effort by a committee of J. H. Oldenbroek, secretary of the ICFTU, Victor Tewson, of the British Trades Union Congress, and Irving Brown, the two federations agreed, on February 7, 1953, to pursue a common economic policy, align themselves with the democratic forces in Italy and in the world, avoid raiding each others' membership, consult with each other before appointing delegates to international conferences, and refuse to cooperate with the communist dominated Italian labor federation.[21]

Greece.

Greece was another country in which the AFL was actively trying to stem infiltration of the communists. In one of his first reports to the AFL, Irving Brown had suggested assistance to the anti-communist unionists then under attack.[22] In a confidential report Brown recommended that the AFL seek the appointment of several labor representatives to the economic mission to Greece. He believed that American labor representatives should establish relations with the Greek trade unions so that a check upon communist infiltration could be made, aid in the modernization of Greek labor law could be given, and advice on the technical problems of labor supply could be made. Brown was emphatic about the necessity of aiding Greek labor to develop sufficient strength to cope with attacks from both the anti-democratic left and the right.

Brown had found considerable hostility toward trade unions among Greek employers. He also found that the communists had entrenched themselves through a series of "illegal" acts during the resistance and liberation. There nevertheless existed a sufficiently large non-communist group to furnish the base for a free trade union movement. Brown noted another problem — government control of some non-communist labor groups. Brown believed the AFL could not work with such organizations "since we stand not only against the domination of the trade union movement by a single type of state but of all states."[23]

Brown recommended that American aid be given on the condition that greater democracy be introduced, although he suggested that the government had a problem of suppressing banditry which should be recognized. He transmitted complaints from Greek labor leaders that American contributions had been diverted to the black markets and to private use, and that there was need of erecting safeguards against these practices. He also recommended that efforts to raise the standard of living of the Greek working people must be made if communist propaganda was to be permanently weakened, that Greek workers should be given the right to organize unions, and that the

AFL should make a determined effort to have unionists and others released from prison for offenses which were not stipulated by Greek law.[24]

While the communists were contained and the Truman Doctrine vindicated, the Greek government did not become a model democracy. At the very time it was receiving aid from the American government and the American labor movement, it enacted "brutal" anti-strike legislation which drew a sharp rebuke from Woll.[25] The AFL continued to assist, and helped finance the reorganization of the General Confederation of Labor, all of which Secretary-General Fotis Makris acknowledged. He praised the AFL for having rendered "precious service" to the Greek labor movement.[26]

Despite the efforts of the AFL, Greece was becoming a more difficult place for trade union activities and for workers in general. In 1953, Irving Brown was able to elicit a promise from the Greek government that it would cease meddling in the internal affairs of its labor organizations. No sooner had the promise been made when it was violated by the Minister of Labor, who had been actively trying to establish government controlled trade unions. On top of these difficulties, was the low standard of living of the Greek working population. The AFL continued its assistance, and the 1954 convention was told that the Greek free labor movement would "never forget" the assistance given by AFL representative Irving Brown "during . . . difficult circumstances."[27] The 1954 CIO convention agreed with the analysis of the AFL in that it found conditions in Greece deteriorating and the country losing its democratic character. It warned that if the trend was not reversed the Greek government would again be a target for communist subversion.[28]

Labor movements can exercise only a moderate influence upon the policies of the government of another country.

Nothing the American labor movement could have done would have reversed the drift to dictatorship by the Greek government. When the reactionary colonels overthrew the legitimate government, the AFL-CIO had no weapons except denouncement, decrying the use of "naked force" by a military dictatorship, and calling upon the United States to "express firm opposition to the reactionary junta."[29]

Spain.

Unlike the other countries dealt with in this chapter, Spain's democratic labor movement did not receive AFL assistance during the struggle against Franco. A resolution warning against the consequences of a victory by the insurgents was referred by the delegates to the executive council.[30]

Although not much attention was given to the Franco dictatorship during World War II, it had obviously revealed its true character. In 1945, the AFL strongly supported the Spanish Republic in exile, which was described as Spain's "most inclusive constellation of genuine democratic elements."[31] The statement praised President Martinez Barrio and the head of the shadow cabinet in exile, Don Jose Giral, for their ability to bring about a "complete democratic regeneration of Spain."[32]

Overthrowing Franco.

In 1948, the Free Trade Union Committee explored the prospects of Franco's continuation in power. At the time, Franco was still suffering from the opprobrium of having been an ally of Hitler and Mussolini, and it was believed that there might be sufficient sentiment among democracies to topple him. Before proceeding with the plan, Jay Lovestone, executive secretary of the committee, approached His Excellency, the Most Reverend Amieto Cicognani, the Papal

Nuncio in Washington, to ascertain the Vatican's views. The Nuncio asked for time to make preliminary soundings, and several weeks later met with Lovestone, Luis Araquistain (a socialist leader living in exile), and Indalecio Prieto (a moderate socialist member of the first cabinet of the Republic and a dominant figure in the Loyalist government during the Civil War).

His Excellency listened to the plans of Araquistain and Prieto and then said: "Gentlemen, the Vatican does not make revolutions, but if you succeed we will not oppose you. We will only ask that we be given a role in the educational system."[33] Without a moment's hesitation, Prieto answered that a revolutionary government could not organize an educational system in Spain without the collaboration of the Church. Upon this note, the conference ended. There was a feeling of restrained hope that the first step had been taken to topple the last fascist dictatorship on European soil. A leading labor reporter sounded out the State Department on the American government's view of the undertaking. He was told that the United States had no interest in disturbing the Franco government, and that Britain fully shared the same view.

There would perhaps have been insuperable obstacles to successful mounting of such a project. We must, however, bear in mind that Araquistain and Prieto were not inexperienced adventurers but politicians with a following in their native land. Outside of Spain, Franco was at the nadir of his popularity, facing resentment of his flirtations with Hitler and Mussolini during the war. Yet, Europe and the United States were tired of bloodshed, and the communists were closer to the putative field of battle.

Since that time, the American labor movement has opposed granting aid to the Franco regime unless concessions to democratic process were given. It protested suppression of the rights of workers' organizations established in defiance of the government. In 1949, it opposed allowing Spain to share in the benefits of the Marshall Plan. The AFL cited the statements of President Truman and Secretary of State Acheson in support of its position, and called upon the United States to warn Marshall Plan countries that it was impermissible for them to allow Spain to profit from arrangements involving Marshall Plan funds or other resources contributed by the United States.[34]

When the question of recognition of Spain arose in 1950, the AFL opposed it and refused to "accept as a premise that in the present explosive international situation . . . diplomatic recognition by the world's leading democracy has no moral implication whatsoever."[35] The resolution, furthermore, pointed out that recognition by the United States would encourage Latin American dictators; "the ones who maintain relations with Franco." The CIO expressed the same sentiments as the AFL.[36]

In 1951, the AFL protested the barring of the *Monthly Bulletin of the General Union of Spanish Workers* from the international zone in Tangier. At this time, George Meany protested the repression within Spain. He told Secretary of State Dean Acheson that no matter how great the danger of communism might be, "free nations cannot afford to tolerate the presence of the Franco regime. . . ."[37] Woll also asked for intervention by the government of United States, which would, in a "memorandum," urge "the restoration to the workers and the people of Spain [of] their rights of freedom of assembly, association and press. . . ."[38]

Secretary Acheson replied that while the United States supported and wished to foster the principles of freedom "in all parts of the world," he was certain that the course suggested by Woll "would be interpreted as direct intervention in the internal affairs of another nation and would, therefore, fail to have the effect you anticipate in your letter." Woll had a more direct opportunity to show his displeasure with the Franco regime. When the Spanish falangist unions sought to arrange reciprocal visits with their American counterparts, he rejected the invitation and said that "no trade union organization in our country could ever accept an invitation . . . or enter into any . . . relations with a labor front. . . ."[39]

The AFL regularly opposed recognition of the Spanish government and the granting of economic aid to it by the United States. When an agreement was made with the Spanish dictator, both the AFL and the CIO insisted that the United States government demand that the peseta counterparts of the dollar aid be used for benefit of the Spanish masses and for improvement of wages and working conditions — especially upon projects in which the United States had an interest. Both federations demanded that the United States use its influence for the restoration of democratic rights to all people of Spain. Both of them reaffirmed their "solidarity with the heroic free trade unionists of underground Spain and their courageous colleagues in exile."[40]

The AFL-CIO has followed its ancestor federations on this issue. In 1965, the AFL executive council greeted the growth of opposition to the Franco regime, the increase in number of strikes, and pledged its aid in their fight for freedom.[41] Again in 1970, as a reaction to the suppression of strikes and public demonstrations by the underground unions, President Meany denounced the Franco regime for its "brutality" which was "reminiscent of the Nazi and Communist terror." He called upon the American government to "bring to bear its full diplomatic and economic pressure on the Spanish tyrannical regime to end its barbarism."[42]

CHAPTER EIGHT

Support for Free Trade Unions in Latin America

THE INTEREST of American labor in Latin American affairs goes back to the early years of the century. In times of trouble or serious need, the relationship between United States unions and those in South America is more visible, and although it is greater at some periods than in others, it has always continued on some level. The depression diverted the attention of American unions from this area, but even in the midst of war, representatives of United States labor — Emil Rieve from the CIO, and Robert J. Watt from the AFL — explored the possibility of an economic conference of the labor movements of North and South America with government participation limited or excluded.[1] Difficulties over financing, and the desire of independent and denominational trade unions to be represented, complicated the problem and no meeting was held.

The AFL or CIO might nevertheless have been asked to intervene on behalf of a Latin American labor organization with the United States government. Thus, Robert J. Watt, speaking for the AFL, requested the government to guarantee a fair price for Bolivian tin so that the operators could pay their miners a living wage.[2] In the same year (1945), the AFL protested the government disbanding of Chile's labor federation, and charged that it was an "irresponsible action inspired by American business interests."[3]

The hope that a democratic trade union movement could be built in Latin America suffered a serious setback as a result of the appearance of the Latin American Federation of Labor (*Confederación de Trabajadores de America Latina* — CTAL). Organized by the talented and ubiquitous fellow traveler, Lombardo Toledano, in 1938, the CTAL sought to weld the communist dominated labor organizations and the free trade union rivals into a united front. Such cooperation was a major policy of the communists at that time, and it was propagandized in many countries as the "popular front." The CIO, whose president, John L. Lewis, was present at the founding convention, did not affiliate with the CTAL, but maintained cordial relations with it for some time.[4]

The AFL had been active in Latin American affairs over the years and, in 1945, it appointed Serafino Romualdi to head its newly established Latin American section. An anti-fascist Italian forced to leave his native land because of his opposition to the Mussolini regime, Romualdi had been a staff member of the International Ladies Garment Workers, had served in Italy in the Office of Strategic Services during World War II, and had contacts in South America. His major tasks were to investigate the possibilities for a free labor movement in Latin America which would be divorced from both left and right, and to enlist assistance for these efforts.[5]

Armed with a sheaf of letters from diplomats and scholars to their Latin American connections, Romualdi toured the Latin American countries and laid the groundwork for the creation of a democratic trade union federation. In the meantime, the AFL was active on another front. Romualdi's article in the *American Federationist* attacking the Perón government drew a protest from the Argentine General

Confederation of Workers (CGT), and an invitation for the AFL to send a delegation to view the beneficent work of the new dictatorship. A committee from the AFL and the Railway Labor Executives Association came and were unimpressed by what they saw. They recommended that no cooperation with the Argentine labor movement should be attempted as long as it was under government control, and that free unions should support the labor organizations which were fighting to prevent their own absorption into the government apparatus.[6]

The appointment of Romualdi provided the AFL with an energetic representative with excellent contacts in Latin America, all of which was valuable for reconstructing a democratic labor movement. In his soundings on the possibility of cooperation from the Confederation of Labor of Ecuador (CTE), Romualdi learned of government plans to dissolve that federation. When informed, Matthew Woll promptly sent a cable to President Ibarra in which he appealed against this plan and said that the contemplated action was a violation of the trade union clauses of "the Act of Chapultepec," which guaranteed freedom of organization to labor in every country of the hemisphere.[7] Other pressures were applied, and the planned dissolution was not carried through.

The first fruit of Romualdi's labors was a conference of free labor unions headed by Bernardo Ibanez, Haye de la Torre, and a number of others. The AFL sent several delegates who, before their departure, were advised by their executive council "not to propose any resolutions but . . . go along with . . . proposals made by other delegations which were in accord with our viewpoint."[8] This self-denying behavior did not exempt the AFL from an attack by Louis Morones, a one-time associate of Gompers who had gone over to Perón. Morones, who was present as delegate from the

Mexican Federation of Labor, charged that the meeting was sponsored by the United States State Department. Romualdi, who was a member of the AFL delegation, demanded an investigation (which found no basis for the charges).

Delegations from seventeen countries were present at the opening session: the Dominican Republic and Venezuela sent fraternal delegates. After establishing the Inter-American Federation of Workers (*Confederación Interamericana de Trabajadores* — CIT), the conference adjourned. The American delegates reported that aid from the United States labor movement whose organizations had been suppressed. Presi-in their efforts to establish viable unions. Only by active participation of the North American labor movement would the heritage of suspicion, in the view of the United States delegates, bred by economic imperialism and the policy of the "big stick" be dissipated.[9]

The AFL was soon called upon to aid the Peruvian labor movement whose organizations had been suppreseed. President Bernardo Ibáñez of the Inter-American Federation of Labor, came to the 1948 AFL convention and informed the delegates of conditions in Peru. President Arturo Sabruso Montoya of the Confederation of Labor of Peru, had been among those "subjected to every sort of indignities and acts of violence."[10] The convention pledged its aid to the Peruvian trade union leaders and their organizations.[11]

Late in 1948, Matthew Woll and David Dubinsky, consultants to the United Nations from the AFL, filed a complaint against the government of Peru for violating the rights of trade unions. The brief summarized the acts committed in violation by the government of Peru. It estimated that about 2,500 trade union officials had been jailed, including all the top leaders. It called for an investigation of the charges and for "proposals for remedy if the above-mentioned facts are proved to be exact."[12]

Following a coup in Venezuela, in November 1948, the scenario for suppression of labor in Peru was faithfully followed. The AFL supported a resolution for an investigation in Peru and Venezuela at the April 1949 meeting of the ILO in Montevideo.[13]

Establishing a Regional Labor Federation for the Western Hemisphere — Organización Regional Interamericana de Trabajadores (ORIT)

It was agreed at the time the International Confederation of Free Trade Unions (ICFTU) was established that regional federations would be set up to facilitate aid and promote the activities of ICFTU members in different parts of the world. As both the AFL and CIO were members of the ICFTU, an agreement was reached on the extent and work of the contemplated organization.

The conference called by the ICFTU met in Mexico City on January 8-12, 1951. It was addressed by Mexican President Miguel Alemán and Jan Oldenbroek, general secretary of the ICFTU. Twenty-one countries were represented by delegates or observers. The AFL, CIO, and the United Mine Workers of America sent delegates. George Meany spoke on behalf of these three organizations. He told the conference that it was the view of American labor "that every country in need of capital investment from abroad has the sovereign right to fix the conditions under which such investment is to be permitted and regulated."[14] He also reiterated an old principle of American labor; that every country has the right to adopt the social and economic organization it holds suitable to its needs. The only qualification would be to deny aid to those who threatened the peace of the world or to countries which consistently violated human rights and suppressed civil liberties.

The Organización Regional Interamericana de Trabajadores (ORIT).

The ORIT was organized with Francisco Aguirre of Cuba as regional secretary. Arthur Montoya of Peru was chosen president. Three United States labor leaders were placed on the executive committee — John L. Lewis, George Meany, and Jacob Potofsky, of the CIO. ORIT became a rallying point for the democratic trade union forces in Latin America, and the AFL-CIO loyally cooperated and supported its efforts. It has continued to be a member of ORIT and still cooperates with it on issues involving South America.[15]

The American labor movement sought to be of assistance to the workers of South America and their organizations whenever issues arose on which it could make a contribution. Thus, the AFL, in 1951, repeated its plea for a higher price on Bolivian tin to prevent the closing down of the mines and enable the operators to pay a reasonable wage.[16] On the other hand, the AFL supported the coup which overthrew the Guatemalan government of Jacob Arbenez Guzman because Guzman had "betrayed the democratic aspirations of the people and had transformed the country into a beachhead of Soviet Russia in the Western Hemisphere."[17] The AFL hoped that the new government would allow for development of free trade unionism, but the plans were not realized for a time and the fight for a movement that could bring relief to the age-old abuses within a democratic framework had to be continued.

In addition to providing direct and indirect financial subsidies, the American labor movement, as indicated above, has often been called on to render aid to workers and their unions in specific situations. In the first strike of the Honduran banana workers against the United Fruit Company, an appeal for assistance was made to the AFL (not financial assistance, but to prevail upon this American company to negotiate terms of employment with its workers, a practice the company customarily followed in the United States). George Meany took the lead, and the CIO and the United Mine Workers of America lent their voices to the call for a negotiated settlement. The Honduran government's commission to investigate the dispute recommended a settlement which was rejected by the company without a counter offer. Meany then called on the State Department and informed it that the behavior of the United Fruit Company was adversely affecting sentiment toward the United States throughout Latin America. An agreement was reached.[18]

The American labor movement also reacted quickly to a plea for aid from Costa Rica during an invasion of its territory in January 1955. The CIO, the United Mine Workers of America, and the AFL each issued statements supporting the invaded country. A joint committee pleaded with the Organization of American States (OAS) to give prompt support to the invaded government. Woll asked for prompt and adequate assistance to enable the democratic government of Costa Rica to repel the invasion.[19] It was provided and the invasion was unsuccessful.

The AFL-CIO Merger Convention.

In the foreign policy statement adopted at the merger convention, the needs of Latin America were recognized as strengthening democracy and raising the living standards of the masses.[20] In June 1956, the AFL-CIO reviewed the trade union situation, found that there was an encouraging growth in democratic trade unionism, and attributed the progress largely to ORIT. The statement, however, warned against attempts in a number of countries to curb union activity by restrictive legislation. The statement also expressed support for the policy of noncollaboration with communist dominated organizations.[21]

In reviewing the dictatorial regimes which have fastened themselves upon a number of Latin American countries, the executive council noted that it was virtually impossible to "mobilize the . . . support of the Latin American people against communist aggression if these people are subjected at home to a brutal aggressive totalitarian dictatorship of their own."[22]

Review of Latin American Relations.

Latin America and its problems have been a constant theme of the conventions of the AFL-CIO, and the meetings of its executive council. Sometimes a short statement was issued to decry a dictatorship or to commend the feat of a trade union or a government servant. The 1957 convention adopted a resolution which touched a number of the important problems in this part of the world, and it gives us a good insight into the views of the federation.

First, the convention recommended an increase in the exchange of trade union visitors and encouragement by the unions of North America of their Latin American counterparts to join their respective international trade secretariats. It was believed that the latter could aid Latin American unions in improving their knowledge and practice of collective bargaining and union administration.

Secondly, the convention noted that Latin America needed capital and technical assistance from abroad for modernization of its productive plant, and suggested the World Bank, other intergovernmental agencies, and private investors as sources of the needed capital. It requested the United States government to guarantee loans for the program of "enlarged economic aid."[23]

The gains of the democratic labor movement in Latin America were noted, but a warning against the threat of totalitarian communism was issued. The convention charged that the "rampant inflation" which plagued many of the countries and the repressive measures of some of the governments against free trade unions were the cause of communist influence. The convention hoped that the government of the United States would "within the limitation of diplomatic propriety and the accepted principle of non-intervention" support those governments in South America which were based on the democratic choice of its people.[24]

The AFL-CIO and the parent federations before it, denounced military dictatorships in every country in which they were established. It denounced the Duvalier regime in Haiti and the "dictatorship of the Trujillo family in the Dominican Republic," and urged the United States not to admit into our country former dictators such as General Batista of Cuba, Péron of Argentina, General Perez Jimenez of Venezuela, or their top collaborators.[25]

Reviewing economic needs, the executive council declared that Latin America must be given aid to free it from the poverty which surrounded its people. The Latin American countries could not by themselves raise sufficient capital, and the AFL-CIO suggested: 1. Establishment of an international-American development bank, in addition to existing lending institutions, to provide funds for economic projects. 2. Substantial expansion of technical assistance. 3. Cooperation in stabilizing trade of key raw materials to avoid severe price fluctuations; this might be achieved by eliminating quotas and tariffs and by aiding in the development of enlarged markets. 4. Encouraging the development of a common Latin American market.[26]

After the policy declarations of President John F. Kennedy on cooperation between the United States and Latin America, the AFL-CIO welcomed the "return to the Franklin D. Roosevelt 'Good Neighbor Policy'," and urged that assistance be given in the development of sound economies, improved working opportunities, and general prosperity. It suggested the granting of assistance for adequate housing and medical care.[27] At the same time, the federation supported "an act to provide for assistance in the development of Latin America and in the reconstruction of Chile and for other purposes," enacted in September 1960. It asked Congress to appropriate funds to carry out that statute. The statement called on the Inter-Development Bank to include in its regulations that funds provided for social development could be used to strengthen democratic unions.[28]

The statement also asked that cooperatives and trade unions be allowed to apply for loans for technical assistance. Finally, the AFL-CIO reiterated its views that policies on loans must be adapted to the repayment capacity of the nation involved, with allowances for differences in economic problems and development levels. However, eligibility for and "terms of, loans should not be determined solely by so-called 'sound' banking criteria, but by the likely contributions the projects involved can make to effective growth. Funds must be made available on a manageable long-term, low-interest basis for social overhead projects to provide the groundwork often necessary for successful economic development."[29]

In 1967, the executive council endorsed the Latin American common market, but also noted the need to expand domestic markets. Moreover, the statement emphasized that a "genuine effort" had to be made to have the benefits of increased productivity go in fair measure to workers and farmers so that the traditional inequitable distribution of the national income not be accentuated.[30]

In endorsing the Alliance for Progress, the federation asked that it be realistic in its purposes and avoid the "erratic and inadequate development activities of the past."[31] It repeated the concern that programs for reform and economic development not ignore improving the position of the masses and thereby fail in the most important objective of the new program.

The American labor movement opposed the Batista dictatorship, and the 1959 convention of the AFL-CIO extended to the Cuban people its best wishes in rebuilding their country's "political and economic structure on the basis of social justice, freedom, civic morality, and human rights." It offered its cooperation in the rebuilding of a democratic labor movement.[32] Several months later the executive council declared that the AFL-CIO had, in the first months of the Castro regime, shared the "misgivings caused by the initial excesses of the revolution," but hoped that democratic process would be restored. It noted that Cuba turned toward a totalitarian regime, with unions as mere appendages of government and the right of collective bargaining abolished. The Communist Party, the statement noted,

> is the only political party which is free to operate today in Cuba. Opposition newspapers have been forced to close. Democratic journalists, who distinguished them-selves in opposition to the Batista regime, have been forced into exile for insisting upon their right to criticize the pro-communist policy of the present government.[33]

In a report to President Meany, the AFL-CIO Community Service Committee said it was prepared to aid in resettling Cuban refugees as it had done for Hungarian escapees. The executive council authorized the opening of offices in Florida and in other communities if necessary. A special grant of $10,000 was made for this purpose.[34]

The Community Service Committee appealed to the central labor unions for help in the relief program, aid in resettling the refugees, and aid in obtaining employment for them. It was found that only in Miami was the problem of aid and employment serious. The executive council recommended that out-patient care should be provided by the federal government (in-patient care was already given), that surplus food be made available by the Department of Agriculture, and that the federal allotment of $85 a month for relief to the refugee family be increased. The executive council noted that the Cuban refugee problem was greater than the problem which faced the United States after the Hungarian revolution, and that it should be regarded as a national problem and not one that could be solved by Miami or Dade County alone.[35]

The 1961 convention denounced dictatorships in Latin America by name, and found the communist "tyranny forced upon the Cuban people" the most dangerous. It repeated Castro's declaration of September 21, 1961, "that he was a communist and that he will be until he dies" as proof of his affiliations and called for the end of the illusion that he was a reformer.[36]

In a review of Latin American problems at the 1971 AFL-CIO convention, the failure of the Brazilian government to restore the rights of its trade unions after the military coup in 1964 was deplored. In a long analysis of conditions in the southern hemisphere, the convention took note of the presence of revolutionary guerrilla bands operating in Uruguay, Argentina, and Brazil, and held them to be a menace to democratic governments. It decried the failure of reforms in Peru, and noted that the domestic reforms of the Allende government in Chile had been "envisioned by former President Frei," but that Allende's relationship to Cuba might constitute danger. On the plus side, the convention found thriving democratic trade union movements in Argentina, Venezuela, Colombia, Ecuador, and Honduras.

The convention regretted that, despite substantial assistance from the Alliance for Progress, the great mass of people in Latin America was still "plagued by widespread social injustice, massive poverty, inadequate housing and educational opportunities, and dictatorial military rule."[37] The remedy prescribed by the convention was the extension of democratic rights, but the statement declared "it would be impermissible and impossible to impose a uniform pattern of economic organization throughout Latin America. In this light, there can be no denial of every country's right to nationalize any of its natural resources or productive undertakings — whether they be domestic or foreign owned. But, however just, nationalization must be accompanied by negotiated compensation, if national credibility and international economic confidence is to be preserved."[38]

CHAPTER NINE

Colonialism and World Peace

THROUGHOUT ITS EXISTENCE of almost a century, the American labor movement has responded to shifts in government policy, both domestic and foreign. As a movement concerned with human and democratic rights, it has always believed that it was obligated to take note of injustice in other regions of the world, even though it might not favor the reaction by the government of the United States. Where the United States was directly involved, the labor movement believed that it had a duty to plead with the government to follow policies consonant with morality and justice. From the beginning of organized labor's history, the United States government was made aware of its views and expectations.

In the first decade of this century, the labor movement was active in international relations, but reverted to isolationism after World War I. However, even in periods when it abjured entangling alliances, it spoke out against gross injustice and violations of human rights. World War II was a watershed for the labor movement. Its leaders recognized that the world was an indivisible whole, and that what happened in the far corners of Asia or Africa would affect the welfare of Europe and the United States. In addition, it looked with satisfaction on the ending of colonialism, a system it had always opposed, and sought to help emerging labor movements of the new countries on the democratic road.

Samuel Gompers believed that the American Federation of Labor was the pioneer advocate "for substantial restrictions of armament and ultimate disarmament."[1] It greeted, in 1887, the Russian Czar's call for reduction of armies and armament, even though the initiative came from a "strange source." The conference which followed did not end the arms race. The nations of the world continued to expand their war-making powers in the face of demands for restrictions on the size of standing armies and the development of weapons. Beginning in 1898 and continuing through 1921, with the exception of the years of war, the AFL annually endorsed disarmament and peace. Gompers ascribed war between nations to "commercial competition . . . and standing armies," and the desire for "opening new markets for our surplus machine-made products."[2] It was the duty of the trade union movements of the world, he believed, to work for peaceful settlement of differences among nations, and to use their influence upon governments and their fellow citizens for establishing a peaceful world. When war engulfed Europe in 1914, the AFL blamed the absence of "methods for peaceful settlement of differences as the chief cause of war."[3]

The AFL's views on disarmament mirror opinions that were widespread in progressive circles, and especially in labor and farm groups. On annexing territories and other imperialistic activities, the AFL took a position that was not held by large numbers of Americans: Gompers and the AFL opposed the annexation of Cuba, an action advocated by many Americans in the late 1890s. He took the same view with regard to Hawaii and the Philippines. He predicted that if the

United States annexed the Philippines, it would have to conquer it "by the force of arms," and deny it "the right of self-government."[4] His forecast turned out to be accurate.

There were other reasons for his position. He feared that the United States would become an exponent of imperialism, which inevitably means foreign entanglements, larger armies, and opening the gates to workers from foreign lands. "Imperialism," said Gompers, "means that the dollar is of more consequence than man, and plutocracy and militarism nobler than humanity." The next convention, in 1899, protested "wars of conquest, whether carried on in Africa [a reference to the Boer war] or the Philippines," and against "forcible annexation to this country of either Puerto Rico, Cuba, Guam or the Philippines."[5]

The objection to acquiring foreign territories, as the AFL saw it, was that it would take the United States in the direction of imperialism and militarism. Such changes were opposed on principle, but there was also concern of their impact on domestic policy. Outright annexation of territory never again became an important issue, although the question was raised whenever intervention in the affairs of Mexico and Latin American countries threatened.

Following the Spanish-American War the United States reverted to its isolationist stance, interrupted only by World War I. With peace the country again took refuge in "seclusion," but was unable to remain aloof during World War II. The outcome of that struggle not only doomed the axis powers, but virtually ended domination by colonial nations over subject peoples.

With the new freedom came danger: released from the tutelage of European powers, the newly created nations might, according to the AFL, fall under the yoke of yet another tyranny. Both the AFL and the CIO spoke out on the question in 1949, in almost the same terms. The AFL called upon the government to cooperate with democratic groups in Asia, and declared: "No imperialist power — regardless of its flag or ideology — must be permitted to exploit for its greedy interests the great upsurge of the masses of Asian people."[6] The statement also enumerated those countries in Africa and Asia which had sought advice and support from the AFL — and received it — during their efforts to end colonial rule.

The CIO saw the issue somewhat differently. It blamed the collapse of the Chiang government on the Chinese mainland on its "corrupt and reactionary policies," and warned the United States that its "power and influence ... will fail throughout Asia unless it supports a forward-looking policy bold enough to hold the imagination of the aroused Asiatic peoples."[7]

In addition to general declarations on broad issues, the American labor movement became increasingly concerned with particular problems facing the trade unions of countries emerging from colonial status or occupied by the United States during World War II. Frequently the concern was generated by appeals for assistance from persons who feared that unless democratic trade unions could be constructed, the game would be won by the apostles of totalitarianism. The AFL was also alert to changes in United States policies that might affect the viability or position of the new governments.

The AFL was anxious that a democratic trade union movement be established in Japan. Even though there had been little exchange of persons or information before World War II, the AFL had some contacts in that country. During the occupation, the Free Trade Union Committee became aware that democratic trade unions were suffering discrimination in the allocation of newsprint. All organizations depended on the decision of the occupation authorities for their allocations. Responding to a complaint from the democratic free trade unions, Woll, in a letter to Secretary of State Marshall, listed the generous allowance to communist groups and the scanty amounts given to the apostles of democracy. "The net effect," said Woll, was to compel "the democratic unions to buy their paper on the black market."[8] This meant "very little printed material by the democratic elements in the ranks of Japanese labor and a flood of communist propaganda." Woll also called attention to the granting of permission by the American occupation authorities for a visit by a delegation from the communist controlled WFTU.[9]

During the occupation, the AFL developed close relations with the free trade unions of Japan and a number of other Asian countries. It established a "Care" program. Even more important were the AFL's endeavors to have restrictions which had been placed on labor organizations and collective bargaining eliminated. In defense of its efforts, the AFL argued that there was a difference between the requirements of a military occupation and "the orders issued thereunder and, on the other hand, legislation intended to establish national policy after military occupation is terminated. . . ."[10] The 1949 AFL convention directed the officers to call upon the United States government to redefine official policy on handling labor disputes in Japan to allow maximum opportunity for the growth of free trade unions. It also asked for discontinuance of repressive policies in the name of anti-communism.[11]

Both American federations welcomed the peace treaty with Japan. The CIO called upon the United States to respect democratic principles of the Japanese government.[12] The AFL made the same recommendation, and asked that all interference with the internal affairs of Japanese labor unions be discontinued.[13] It also asked that agrarian reform be preserved and that the United States champion the "well-being and social progress of the Japanese people."[14]

Although there were few contacts or exchanges between the unions of Japan and the United States prior to 1945, the assistance given to Japanese democratic labor organizations cemented a friendship which flowered in the immediate postwar period. With increasing strain, arising largely from competition of goods, the AFL-CIO and the Japanese Confederation of Labor (DOMEI) decided to set up, in 1971, a permanent joint committee for periodic discussions of common problems. Meetings are held alternately in each country.

The AFL-CIO and DOMEI recognized that the first duty of each labor federation was to protect the economic interests of its own members. In the first joint statement, a warning against the use of low-wage labor was issued, and the organizations agreed to cooperate in problems that mutually affect them. In addition, the AFL-CIO stated that it would cooperate with the DOMEI if problems arose during negotiations between the governments of the United States and Japan over Okinawa.[15] Finally, the joint statement noted:

> The Domei and AFL-CIO strongly feel the need for closer ties and more frequent meetings between them with a view of immediate and timely solution of mutual problems. Both organizations consider it worthwhile that their affiliated unions related to subjects under discussion should also be invited to participate in such meetings as occasion requires.[16]

Korea.

American labor's interest in Korea arose as a result of fear of attack by the communists, who controlled Korea's northern areas. There were also efforts to encourage a trade union movement in South Korea. When an announcement of the plans for withdrawing American troops from South Korea was published, Woll wrote identical letters to Secretary of Defense Louis Johnson and Secretary of State Dean Acheson suggesting, on behalf of the AFL, "that our government should not withdraw all troops from South Korea," but that "a token force be sent from Japan who would symbolize the determination of the United States to safeguard the area from hostile attack."[17]

Secretary Johnson informed Woll that the disposition of troops was in the hands of the State Department. Secretary Acheson wrote that the United Nations General Assembly had, on December 12, 1948, adopted a resolution that the occupying powers withdraw their troops as soon as practicable, and that the date for withdrawal had been set for June 30, 1949. Prior to withdrawal, Acheson noted, "every effort was made to strengthen the security forces of the Republic of Korea to the point where they can serve effectively as a deterrent to external aggression. . . ."[18] He assured Woll that adequate steps had been taken to guarantee the safety of South Korea, including retention of an advisory group of 500 United States officers and men to continue training the native constabulary.

Conditions in Korea soon changed. In 1950, one year to the day of Woll's letter pleading for a token force, the Republic of Korea was invaded by troops of the communist government of North Korea. The United States appealed to the United Nations against the aggression. The UN Security Council directed the aggressors to withdraw their forces to the boundary separating North and South Korea — the 38th parallel. When this request was ignored, the United Nations called upon its members to repel the attack. Although the dispute nominally involved the United Nations, the war was carried on mainly by American forces under the command of General Douglas MacArthur.

The AFL unanimously endorsed the American policy,[19] and the CIO welcomed the "occasion to reaffirm its complete support of our government and the United Nations in the struggle against Communist aggression in Korea. After the conclusion of the fighting in Korea, a great task lies ahead for thoroughgoing measures which will make the reconstruction of Korea an example and inspiration for all Asia. The false promises and dictatorship by the Communists must be replaced not by a discredited feudal regime but by ... freedom under a United Nations Commission."[20]

When negotiations for a truce began, the CIO welcomed the end of the fighting, but warned against rewarding aggressors.[21] The Free Trade Union Committee was anxious over the fate of civilians and POW's who expressed a desire to remain in non-communist areas.[22] It cautioned the United States government to eschew proposals by several countries which would lead to "opening the backdoor to forced repatriation at a later date."[23] Subsequently, Major General William K. Harrison, chief UN negotiator at Panmunjom, declared that: "The stunning blow struck on June 21, 1952 against communist opposition to voluntary repatriation of war prisoners in Korea was based on evidence produced by the historians of the American Federation of Labor."

China.

Up to World War II, the American labor movement was, like most other American organizations, not greatly concerned with China or its people. An undated memorandum to President William Green of the AFL, from legislative representative Roberts, quoted the head of the Far Eastern Bureau in the State Department to the effect that Secretary of State Kellogg favored a neutral policy toward warring Chinese factions.[24] In another memorandum, the legislative agent stated that "the bolshevik movement into which the Chinese workers have been led was entirely foreign to the Chinese idea."[25] However, he added that the Chinese were in favor of change and that the nationalists "were willing to accept any aid from any direction that will make it possible for them to obtain control of the country."[26] Roberts also reported that the dominant opinion in the State Department was that the Chinese were "not liable to fall for bolshevism," but that they were "using Moscow as a means to an end."

The evaluation appears to have been a correct one, but Chiang Kai-shek, who eliminated the communists during the 1920s, was unwilling or unable to introduce the necessary reforms to prevent an eventual communist takeover. In addition, World War II, with its catastrophic changes and dislocations, was not even on the distant horizon. It might also be observed that the AFL had never been interested in China on a continuing basis, and that these memoranda may have been sent in response to an infrequent request for information.

When Japan invaded China in the late 1930s, Walter Citrine, secretary of the British Trades Union Congress, asked the AFL if it would use its influence with the United States government to declare an embargo against Japanese goods until Japan ceased its aggression against China. The AFL appeared to be in a dilemma: the convention had already voted to boycott Japanese goods because of warlike acts. The executive council, however, directed Green to inform Citrine of the boycott and that it was "reluctant to make representations as you suggested. . . ." The AFL would not send delegates to an international conference on the Japanese embargo.[27]

The AFL and its successor federation have always recognized the difference between actions of a private organization in a free democratic country and those of a government. The AFL could boycott goods of another country, and there was nothing the government could do about it. In fact, the government had no responsibility for such actions. An embargo on goods of a nation is another matter. It is an unfriendly act the consequences of which could be serious for the nation imposing such a restriction. Consequently, the AFL could find no justification for exerting pressure on the United States government to take steps that would exacerbate relations between Japan and the United States and might have serious consequences for world peace.[28]

With the onset of war in 1939, China became an ally of the United States. It was the government of Chiang Kai-shek which became a member of the Big Four. With the end of World War II, China saw its own civil war dangerously expanded to a point which eventually led to the communists taking over the Chinese mainland.

The AFL was against placing blame on any particular group or person because the situation was too critical "for engaging in recriminations for past errors or in allocating blame."[29] The 1950 convention simply called for help to the Chinese people.

Admission of Red China to the United Nations.

The AFL consistently opposed the admittance of mainland China to the United Nations.[30] The CIO also opposed recognition of Communist China, but emphasized the need for "massive aid to improve the standards of living of the Asian people."[31]

On July 20, 1954, the Free Trade Union Committee issued a statement urging denial of admittance of Red China to the United Nations. Sent to every member of the UN General Assembly, the statement elicited a reply from Osten Unden foreign minister of Sweden, which was followed by a rejoinder from Matthew Woll. For the foreign minister, the issue of admittance was a political question; a question of whether a State is or is not willing to recognize a new regime in another State which has been established by revolution. He argued that China was already a member, and he saw the problem as "exclusively one of determining which government should be recognized as the government of China."

Woll argued that admission of a government to the UN should be based upon its meeting "the qualifications for membership set by the Charter."

In the early 1950s, the AFL's foreign policy statements began to refer to the "Kingdom of Laos" and Vietnam. Discussing the review of foreign policy attitudes at the 1953 AFL convention, Woll noted that "colonialism is the most dangerous agent of and virulent force for the Communist fifth column . . . in all countries aspiring to national freedom and independence."[32] He noted that "French imperialism has provided the communists . . . with the excuse for their unprovoked aggression against the Kingdom of Laos . . . and to the national sovereignty of Thailand, Burma, and other peoples of Asia."[33]

Vietnam.

Vietnam was first noted by the AFL in 1951, when it described Ho Chi Minh as a communist tyrant whose purpose was to lead the country toward communist dictatorship.[34] The characterization followed speculation in the western press with regard to the loyalty of Ho Chi Minh to communism or to some type of democratic radicalism. The AFL hoped to alert the American public to the true nature of the movement he was leading.

As the war in Indochina became a matter of serious concern, the executive council, in 1954, called for a special session of the UN General Assembly to "mobilize maximum world support for ending the war in Indo-China . . . and aiding its reconstruction."[35] Although the AFL sought an end to the Indochina war, it was disappointed with results of the Geneva convention which settled the conflict. In reporting to the AFL convention in 1954, the council claimed that democratic powers had allowed events to overtake them, and that they threw away their last chance "to have France break with colonialism in Indo-China. . . ."[36] The council advised that it was necessary to "rally the people of Vietnam to fight for their own freedom,"[37] that the democracies had made far too many concessions in "the Indo-China armistice," and forecast that the Ho Chi Minh apparatus would destroy the opposition as a prelude to any elections. Moreover, while the North of Vietnam was "inviolate from attacks," the armistice terms permitted the communists "full freedom to attack the South."[38]

The council was critical of concessions to North Vietnam, and said that Britain and France, at Geneva, had no more right to give away territory to the North than they originally had in taking possession of the whole country.

Probing actions against South Vietnam were gradually transformed into outright campaigns of conquest. The 1963 AFL-CIO convention warned that "Guerrilla warfare against Vietnam has been stepped up by the Communists."[39] In the meantime, American advisors and supplies were increasing. As the United States became more involved in Vietnam, the AFL-CIO pledged its support of measures needed for "safeguarding the independence and freedom in Vietnam."[40]

The 1965 AFL-CIO convention followed the sending and promising of several hundred thousand additional American troops for war service in Vietnam. Emil Mazey, secretary-treasurer of the United Automobile Workers, then an affiliate of the AFL-CIO, told the convention he was "worried about our foreign policy . . . probably the most difficult single subject to discuss. . . ." While critical of the Vietnam government, he found it necessary to give "support to President Johnson in his efforts to negotiate. . . ."[41] He told the convention that the leadership of the United Auto Workers was united in the belief that the United States must intensify its efforts to find an "honorable . . . settlement of the Vietnam situation."[42]

Walter Reuther was more outspoken in his defense of the government's policy than his colleague Mazey. Reuther questioned the judgment of those Americans "who would have us pull out of Vietnam on the theory that this is a civil war, it is an internal matter that the Vietnamese people should resolve themselves, and therefore we ought to bring the American troops home. I reject this, as does this resolution, as does American foreign policy because such a policy would create a vacuum which the communists would fill. . . ."[43]

Reuther claimed that withdrawal would lead to a "chain reaction" which would endanger every country in Southeast Asia, none of which would be secure against future subversion.

These views were reiterated by virtually every meeting of the executive council and the conventions. Mazey and others, like many Americans, changed their opinion and advocated a pullout of all troops in a "cut your losses" attitude. In February 1966, the executive council reiterated support of President Johnson's policies in Southeast Asia.[44]

In the meantime, Walter Reuther's views had undergone a significant change. After public criticism of the AFL-CIO position, Reuther asked for a review of all its policies with respect to foreign affairs. A meeting was scheduled of which Reuther, claiming the necessity to attend important contract negotiations, was not in attendance. The meeting found no reason to revise past positions. In a left-handed compliment to Tito, the meeting noted that he had abandoned the expansionist policies he cherished in 1948 — the support of Greek armed guerrillas and the claim to Trieste. In contrast, the meeting added that Ho Chi Minh sought to conquer South Vietnam, Cambodia, and Laos and weld them into a unified Indochina.[45] The meeting noted that the United States did not seek destruction of the North Vietnamese government, but merely the end of aggression.

The AFL-CIO described the Tet offensive action as the "latest escalation of terrorist warfare by Hanoi . . . of sinister international significance."[46] While recognizing the ability of the Vietcong to mount an effective offensive, the executive council affirmed its previous positions and called for strengthening of the President's hand so that he might seek a just settlement.

A resolution calling for the reduction of American involvement in Vietnam came before the 1969 convention. It was introduced by Arthur Carter, the delegate from the Contra Costa Central Labor Council of California. Carter also spoke in favor of the resolution. He was answered by President Meany. The resolution failed to get any support whatsoever from the convention.[47]

To what extent does a convention of delegates of the AFL-CIO reflect the views of the rank and file? Implied in this question is that the rank and file members of unions perceive issues in a manner different from the delegates and officers. This problem is common to all representative assemblies: does Congress reflect the opinions of the voters or do its members only register their own biases? There is no way to tell, and neither voters nor union members appear ready to turn issues over to the pollsters for determining a majority view on questions that affect them.

Delegates to AFL-CIO conventions are chosen at conventions or by referenda of the affiliated organizations, and in some instances — in the cases of city central bodies — by regular or special meetings. It has to be assumed that those elected will reflect the views of the membership, although it is possible that in a particular case they might not. There is no evidence, however, that the official views of the AFL-CIO evoked massive protests. Few leaders disassociated themselves from positions taken by the AFL-CIO or its executive council. Nor did the labor papers show widespread criticism.

We can assume that the unanimity of the convention did not truly reflect the number of union members who opposed the view. What nevertheless stands out is that few union officers registered opposition. There were some dissidents, of course, but not in large numbers until the last two or three years. Even then there were only a handful in the top ranks.

Perhaps, if Reuther had lived, he may have been able to rally a larger opposition. Such a possibility is by no means certain, since loyalty on the picket line does not necessarily mean acceptance of the social and political views of the leaders. The large vote for George Wallace in Michigan, and the opposition to busing (on which the leaders' views seem to be the opposite of the members), should warn us against believing that a leader even as eminent and gifted as Reuther can reverse the deeply held opinions of his members.

It appears that George Meany is closer in turn to the rank and file than some of those who are applauded in the press. Of course the majority may be wrong, and the minority on the side of the angels. The logical difficulty inherent in such a view is that it is self-righteous and assumes majority opinion is inspired by the prince of darkness. Even if we grant the opponents of the war in Vietnam the greater virtue, it would by no means demonstrate that they reflected the opinion of the rank and file union member.

CHAPTER TEN

Africa and the Near East

WITH THE ENDING of colonialism in Africa and the Near East, the American labor movement was anxious that democratic forces be encouraged and that there not be a reversion to some form of totalitarianism. An anti-colonial attitude had always been held by American labor, and while the people of these regions had been able to rid themselves of their colonial guardians, it was a much more difficult task to discover the democratic way and hold to it against both internal and external pressures for more autocratic rule. Federations of labor do not dispose of armies nor are their resources of such magnitude that they can finance large-scale programs of economic development. They nevertheless have considerable moral and some political influence, since they can obtain the ear of high officials in our government and even evoke the attention of foreign governments.

In keeping with historic anti-colonial tradition, both federations joined in criticism of the refusal of the United States' delegation to vote for placing the Tunisian question on the agenda. This refusal of support, the statement noted, was a break with the traditional position of the United States government which favored discussion even when it was critical.[1]

209

The AFL established close relations with leaders of the Tunisian Federation of Labor in the hope that it would serve as a spokesman for the wage earning population and seek to obtain for them a fair share of the fruits of economic progress. The leader of Tunisian labor, Secretary General of the Tunisian General Union of Workers Farhat Hached, was murdered by terrorists and his close co-workers interned by the French colonial authorities. Hached had visited the United States under the auspices of the two federations, and had assured the American people that the "Tunisian National Movement is neither communist, anti-foreign, anti-Western, fanatic, or feudal."[2]

George Meany and Matthew Woll denounced Hached's murder, and Woll told French Ambassador Henri Bonnet that, if the French government had allowed Hached to come to New York for the meetings of the United Nations, he would not have become the victim of an assassin's bullet.[3] On Human Rights Day, proclaimed by President Eisenhower, Woll again raised the question of releasing the interred leaders of Morocco and Tunisia. He told Ambassador Bonnet that such an act of generosity by the French government would enhance the prestige of France and the democratic nations associated with it. Bonnet promised to forward the message to the French Ministry of Foreign Affairs.[4]

In September 1953, Woll, speaking on behalf of the Free Trade Union Committee, denounced the United States delegation to the United Nations for supporting the refusal of the General Assembly to discuss the deportation of Sultan Mohammed V of Morocco. Woll denounced this as a "stain on the American government" and contrary to the overwhelming opinion of American people as reflected in the nation's press. Woll claimed the refusal to permit the United Nations to hold a hearing on "this outrageous crime of French imperialism is bound to antagonize the laboring

people of Morocco."[5] The Sultan was subsequently rein-
stated and, on his first visit to the United States, he was
asked by his State Department host whom he would like to
visit. First on his list was the organization which had spoken
out in his behalf. After a call from the State Department, a
reception was prepared for the Sultan at AFL headquarters.[6]

The AFL believed that to support colonial governments
was harmful to the prestige of the United States among the
less developed areas; those areas to whom a more positive
policy by the United States would mean assistance in
achieving "full national freedom." American initiative and
world leadership, the statement charged, had been damaged
by the government's policy of "overt and covert support of
the colonial interests of our allies."[7] In supporting the
colonial powers against nationalist forces in Africa, the
United States was deviating from American ideals.

The merger convention of the AFL and CIO called upon
the United States to help the people of Africa achieve
independence. Those subjected to the "yoke of alien
despotism," declared the convention, should be aided in their
efforts to "regain the right of self-determination . . . choose
the form of government they desire and enjoy national
sovereignty and the fundamental human rights proclaimed in
the Charter of the United Nations."[8] Subsequently, the
AFL-CIO called for the withdrawal of troops from Algeria,
which drew a defense of French colonialism from Jacques
Soustelle, former administrator for the French government in
Africa. The AFL-CIO then appealed to trade unions in
countries still practicing colonial rule to demand that their
governments withdraw from dependent areas and allow the
native populations to control their own destinies.[9]

Apartheid.

The absolute legal separation of races has been the

ideological justification for brutal exploitation of the native black people in South Africa, Rhodesia, and Nyasaland. A monstrous system of laws forbids them to enjoy opportunities which are their natural right on their native soil. The exclusion of millions of people from economic and social advancement violates every principle cherished in democracies. Involvement in African affairs made consideration of this system of injustice and brutality inevitable. When a group of men and women were brought to trial in South Africa for treason because they refused to follow the racial code, the AFL-CIO expressed solidarity with them.[10]

Later, the AFL executive council took note of the miserable exploitation of black workers and the "systematic destruction of union organization." Employers aided by the government were denounced for the miserable wages they paid. As black workers are not permitted to form unions, they are nominally protected by government appointed wage boards. The example of nine dollars per month as top wage in rural factories was cited by the executive council as how these boards functioned. The council called upon labor in the United States and Canada to rally to their assistance.[11]

In 1960, the executive council reviewed the results of its protest against the racist policies in South Africa. Despite condemnation by the United Nations, among others, the council approved a boycott of raw materials and manufactured products imported from the Union of South Africa. It directed the department of international affairs to cooperate with citizens' committees organized for a boycott of South African goods. It also directed them to explore the possibilities of extending the boycott to other commodities.[12] The 1963 convention denounced the destabilizing effects of apartheid, and endorsed the boycott of the Longshoremen's Union in New York City against South African imports. It urged the International Confederation of

Free Trade Unions and the International Federation of Transport Workers to consider extending the pressure of the boycott upon South Africa.[13]

When Ian Smith led his government into the quagmire of racial injustice, the AFL-CIO denounced his "racist clique" and urged the United States to initiate steps to quarantine that regime.[14]

Throughout discussions on the problems of Africa, stress was placed on the need to develop trade union organizations for effective protection of workers' rights. In 1960, the executive council expressed willingness to aid these organizations with funds and other forms of help.[15] The federation opposed, however, any plan to impose upon the "workers of Africa any American or European pattern of trade union organization."[16] The 1961 convention called the attention of the delegates to the bitter strikes "so cruelly repressed in Ghana and Libya," which convinced the native leaders of the importance of independence from government control of their labor organizations.

The AFL-CIO was aware that, while some African nations recognized the potential of trade unions for a nation's economic development, a number had resorted to the worst totalitarian methods and suppressed all independent organizations. Regimentation, the resolution warned, spells lack of individual initiative, poor quality of work, waste, and large labor turnover. It regretted the failure of some African nations to learn this lesson.[17]

When the Ghanian dictatorship was overthrown, the AFL-CIO expressed its satisfaction. At the same time it urged more aid to African nations so they would be able to develop their economies. It praised the aid given by the United States to the Mobutu government in the Congo as the "timely assistance" which prevented foreign intervention and the conversion of the Congo into another international battlefield. Another source of satisfaction was the growth of unions independent of the government, whose primary purpose was the protection of the economic welfare of their members.[18]

The Near East.

American labor has been a leading supporter of Israel from the beginning of that country's history. It knew of the terrible persecution of the Jews during the Hitler era, and was among the first organizations to raise a voice in protest. It was also aware of the rejection by European countries and the United States of the thousands of refugees uprooted by Nazi terror and of the discrimination and persecution by the "people's democracies". It hoped that Israel would be allowed to live in peace. The 1954 AFL convention asked Israel and the Arab states to recognize "each other's existence."[19] The merger convention advocated signing mutual security pacts with both Israel and the Arab states by the United States, the development of a program for settling Arab refugees, and economic and military aid to make the area self-supporting.[20] At its winter meeting in 1956, the council again gave attention to conditions in the Middle East, and blamed the Soviet Union's shipment of arms to Egypt for deteriorating conditions in that area. It called on the free world to offset the threat to Israel by immediately supplying it with the needed "defensive weapons."[21]

The AFL-CIO had continued support of Israel, although it described the Israeli invasion of Egypt in 1956 as a violation of the UN Charter. However, it blamed the outbreak of armed conflict to Soviet arms shipments, the blockade of Israeli shipping, the arbitrary seizure of the Suez Canal, and constant sniping and infiltration on the borders. In the following year, the AFL-CIO endorsed President Eisenhower's proposals, but expressed doubt of their effectiveness for keeping peace because they lacked a real program for settling the Arab-Israeli conflict.[22]

After an armistice had been established, the AFL-CIO recommended maintenance of the territorial integrity of all nations in the area, and non-interference in their internal affairs.

Resolutions calling for a peaceful settlement were adopted at almost every meeting of the AFL-CIO. They, however, had no more effect than proposals of the United States government. The Arab states were not ready to adopt an agreement which guaranteed permanence to the Israeli government. When open warfare was temporarily renewed in 1967, the AFL-CIO convention blamed the war on Soviet shipments of arms to the Arab states, and urged the United States to offset these supplies by making available the arms needed by the Israelis. In addition, the convention called for direct negotiations and secure borders as first steps toward solving the refugee problem and developing the area's natural resources for the benefit of all people in the Middle East.[23]

CHAPTER ELEVEN

The American Institute
for Free Labor Development

THE DEVELOPMENT OF LABOR INSTITUTES for the training of trade union activists and leaders, and the provision of financial aid for housing and other projects, was recognition that labor movements in less developed areas required positive assistance if they were to remain democratic. The first institute of this kind was the American Institute For Free Labor Development (AIFLD), established in August 1960 for providing training and education for Latin American labor leaders. At this 1960 meeting, the AFL-CIO executive council approved the project, and directed that twenty-five Americans from labor, management, and the academic community be appointed to investigate its feasibility. Funds for the study were appropriated.[1]

Subsequently, the executive council voted to support the program financially and to seek additional funds from business and government.[2] AIFLD was incorporated in Delaware and a board of directors elected; George Meany was chosen president, and Peter W. Grace of W. R. Grace & Co., chairman of the board. Of the thirty members of the board of directors, twenty-one came from labor organizations. Serafino Romualdi was appointed executive director, and served until his retirement in 1965. William C. Doherty, Jr., who had been head of the social projects department, took over his post. AIFLD was granted tax exemption.

Romualdi was confident that funds could be gathered from private foundations, but his hopes were never materialized. A grant of $100,000 was obtained from the President's emergency fund by Secretary of Labor Arthur Goldberg,[3] and the problem of permanent financing was brought before the newly established Labor Advisory Committee of the Alliance for Progress. At the suggestion of the latter, a social projects department was established. This department was to assist labor organizations in establishing low cost housing, credit unions, cooperatives, and vocational and adult educational classes. It was to "rely upon the U.S. Agency for International Development (AID) for the major part of its funds on a project basis."[4]

Allowing employers to participate in the management and financing of the program gave rise to criticism from American labor educators and from some labor union officers. Employer membership on the board of directors and acceptance of contributions from them, it was claimed, tainted the program and made it subject to suspicion. Romualdi rejected this line of criticism. He pointed to the various levels of cooperation between unions and employers, and said that he saw no reason for rejecting cooperation in this area.[5] He also believed that employers could make an important contribution; they were aware of the problems in Latin America and could help in their solution.

As a result of financing by the government through AID, charges have been made that AIFLD tends to favor existing regimes, that it carries on subversive activities within host countries, and that it is an arm of the Central Intelligence Agency (CIA). These charges have all been denied. They were based on the fact that former students sometimes engaged in activities against their government. But no educational institution, in Latin America or the United States for that matter, can underwrite the behavior of its students or graduates. No one has ever provided evidence that AIFLD has received CIA funds, and the Dockery report, which was critical of some of its activities "did not find any undisclosed AIFLD funding or secret agreements. We did become increasingly aware, however, that AIFLD was deeply involved in the development of a free democratic trade union movement in Latin America."[6]

When questioned on differences between the United States and Latin American countries, George Meany stated that diversity in institutions must be taken into account. Moreover, he denied that the AFL-CIO had sought to have the unions of Latin America become copies of their United States counterparts. Instead, Meany said that he hoped they could develop in accordance with the conditions and needs of workers in their own countries.[7]

Under Title I, section 2351 (a), of the Foreign Assistance Act of 1961, as amended, the policy of the United States has been to encourage in the recipient countries the development of self-help organizations — cooperatives, credit unions, loan and savings associations — to "strengthen free labor unions." Some objectives of AID were effectuated through contracts with universities, institutes, and the self-contained business enterprise which provided technical and professional assistance to counterpart institutions in foreign countries. Such a type of contract was devised because of the joint recognition of the need to strengthen trade unions in Latin America.[8]

AIFLD has engaged in a variety of programs. Its educational activities have been directed to training large numbers at the local level, with the more promising students being given more intensive training at national centers in Latin American countries and in Front Royal, Virginia.[9] In addition, short-term seminars, called "basic-in-country" programs are provided in the interior towns and villages. They are tailored to the needs of the sponsoring organization, and cover such subjects as trade union problems, history, structure, and government, union finance and administration, and collective bargaining and labor legislation. The courses are intended to develop an informed membership and to foster leadership skills.

An advanced training school is maintained at Front Royal, Virginia. It is attended by advanced students selected in consultation with the labor officers of the country from which the student is sent. Courses in economics are provided by Georgetown University, Washington, D.C. Some of those who complete their course work may also receive internships in their own country.[10]

AIFLD operates a social projects department which provides technical assistance to labor unions sponsoring low cost housing, erection of community facilities, cooperatives, labor banks, and smaller projects. These undertakings are financed by funds provided by AID.[11]

Between November 1964 and April 1971, the AFL-CIO contributed $500,000 in no-interest loans and grants to twenty-two Western hemisphere countries. An estimated 301 projects have been developed or completed.[12] They are financed by interest-free loans or grants up to $5,000, provided by the AFL-CIO to promote small undertakings such as refurbishing a primary or secondary school, providing electricity or sanitary facilities for residents of slums, or for people in remote areas. "Cooperatives of all kinds have been formed which meet the pressing needs of less privileged, lower-paid and left-out workers."[13]

The program has been under attack from journalists and Senator J. W. Fulbright, among others. When the Senator said publicly that AIFLD was being supported financially by the United States Agency for International Development as the "price we paid for Mr. Meany's support in Vietnam,"[14] Meany asked that either proof of the allegations be presented or that they be withdrawn, and he was invited to present his position before the Senate Committee on Foreign Relations. After Meany testified, Senator Fulbright conceded that "language perhaps overstates it. I didn't put it quite that way."[15] What the Senator meant, he claimed, was "that when one is friendly with the President of the United States it is usually very helpful."[16]

Meany was his usually frank self. He told the Senate committee: "I was here to find out why you took the position that we were receiving a political payoff from the previous administration."[17] Needless to say, there was no proof presented because proof did not exist, and no man who occupied a high post in the labor movement would "sell out" his organization or his members on an issue as vital as a foreign war. It is easy to make charges, but one should expect more complete documentation from a scholar-politician. What followed was almost ludicrous. The Senator placed in the record a sheaf of articles from what might generously be called "mixed" journalistic sources. The articles were put into the record, but Senator Fulbright did not vouch for their accuracy. Since they appeared in, according to the Senator, "generally speaking, reputable publications," they were submitted "for the record simply as background material for the information of the Senate and the public."[18] The articles were not serious studies or investigations. Fulbright's own committee had published a study by R. H. Dockery which was critical, but made none of the charges against which Meany objected. In fact, the articles were largely based on snippets and rumors emanating from a single source.

When Meany strongly objected to the use of uncorroborated statements, Senator Fulbright virtually withdrew his charges: "Well, it all depends on how you do it, and I am not saying positively here what you have done is against our interests, but it certainly is worthy of very serious consideration that these activities may not have aroused opposition because people are often very sensitive to intrusion from abroad in their domestic affairs."[19] This was a proper question but was a few thousand light years from the original charges. Meany answered that the AIFLD stood ready to depart if a government objected to its activities.

Who financially supports AIFLD's activities? Educational programs are largely supported by the AFL-CIO or business enterprises. The social projects department was established to carry out some activities of the Alliance for Progress. The AFL-CIO took the view that, if funds were to be provided for aiding a variety of groups and institutions in Latin America, the American labor movement was capable and could provide the skills for projects that would benefit the working population.[20]

Moreover, projects which required substantial investments could not be financed by the American labor movement. Unless AID was willing to guarantee the monies provided from the pension and welfare funds of the unions in the United States, projects costing millions of dollars could not be undertaken. Under existing conditions, AID guarantees the funds, and they are made available at below market rates of interest. An example given by George Meany was the $10 million loan to finance a housing project in Mexico City at an interest rate of 5½ per cent.[21] The Mexico City project provided homes for 20,000 people, and repayments were on schedule.

From June 1962 to December 1969, AIFLD trained 128,515 students at resident centers and regional seminars in Latin America, and an additional 818 completed advanced courses at the institute in Front Royal, Virginia. In addition, fifty-five students were given advanced training in labor economics at Loyola and Georgetown Universities. All graduates in labor economics returned to their home countries and are working in their field or are preparing to do so.[22]

AIFLD planned the construction of 18,042 housing units in four countries. Of the total number, 14,971 units costing $65,115,510 have been completed and 3,077 costing $12,175,165 are in various stages of construction.[23] It also encouraged the development of credit institutions, including a workers' housing bank in Peru.[24]

Sources of Funds Expended by AIFLD[25]
1962-1969 (000 omitted)

Calendar Year	Labor	Corporations	AID	Total
1962	110	133	397	640
1963	139	159	954	1,252
1964	211	165	2,148	2,524
1965	200	164	3,472	3,846
1966	200	141	4,802	5,143
1967	200	136	5,293	5,629
1968	200	134	5,252	5,586
1969	200	122	5,768	6,090
	1,460	1,154	28,086	30,700

Closer Monitoring.

Criticism of AIFLD's accounting practices have been made by the general accounting office, but no charges of fraud or irregularities have been raised. The basis for complaint is the excessive flexibility AIFLD supposedly enjoys. While not advising basic changes, the general accounting office suggested that AID monitor the activities of AIFLD more closely.[26] Part of the complaint is the bureaucratic literal mindedness of the accounting office. Obviously, the accountants have not the remotest notion of the problems of operating a labor program in a Latin American country.

An example of the undesirable flexibility cited in the report is the change of a seminar scheduled for four weeks for 30 students to a one week seminar for 136 students. As pointed out by AID, the

> labor situation is so volatile, AIFLD programs are subject to frequent change and it is AIFLD policy to advise AID . . . of the need for changes and to obtain, in writing, the authority to deviate from the task order.[27]

The general accounting office also objected to the inclusion in the AIFLD program in Brazil of

> a small agricultural education project — how to plant and care for crops on small plots of land — for Northeast Brazil union members. Although we do not doubt the humanitarian benefits derived from this project, we do feel that this is rather far afield from the purpose of AIFLD's union activities.[28]

This view was challenged by AID, which claimed

> the unionized peasants which form part of the Brazilian labor movement do not bargain collectively and must look to their union organization to afford them services of a different nature entirely, including assistance in forming cooperatives and increasing production of land.[29]

Funds provided by the United States government, although by far the greater part of AIFLD's budget, are not a great portion of the funds appropriated for foreign aid. A variety of objectives have stimulated the foreign aid programs from the Marshall Plan through Point Four up to the present; philanthropic, diplomatic, and military motives have played a role. The mix of motives is not a constant one, and there is a tendency to respond to needs and changes within and without the United States. The results are not easy to calculate, and failures as well as successes are inevitable. It is often difficult to measure results because many are intangible and involve attitudes and behaviors that are multi-causal.

Educational programs may produce more enlightened union members who are a factor in the increased stability of their organization, but how is such success to be discovered? The social projects are visible and, from some points of view, their value can be estimated. Certainly, a successful housing project will provide shelter, but there are no guarantees that the occupants will appreciate their organization or the AIFLD for its services. Yet this may be the only road by which workers can be led to understand the value of labor organizations. Considering the level of overall expenditures for foreign aid, one objective of which is to improve the relationships of the United States with the governments and peoples of other countries, the appropriation to AIFLD appears small indeed.

CHAPTER TWELVE

African-American Labor Center

IN 1964, the AFL-CIO began consideration of the formation of the labor center for Africa which began functioning in the following year. George Meany was chosen president and a number of members of the AFL-CIO executive council were elected to the board of directors. Irving Brown was appointed executive director. From the beginning, it was decided that maximum effort would be expended on workers' education, vocational training, the establishment of cooperatives, health clinics, and low cost housing. Technical aides were recruited for programs in specific areas. A center to develop cooperative relations with the United Nations Economic Commission for Africa, the Trade and Development Department of the United Nations, and with non-governmental bodies concerned with African development was envisaged.[1] Activities have been financed by funds from the American labor movement and contributions from the Agency for International Development (AID). Over $5 million had been contributed by the above sources up to December 31, 1969.[2] In 1971 there were 125 projects in thirty-three countries. Since 1970, AALC has developed thirty new impact projects — the kind that stress small-scale assistance in towns and rural areas.

To administer its projects, the AALC has a staff of thirteen in New York, and seventeen in Africa.

The AALC also employs approximately 100 African educators, vocational training experts, and trade unionists. Most often, they administer or teach in one or more of AALC's educational programs.[3]

The Center estimates that, in a two-year period, almost 2,200 trade unionists, including 20 percent of all Congolese shop stewards, participated in one of forty-six education seminars. In Ethiopia "it is planned" to hold courses for 1,000 workers annually over a four-year period.[4] Eight Ethiopian trade unionists have been trained to administer the program. In addition, the AALC helped finance the construction in Addis Ababa of a $350,000 headquarters for the Confederation of Ethiopian Labor Unions. Labor education programs have been established in Nigeria, Ghana, the Congo, and Ethiopia.[5] The Ghana Labor College, opened in 1971, will be operated by a Ghanian staff trained in the United States.

The Trade Union Institute for Economic and Social Development was founded jointly by the United Congress of Labor (UCL) and the AALC in 1966. The Ghana Labor College in Accra was organized in 1967 with a national representative of the United Steelworkers (a graduate of Brown University), Nate Gould, in charge. More than 6,000 Ghanians have taken advantage of its programs. It is hoped that a number of faculty members will soon assume major responsibility for operation of the school.[6]

In the Democratic Republic of the Congo AALC provided training for almost 300 officers and members of the *Union Nationale des Travailleurs Congolais* (UNTC) and, in another program, made courses available to about 2,200 trade unionists, including almost 20 percent of the shop stewards in the Congo. In 1970, AALC provided a specialist in labor education to Botswana who, with the support of the government, was to establish a trade union center.

Since 1966, an AALC technical advisor has directed the Institute of Tailoring and Cutting in Nairobi, founded in 1965 by the AFL-CIO. Maida Springer, a black woman on the staff of the International Ladies Garment Workers' Union, conceived the idea and, with the help of her union, established the institute. It is engaged in training Kenyans for employment in the garment industries. Curriculum and facilities have been expanded, and the enlarged staff now contains nine Kenyans, two of whom received advanced training in the United States. The student body has been expanded from twenty to 150, and it is hoped that the school will soon be operated by Kenyans. The AALC is planning to set up a second tailoring school in West Africa.[7]

In cooperation with the Central Organization of Trade Unions and the Kenya printers union, a regional project for training East Africans in the printing trades has been established at the Kenya Polytechnic Institute. In 1970, AALC donated a fully equipped lithography laboratory. Similar to the tailoring program, the Kenya project is the only one in East Africa to train printers.[8] Since 1965, the head of Motor Drivers and Maintenance School in Lagos, Nigeria, has been supplied by AALC, which has also paid the salaries of instructors and the cost of maintaining driving fields and vehicles. About 300 students have been trained in this institution.[9] An in-service vocational training program was also launched in Addis Ababa, Ethiopia. In cooperation with the Confederation of Ethiopian Labor Organizations, a program for improving the skills of building tradesmen was started. This program offered courses in electrical work, masonry, carpentry, and plumbing. In addition, the AALC started courses in building maintenance and in the training of automobile mechanics.[10]

A training program for rural craftsmen was begun in 1968 by AALC in Nigeria, in cooperation with local unions. Over an eight-month period, fourteen workers from each of three villages were given training in blacksmith's skills and the repair of farm implements. The villages in question are "pilot centers for agricultural development and serve as models for other craft workshops."[11]

AALC has sought to develop cooperatives on the theory that such institutions would be of assistance to the African labor movements and their members. With the aims of fostering such activity and training personnel able to administer cooperative enterprises, the AALC established, in 1969, the Pan-African Cooperative Training Center in Cotonou, Dahomey. This center should enable Africans interested in cooperation to obtain needed knowledge and skills without going to Europe or North America. In addition to reducing the expense of training, it makes possible greater emphasis on the problems and needs of Africa. The Center is governed by a board of directors composed of representatives of African trade unions, governments, cooperatives, and the AALC.[12] It trains students from French-speaking Africa. A comprehensive training program for English-speaking Africans was inaugurated in 1969 at the cooperative school at Ibadan, Nigeria. Trade unionists from Cameroon, Gambia, Ghana, Liberia, Nigeria, and Sierra Leone have completed the nine-month program given at this school.[13]

As an adjunct to AALC's program of workers' education and vocational training, literacy courses have been given in Chad, Ethiopa, Ghana, Nigeria, and Upper Volta. It was believed that the labor college in Ghana would provide the equivalent of elementary school literacy to most members of the Ghanian labor movement.[14]

AALC has also sought to improve medical services available to trade unionists and their families. Two mobile medical clinics have been provided, with each equipped with a medical vehicle (car or jeep), surgical instruments, and medical supplies. A clinic given to the Ghana Trades Union Congress in 1968, was utilized for rural health programs as a combination walk-in examination infirmary and laboratory and mass organization center; a similar clinic was given to the Congolese labor movement.[15]

AALC also sponsored study tours in the United States for African trade unionists. Under this program, ninety African trade unionists from thirty-four countries visited the United States. Training courses in Harvard University's Trade Union program, financed by AALC, have been made available to seventeen trade union officers from eight countries.[16]

Impact Projects.

Impact projects are one of the more popular programs of American labor in economically underdeveloped countries. Requiring, as a rule, only modest expenditures of funds, these projects entail small risk, and can be carried on in a variety of areas and for many purposes. The seventy-four projects in twenty-four countries that have been financed by the Impact Fund Agreement, were carried on by funds totaling $881,254.91:[17]

> The Impact Fund has enabled us to focus on the specific needs of the unions in individual countries, discuss potential approaches, get necessary agreements both from the host country and the U.S. Mission, and act expeditiously.[18]

The impact projects have been the means of introducing AALC to many African nations, and in a number of instances they have been the beginning of broader regional programs.

The activity involved in impact projects may be more effectively noted by a description of several typical ones of the 110 described. AALC provided the *Union Nationale due*

Senegal (UNTS), with a variety of office and business equipment for its central office in Dakar. In addition, typewriters and duplicating machines were donated for the use of the regional offices. AALC appropriated $3,215 for this project.

Training equipment for the advanced vocational training course in the Republic of Niger was made available by AALC through a training grant of $5,150. The project was designed in cooperation with the *Union Nationale des Travailleurs du Niger* (UNTN). The equipment was used to train welders, auto mechanics, and electrical and woodworking methods. Four workshops were established at the training center in Niamey. The project had the cooperation of the Nigerian government through the Ministry of Labor. The funds were used to purchase equipment.[19]

Another project was providing transportation to the *Confederacion Nationale des Travailleurs Gabonais* (CNTG). AALC purchased a car which enabled the CNTG to develop programs outside of Libreville, and to maintain closer connections with its regional branches. It was believed that the improved contacts would make for more effective administration of the unions.

The construction of a workers' education center is another type of impact project. Such a center is being built by the AALC in Upper Volta on land offered by the government. It will serve to train union personnel and trade unionists throughout West Africa. Courses on organizing, union finance, and economic and social research will be given. Fifty thousand dollars was allocated for this project.[20]

AALC also underwrote the travel expenses of educational administrators of the Confederation of Malagasy Workers under an impact project. Five seminars were conducted, and the operating costs — $600 — were covered.[21] Another impact project distributed fifty kits containing basic materials needed for labor education programs to twenty-four countries;[22] thirteen of which were French-speaking and eleven English. A manually operated mimeograph machine with instructions and supplies, a portable battery operated public address system, and a portable tape recorder and supply of tapes were included in the kit.

This project was originally developed at the request of African trade unions, who lacked the basic materials necessary for launching a labor education program. It was also hoped that the project would strengthen relations between AALC and trade union organizations in Africa.[23]

Impact projects have also been used for more mundane purposes. One grant provided a roof for a metal workshop of a producer cooperative specializing in the construction of houses and schools and the making of furniture. The grant allowed for completion of a metal workshop. It was the view of the AALC officers that the effectiveness of such small but useful projects resided in their "demonstration effect"; the encouragement they offered and the example they set for other union groups. The report noted: "The development of small scale industries of this kind throughout the developing world is . . . of primary importance."[25]

In the same direction, but involving a larger expenditure — almost $7 million — the AALC provided the Fishery Cooperative of the Confederation of Malagasy Workers (FMM) with a deep-sea fishing boat. In addition to the cost of the vessel, $3,000 was allocated for renovation. The project was supported by the Government of Malagasy, the AID director, and the United States embassy. The union had sixty members, half of whom were experienced deep-sea fishermen. They were compelled to pay high rental fees for their vessels, and the AALC purchase enabled them to make considerable savings.[26]

Purpose of Impact Grants by AALC[27]

	Number
Purchase of office equipment, vehicles, fishing boat[28]	27
Construction of cooperatives, low cost housing, union buildings, and educational centers	8
Training of union leaders, cooperatives, and rural leaders	11
Seminars and classes in workers' education and training	14
Scholarships in American universities and visits of trade union leaders to the United States	7
Supplying educational kits and buttons	4
Supplying of mobile medical and dental clinics and medical material	5
Total impact projects	75

Cost of 76 Impact Projects[29]

		Number
Less than $	2,000	11
	4,000	15
	6,000	11
	8,000	4
	10,000	3
	12,000	5
	14,000	2
	20,000	6
	25,000	6
	30,000	6
	50,000	5
Over	50,000	2

Expenditures ranged from $127 for the purchase of union membership buttons and graduation certificates for the students of the Mauritius Labor College, to the allocation of $64,000 for support material and an advisor for a labor education program in Botswana. The next highest expenditure ($50,000) was allocated to a low cost housing project in Ghana. Expenditures of several thousand dollars or more are generally for some kind of equipment needed by a union or a cooperative. Amounts of less than $2,000 are generally used for conferences or the purchase of supplies of some kind. Supplying medical and dental clinics requires larger than average sums.

North Africa.

The AALC has reestablished relations with the Tunisian labor movement in North Africa, mainly as a result of the return of General Secretary Habib Achour. The AALC provided Tunisian unions (UGTT) with a mobile clinic, four ambulances, and an audio-visual educational unit. Since 1969, planning of new programs and evaluation of the old have been conducted by a consultative committee upon which labor leaders from Nigeria, the Congo, Ghana, and Ethiopia serve. In addition, the committee deals with broad problems of the African labor movement.

As one reads of the aid and the effort expended by the AFL-CIO, it is clear that its aim and hope is to build a labor movement that will be free, independent, and willing to defend the rights and interests of its members. There are no grandiose plans, and the work is carried on at the grassroots level. Many of the contributions in money or goods are modest, but they are given directly to unions and their members. No effort is made to dominate, but the message of an independent labor movement is taking hold, and the report of a writer and old African hand is more significant than argument. "Thanks to an AFL-CIO team," the author tells us, "the Congo has nearly 800,000 unionists paying by the check-off system." Andre Bo-Boliko, we are told, is "the university trained labor leader who wants to restore the 45 percent of purchasing power lost since 1960 and then peg wages to the cost of living."[30] An independent, viable, and democratic labor movement will cooperate in economic development which is vital to Africa, but it can also see that the interests of workers are not completely swallowed up by ambitious programs which ignore or downgrade his needs.

The African labor movements are at the beginning of their history. Because the governments are of recent origin, hostility between the labor movement, the government, and the community — which developed in many countries — may not arise or may never be severe in others. The labor movement could play an important role in the progress of the economies and societies of the African states. Not only could they offer protection, but they could be a source for leadership and administrative talent which could serve the entire continent.

CHAPTER THIRTEEN

Asian-American Free Labor Institute

THE ASIAN-AMERICAN Free Labor Institute is the most recent one established by the AFL-CIO. The institute was the direct result of a request for assistance directed to George Meany from Tran Quoc Buu, president of the Vietnamese Confederation of Labor (CVT). His organization needed help to become more effective as the representative of its members.

After a feasibility study by a committee from the AFL-CIO executive council, it was decided, in 1968, to set up the Asian Institute. AAFLI in general follows policies and engages in activities similar to those carried on by other foreign labor institutes sponsored by the federation. Its major purpose is to aid the workers and their organizations to develop free and democratic trade unions able to survive within the economy and society in which they operate. Specifically, AAFLI tries to devise programs to train union administrators and active union members in the jobs and needs of their organizations. It tries to improve skills, and provides finances for training programs for the development of cooperatives which would benefit the union member, the community, and the nation.

In structure, AAFLI resembles the other two institutes.

George Meany is its president, and AFL-CIO Vice President James Hunter Wharton is the secretary-treasurer. The board of trustees is made up of presidents of AFL-CIO unions.

Funding comes from three principal sources: the AFL-CIO, the affiliated unions of the federation, and the United States Agency for International Development (AID). AID funds are provided under a technical assistance cost reimbursement contract. This contract includes a description of any particular program and its cost. Policies are determined jointly by the AFL-CIO and the particular national center of the country in which the program will be developed. The location, size, duration, and nature of the program are also determined by the AFL-CIO and the national center.

The independence of the AAFLI is recognized in the basic agreement with AID. Under its provisions:

> the unique capabilities of the American Federation of Labor-Congress of Industrial Organizations (AFL-CIO) as represented by the Asian-American Free Labor Institute (AAFLI) to furnish expert advice and assistance in the development and administration of trade union programs and labor related endeavors, the Government of the United States, through the Agency of International Development (AID) has requested the AFL-CIO to provide the following services under Task Orders which may be issued pursuant to the terms of this Basic Agreement.

Programs are undertaken only at the request of the host country trade union centers and are designed to aid all trade union centers in the particular country. The programs are jointly conducted by the institute and trade union centers and an effort is made to utilize, whenever possible, the local trade union leaders as instructors and administrators. Programs are developed in accordance with local customs, practices, and laws, and stress is placed on self-help with a maximum contribution of manpower, facilities, or funds by the trade unions or social agencies within the recipient country. Joint program cooperation and assistance of other national centers within the region is encouraged.[1]

Requests for a program are made to the AFL-CIO. As a first step, AAFLI makes a feasibility study in cooperation with the requesting trade union center. When an agreement is reached on the contents of the union-to-union program and the host country's labor ministry cooperates, a formal contract is made, and the program started.

In Vietnam, AAFLI has provided financial aid and staff for education and training in a variety of trade union functions. More than 2,700 union members have participated in this program, and activities have been conducted in fifteen provinces. The institute has also provided machinery and equipment on a "revolving fund" basis that makes possible the purchase of additional machinery through repayment of the original purchase price. Office equipment, garden and farm machinery, have all been donated for the use of the CVT. There is a hope to expand the social centers, and speed up the development of cooperative farming and fishing by making credit more readily available and by improving marketing.

The Philippines.

AAFLI has assisted the Trade Union Congress of the Philippines (PMP) through a number of impact projects such as assistance to the Federation of Free Farmers in its development program in central Luzon. In addition, 168 participants have completed courses in a trade union leadership program and in the administration of farm cooperatives. Through the "revolving fund" concept, AAFLI has purchased fertilizer, irrigation pump systems, and tractors with rice farming accessories. For the future, AAFLI intends to expand its program of education in the Philippines.

Indonesia and Taiwan.

A series of educational classes and seminars have been conducted in Taiwan. In late 1970, the institute met with leaders of the Indonesian labor movement in the hope that assistance could be given. A variety of office equipment has been presented, and the institute's hopes for enlarging activity are high.[2]

CHAPTER FOURTEEN

The International Labor Organization

IN THE FIRST YEAR of World War I, the AFL suggested that a meeting of representatives of labor should be called at the same time and place as the eventual peace conference. This meeting would concentrate on a program for the permanent ending of war and the promotion of social justice. President Woodrow Wilson was informed of the resolution and his support for the enterprise was solicited "in the event that a Peace Congress shall be ultimately called."[1]

Despite initial scepticism, the program was eventually endorsed by labor movements of the allied countries, and was submitted to the British Prime Minister by the British Trades Union Congress.[2] In response to several requests, the Council of Ten — representing the five major governments on the allied side — appointed the Commission on International Labor Legislation to draw up a labor program to be embodied in the peace treaty. "Permanent peace," the council believed, "can be established only if it is based upon social justice." Another consideration influencing the establishment of the commission was the belief that "hardship and privation of large numbers" tended to produce unrest within nations and could become a force to imperil the peace between nations.[3]

The major debate within the commission centered around Gompers' proposal that the workers' delegates should be granted full freedom to discuss and vote on proposals coming before the conferences of the projected labor body. Because Gompers believed that the views of labor did not always coincide with those of government, he believed that the labor delegates should be untrammelled by governmental influence. After a long debate this view was accepted. The commission reported that if the annual conferences were in fact "to be representative of all those concerned with industry and to command their confidence, the employers and workpeople must be allowed to express their views with complete frankness and freedom. It was accordingly thought that the employers' and worker/peoples' delegates should be entitled to speak and vote independently of their governments."[4]

The report of the Commission was accepted and, under Part XIII of the Treaty of Versailles, the International Labor Office (ILO) was established. This organization was placed under the general direction of a governing body whose members were to be chosen at a conference. Its operations were to be carried out by a director, chosen by the governing body, who was authorized to assemble the requisite staff. The ILO is still active on two levels: (1) It collects and dissemenates information on all phases of industrial life and labor. (2) It is also required to hold one, and if warranted more, conference a year at which members' proposals are considered. Such proposals can be adopted by the conference at which they are submitted, or a draft international convention may be approved for the members' ratification. The latter requires a two-thirds vote by delegates present. Delegates are obligated to bring the recommendations of conferences or draft conventions before competent author-ities of their country. If the draft convention is ratified, the

ILO must be informed of this action and the steps taken to enforce the provisions.

When the AFL considered a resolution endorsing the new international organization, Andrew Furuseth, president of the International Seamen's Union, attacked the ILO constitution and warned the delegates that the labor movement and the United States were in great danger from the "super-legislature" spawned by the peace conference. He was answered by Matthew Woll, William Green, and Gompers. In the end, the convention overwhelmingly endorsed the work of the labor commission, and appointed a special committee to cooperate in preparing the first meeting — scheduled for Washington in October 1919.[5] Although Gompers participated in discussions about the Washington ILO meeting, American delegates were not formally present at ILO conferences until 1934. As the United States did not join the League of Nations, it was assumed that it could not affiliate with the ILO.

Joining the ILO.

In 1933, the United States government sent four observers — one of whom was recommended by the AFL — to the annual conference of the ILO. On June 16, 1934, Congress, by joint resolution, authorized the President to accept membership in the ILO without assuming obligations under the covenant of the League of Nations. The AFL approved the government's step, and recognized its own "special responsibility:" the workers' representative was to be chosen "in agreement with the most representative organization of the working people."[6]

Satisfaction with the ILO was annually expressed by the AFL, members of which were chosen as the delegates from the United States. The only discordant note came from the

CIO, which also sought to be represented at ILO conferences. President Franklin D. Roosevelt sought to have the AFL share with the CIO the right to represent the workers of the United States. He pointed to the ILO constitution, which specified that the worker delegate be appointed by government upon the recommendation of the "most representative organization" of labor. The AFL offered to submit its records to government inspection if the CIO would accept the same procedure: the request was forgotten.[7]

The governments of Eastern Europe join the ILO.

Soon after the affiliation of Eastern Europe, the representatives of the workers' group on the ILO governing body and the International Confederation of Free Trade Unions (ICFTU) objected to the seating of the workers' delegates from the USSR and other eastern bloc countries. The challenge was based upon the view that these delegates were not free to represent the interests of their constituents. The AFL executive council shared this view, and in a statement called for the amendment of the ILO constitution to prevent government selection of workers' and employers' delegates.[8]

The ILO responded by appointing a commission to consider whether representatives from the Eastern European countries were authentic spokesmen for their constituents, or agents of their governments. In its report, the commission noted that it had been the insistence of labor, after World War I, which led to the adoption of the tripartite principle. As labor claimed the right to an independent voice upon industrial matters, members of the original labor commission believed that to "ensure a just equilibrium it was necessary that the employers should likewise be represented."[9] The tripartite structure was the means by which those objectives could be realized. (Tripartite representation is the method by which both workers and employers can influence and contribute to the discussion of industrial issues.) It followed that this "could only be achieved if the delegates representing workers and employers respectively were independent of their governments and free to speak the minds of their constituents. The tripartite structure is, in the words of the resolution of the Governing Body under which they were appointed, 'a unique feature' of the International Labor Organization."[10]

The AFL found that affiliation of the Soviet bloc countries called for increased participation and greater activity for the free nations in the ILO. It objected to efforts to weaken the ILO's autonomy and opposed attempts to bring the ILO under control of the United Nations.[11]

After the merger of the AFL and CIO, the ILO was subjected to a mendacious attack by several employer organizations in the United States. The AFL-CIO denounced these assaults and officially reiterated its "full and unqualified support of the ILO and of United States membership and participation therein."[12] The following year, the executive council again denounced the criticisms of the ILO and called for its support.[13]

In 1959, the AFL-CIO criticized the employers' delegate to the ILO conference for his opposition to "virtually all of the constructive and forward-looking actions of the ILO," and the two government delegates for failure to support "most of the standard-setting actions of the ILO."[14]

From the first year of its affiliation, the AFL, and the AFL-CIO after it, firmly supported the ILO when it carried out its activities in accordance with its principles. It has, however, not been willing to close its eyes to unfairness and the oversights of basic violations of ILO standards by Eastern bloc countries. The ILO mission which investigated the trade union situation in the Soviet Union was criticized for failing to adhere to the guidelines laid down by the ILO governing board, and for not providing an adequate picture of actual conditions which affected freedom of association. It found the mission's report lacking in objectivity: "Under cover of 'neutrality' it shut its eyes to the Soviet communists' continuous contempt for the flagrant violation of the right of freedom of association."[15]

In contrast, the ILO commission studying trade union practices in the United States found much to criticize. Inevitably, such differences in treatment could scarcely be regarded as fair by the labor movement of the United States.[16] Other developments were equally serious. The use of the ILO as a forum for political discussions and for attacks upon the United States was in disregard of the principle that the ILO would not concern itself with political matters. The continuing and increasing pressure of the communist bloc was resented by Rudolf Faupl, the workers' delegate from the United States, and, in 1965, he reported his concern to the AFL-CIO executive council.

At that meeting of the executive council, George Meany was authorized to take any action he deemed necessary after discussions with the United States government. In a discussion with Secretary of State Dean Rusk, Meany and Faupl reported their concern over events at the ILO. They emphasized that they were especially concerned with the use of the conferences and resolutions of the ILO as instruments of political propaganda. Such actions violated the rules of the ILO and the purposes of the organization. Speaking for the AFL-CIO, President Meany told Rusk that such conduct was intolerable and that its continuance would lead to a refusal of the AFL-CIO to cooperate.[17] Secretary Rusk assured Meany and Faupl that the government delegate would work more closely with the workers' representative in an effort to eliminate political discussion and to preserve the tripartite character of the ILO.

Despite assurances, attacks upon the United States, introduction of political discussions, and the breakdown of genuine tripartite representation continued. The strength of the communist bloc was demonstrated by the election of a Polish national to the presidency of the 1966 conference. As a sign of displeasure, the United States workers' representative, Rudolf Faupl, temporarily withdrew from the session. The act was an established method of protesting a decision. It was nevertheless sharply criticized by the late Walter Reuther, a member of the AFL-CIO executive council, who questioned whether a decision of this kind could be made without consultation with the council.

The executive council had authorized President Meany to take the action he deemed necessary, but Faupl had made the move on his own. The executive council was called into session on June 10, 1966, to consider Reuther's complaint. Faupl, who was present, defended his protest as "within the constitutional procedure and the traditional practices of workers' representatives in the ILO."[18] The issue was discussed, after which Vice President Roy Siemiller proposed:[19]

> The AFL-CIO Executive Council fully supports, and endorses the position of the President of the AFL-CIO and the recent action of the United States Workers' delegate to the International Labor Conference and his advisors. Through their demonstration protest which was not a withdrawal from the ILO — they used the most effective means available to indicate the reaction of the free workers of America to the election as President of the Conference of a representative of a totalitarian regime whose record and practices are a standing denial of everything the International Labor Organization stands for and was created to achieve.[20]

The resolution was approved by a vote of eighteen to six, with five members of the council absent.

The American labor movement wanted the United States to remain a member of the ILO. It will remain only if the ILO adheres to its original purpose — promoting policies in industrial matters that will improve the lot of the workers of the world, and avoiding political polemics. At the 1967 conference, the American workers' delegate protested against the "vicious, slanderous attack on the policies of the United States and several other countries."[21] The AFL-CIO, at the same time, extolled its positive achievements. At the celebration of the fiftieth anniversary of the organization, President Meany praised the standard-setting activities of the ILO and urged the United States Congress to ratify the ILO conventions. He also noted that the ILO had not vigorously insisted that the ILO convention on workers' freedom of association be obeyed in the countries of the Soviet bloc.[22]

Complaints about the differences in treatment of the free countries and those in the Soviet bloc continued. Tendentious articles began appearing in the publications of the ILO. An article, "Lenin and Social Progress," in the *International Labour Review* (April 1970), sought to demonstrate that the historical methods of reform used and advocated by the founders of the ILO and by the organization itself were exercises in futility. The solution, the authors proposed, was a revolutionary program capable of eliminating the contradictions in the system. Irrespective of the merits of the article, its publication was a deviation from the standards of objectivity which has been a hallmark of the ILO.

The United States contribution to the ILO.

The complaints against the ILO were reviewed by a subcommittee of the House Appropriations Committee before whom President Meany, the employers' representative, and officials of the State and Labor departments testified. All witnesses agreed that the ILO had deviated from its principles. Lack of consultation with United States officials was another complaint. In his testimony, President Meany said: "We in the American Trade Union Movement believe in the ILO and its purposes." At the same hearing he added: "No, I do not want to destroy the ILO." Nevertheless, he strongly objected to the political road the ILO had taken. It was only after Undersecretary of Labor for International Affairs George Hildebrand complained that the appointment of a Soviet national as assistant director had been made without "consulting with us," and that the subcommittee discussed the withholding of funds from the organization.[23]

Because funds were subsequently withheld by Congress, the AFL-CIO executive council said: "We have no desire to destroy or withdraw from the ILO."[24] The problem of restoring the funds that had been withheld was discussed by President Meany in a press conference on May 11, 1971. His position was that the United States government owed the money to the ILO and that it should be paid. He explained that the AFL-CIO, "because of the strenuous opposition in Congress," had "gone along with a suggestion made by the employer representatives and approved by the State Department that we should pay up all our obligations immediately, and, at the same time, file an official notice of withdrawal from the ILO two years hence."[25]

Reaction of the ILO.

The active opposition of the American labor movement has not been in vain. The 1971 conference reasserted the tripartite principle by electing a French employers' representative as president. There was also less inclination to overlook the failures of the communist bloc to live up to the ILO convention on freedom of association and discrimination in employment: discussions on these subjects were not avoided. The staff was also instructed to maintain objectivity in the treatment of industrial questions and to avoid propaganda. The AFL-CIO executive council greeted these changes as signs of progress, and hoped that the ILO would concentrate upon its historic mission of improving the lot of the workers of the world.[26]

What of the future?

The future of the ILO, at least in its present form, rests on the ability of nations with different ideologies and economic systems to cooperate in the promotion of the well being of the toilers of the world. Cooperation for this kind of purpose is basically different from and more difficult than collaborating politically. Nations must recognize each other's existence irrespective of differences in ideology or political organization. Promotion of reform requires a common outlook on the utility of measures for improvement in the position of the millions who work.

Tripartism poses an even more severe problem. This principle is the cornerstone of the ILO edifice. It assumes independent workers' and employers' representation able to vote against and advocate policies which the appointing government opposes. The workers' delegates from England, West Germany, France, the United States, and other free countries can take independent positions. Such a right is not enjoyed by the non-governmental delegates from the Soviet bloc. Human ingenuity is diverse and endless, and it may be possible to devise a formula for long-run cooperation of all members. As a first step, the free nations have to take the ILO seriously, and cooperate vigorously to enlarge the freedom of workers and all men and women and for the betterment of all peoples of the world.

CHAPTER FIFTEEN

Final Observations

THE INTEREST OF AMERICAN LABOR in foreign affairs and in the prosperity of labor movements of other lands reaches back more than a century. As in the country at large, there have always been minorities, and on occasion majorities, which opposed close alliances with the labor movements of other countries. An exception to the policy of "nonintercourse" was made with regard to the British Trades Union Congress, with which Americans have, since the middle 1890s, annually exchanged fraternal delegates. In the last four decades, concern and expenditures of money and effort in these areas have vastly increased. To some extent these changes reflect the global activity of the United States in other areas, but the main reason is that communist penetration through "innocent" fronts and direct assault could only be countered by greatly expanded activity in what can be broadly described as "foreign relations."

The increased attention given to foreign affairs has not always evoked applause from those who have traditionally preempted the field. In their view, the arcane subject could only be penetrated by persons trained in eastern or English universities. A concession might grudgingly be made to those who mastered the mysteries through government service, but no such allowance was ever extended to officers of labor organizations. Elected officials might feel grateful for support, but journalistic and academic intellectuals have always resented the independence and initiative shown by leaders of labor in matters touching on foreign policy.

It appears, however, that foreign policies of democratic governments will be increasingly influenced by broadly based organizations representing masses of citizens — labor organizations, political parties, chambers of commerce, and other types of popular associations. In the future, it might be more profitable for the diplomat to be acquainted with the views of labor than with the dynastic rivalries that rent old Europe or with the works of a Metternich or a Talleyrand.

The attempts of labor organizations to influence foreign policy have not received an enthusiastic reception from politicians suffering from the conceit that they are masters of the area or from writers or teachers who tend to charge that the views of the AFL-CIO are determined by the government of the United States or one of its agencies publicly unpopular at the particular moment. It is futile to review the misinformation and the half truths that have been circulated by certain members of the liberal intellectual community. They are neither new nor novel. This self-satisfied group has always regarded the views of organized labor with extreme disfavor. It has never sympathized with the American labor movement's opposition to all forms of totalitarianism.

The intellectual liberal community has never been able to understand how persons not trained in graduate schools could have the temerity to make independent judgments. It has been too lazy and arrogant to examine labor's views, and has frequently presented caricatures of opinions of the AFL-CIO and its predecessor federations. One of its favorite devices has been to attribute labor's views to some sinister influence — without noting that the opposition to all forms of totalitarianism has been a consistent position from the time when this monstrous evil saw the light of day.

Policy in the AFL-CIO and its predecessor federations has always been made by the conventions. Despite views to the contrary, the dicta of the convention are not lightly regarded by the executive council or the executive officers.[1] The executive council determines policy between conventions, and debates issues in executive sessions. (Minority reports were never issued by members of the executive council during the time of the old AFL.) With a tripling of the membership of the executive council, one might expect greater variation in views. Yet there has been little difference on essential policies of the executive council, the members of which are generally heads of autonomous unions.

The executive council is made up of members with an independent base. Over the years they have not always gone along with the recommendations of the head of the federation. Gompers' experiences illustrate this point. Virtually all leaders of organized labor in the United States, with the exception of a minority that has been severely reduced since the 1950s, have shared an abhorrence of communism and were denounced by groups similar to those more recently attempting to destroy the influence of American labor in this area.

In the late 1930s, the AFL rejoined the International Trade Union Federation. Reaffiliation was due to the influence of President Green, Matthew Woll, and David Dubinsky in spite of strong isolationist sentiment in the ranks.

Soon thereafter, the AFL faced a dilemma as a result of pressure by the British Trades Union Congress to bring Soviet unions into affiliation. The AFL warned that it would immediately sever its relationship with the International

Trade Union Federation if Soviet unions were admitted to the ranks. The same rule (non-cooperation) has been followed by the federations of labor in the United States toward unions in all totalitarian countries. The principle has also been applied to unions in Franco's Spain and in Yugoslavia.

A challenge to the principle of non-cooperation was made in 1942, when representatives of the British Trades Union Congress sought to have the AFL join the Anglo-Soviet labor committee. Despite this pressure, and more than a nudge from the White House, the AFL refused to join. This policy has been followed by the AFL-CIO since the merger. It is true that the CIO decided to follow its own course after the AFL refused to go along, but the experience of the CIO leadership with the communist controlled World Federation of Trade Unions — organized in 1945 — convinced the CIO that cooperation with communist federations of labor was infeasible, and could only lead to frustration at best. Consequently, the leaders of the CIO held the same views on cooperating with union federations in totalitarian countries as did the AFL, and the issue was never a matter of debate during merger negotiations.

In the early years of Hitler's power, the CIO was establishing its great unions, some of which faced serious factional divisions. Moreover, the internal situation of the CIO did not allow that organization to pursue a foreign affairs policy. The communist bloc, which was ready to sabotage the election of Harry Truman would not have recoiled from splitting the CIO asunder, if such tactics had been indicated.

With the end of the war the CIO was four years away from openly challenging the communist bloc in some of its own unions. By 1949 its leaders were convinced that the CIO could retain membership within the World Federation of

Trade Unions (WFTU) only on the basis of accepting the objectives of the communist leaders in control of the WFTU's apparatus.

The AFL, because it never operated under the disadvantages of the CIO, which were accidental and a result of the conditions under which the CIO arose, was able from the beginning to recognize the danger to the free world in the rise of Hitlerism. But it was never deceived that the heroic defense by the Soviet armies of their native soil converted their government into a democracy. Demands for second fronts did not come on the floor of AFL conventions. The leadership recognized that the end of the war would require reestablishment of the labor movements of Germany and the occupied countries, and it sought to assist in this task. Leaders of European labor were brought to the United States and others were aided in their native lands or in the countries where they had found temporary refuge.

The Marshall Plan, unprecedented in purpose and scope, had serious repercussions on the international trade union federations. A program which had for its aim the industrial reconstruction of Europe through American aid, its presentation to the world by President Truman created a dilemma for not only the communist bloc unions in the WFTU but also for their followers within the free world. Soviet ideologists had forecast a crisis of capitalism, a catastrophic depression which would seize the economies of the free world as soon as the pent-up demand unsatisfied during the war had been met. The communist theoreticians were convinced that the inevitable postwar depression would add to disillusion with the results of war and would lead the European masses to accept communist solutions. They, after some hesitation, recognized that their hopes would be shattered by a successful Marshall Plan. As soon as the signal was flashed from the leaders of world communism, the faithful fell in line. The non-communist leadership of the CIO rejected the anti-Marshall Plan maneuver, seeing it for what it was — a plan to prevent the reconstruction of a free Europe. With the exclusion from the CIO of unions loyal to the communist line and with the erosion of communist influence in other CIO affiliates, the CIO, in common with federations from other free countries, withdrew from the WFTU and ultimately established the International Confederation of Free Trade Unions.

The view of the AFL and the CIO, as well as that of the merged AFL-CIO, was that the unions of the free world had to oppose communist totalitarianism because it denied men the right to choose their governors, their organizations of labor, and took away the rights of freedom of association, speech, and press. Those who have attacked the American labor movement for its views and for not always falling in line behind the United States government forget that the federation, like its predecessors, is not a government agency and that it is the critics rather than the AFL-CIO who expect the labor movement to accept a tyranny that is politically and economically viable just because the United States government finds it expedient to deal with it.

Organized labor in the United States has never been beguiled by totalitarian tyrannies which control means of production and distribution. Its adamant opposition to exchanges with the "unions" of the eastern bloc has always been based upon the view that these organizations are neither autonomous nor independent, and that nothing can be gained by meeting with what are in fact government controlled organizations. The "unions" of the eastern bloc are not singled out, since the same criterion has been applied to the "unions" in Spain and in Argentina during the Peronist period. There are those who, because of their socialist sympathies or other reasons, seek to distinguish between totalitarianism in socialist clothing and the fascists. American labor has, on the whole, not been receptive to these distinctions, and it finds both types of dictatorship evil and repulsive.

Like other institutions, the labor movement has adopted its program to changing needs and circumstances. A policy which was effective at one place or time might no longer be applicable to other parts of the world. It must always be recognized that the labor movement is not sponsoring or promoting what might be described as realpolitik, which is the task of governments, but democracy and social and economic justice. It is not obliged to shake the bloody hand of the tyrant even when the American government finds it necessary to do so.

The difference between the government and voluntary private organizations must always be borne in mind. The latter are not obliged either by law or morals to be in tune with government decisions at any moment. An arrangement may be repugnant to an organization, and it enjoys the right in a democracy to express its views without fear or favor.

In pursuance of this aim, the federation has established several institutes to aid in training both leaders and the rank and file. These institutes have carried on projects in workers' education, vocational training, assistance to consumers' and producers' cooperatives, and in some instances large-scale housing developments. Of the three institutes operated by associations founded by the AFL-CIO, the American Institute for Free Labor Development is the oldest and carries on the most extensive program. It is also the one which has been subjected to the most severe criticism. Its character could best be judged by reading several articles and President George Meany's testimony before the Foreign Relations Committee.

Obviously there will be differences of opinion on the

desirability of a voluntary private organization of the United States engaging in certain types of activity abroad. This type of criticism differs from charges repeated by a variety of journalists, without proof, of CIA financing. Funds for projects are provided by the AFL-CIO, individual unions, employers, and by the federal government through AID. The government allocations are made openly and are subject to the same audits as funds for programs operated by universities and similar institutions.

The African-American Labor Center was, in a broad sense, organized for the same purpose as AIFLD. It is operated on a more modest scale because the skills it is trying to generate are more elemental than those needed in the Latin American countries, with their established labor movements. Vocational training, housing, and schooling in the administration of cooperatives and labor organizations have all been important parts of the curriculum.

The most recent institute, established for the Asian countries, aims to provide the same types of general assistance. It is hoped that it will in time provide the same general aid to urban and rural workers as the other institutes. It is hoped that the institute can contribute in a modest way to the training of activists and leaders of democratic labor movements that will be independent.

American labor has been concerned with the problems of Indochina since the 1940s and 1950s. In contrast to many other observers, the AFL identified Ho Chi Minh as a communist agent and also warned the United States against supporting the French colonial regime. After the end of the Vietnam war, the AFL stressed that the Geneva conference had failed to meet the problems of the area and that the settlement would not lead to the establishment of peace. The AFL predicted an increase in subversion and open conflict. It supported President Lyndon Johnson's intervention on the grounds that the Viet Cong invasion represented a communist attack upon a peaceful government and its people.

Beginning in 1965, the AFL-CIO urged its members to help in the campaign for the resettlement of "hundreds of thousands of Vietnamese men, women, and children who have become refugees in their own land." The council also noted that the "Vietnam Confederation of Workers has a decisive role to play in ensuring social justice and safeguarding freedom in this heroic country." The December 1965 convention declared the "communist enemy can never be defeated by military means alone. Along with adequate measures, there must be sound large-scale programs for improving the conditions of life and labor and for developing democratic institutions. But even the best programs are useless without people. In this connection, the unions of the workers and peasants can play a decisive role. The convention, therefore, reiterates the AFL-CIO plea for appropriate and adequate assistance to the Vietnam Confederation of Workers (CVT), which has emerged as an invaluable force for democratic regeneration and social justice in the land."

The American labor movement has always regarded the expansion of communist power as dangerous to freedom. It has opposed communists whether they were in Europe, Africa, or Asia. The major activity of the AFL-CIO, as of other organizations of labor in the United States, is the protection of the workers' interests on the job, and the seeking of state and federal legislation that will advance them. It has never made foreign affairs its principal activity; neither has the government of the United States. There are many problems facing the labor movement and the country, and some of them involve relations with other lands. No one will contend that, on issues as complicated and difficult as some of these, the membership and the leaders are unanimous in their views.

If the past is any guide to the future, one will note the importance of the views of the membership and leaders upon policies. Men like Dubinsky, Woll, George Harrison, George Meany, and many others believed that the American labor movement must pursue an active anti-totalitarian policy. It is conceivable that many of the questions which divide the Western powers from the governments of Eastern Europe will in the near or distant future be settled or minimized. Such changes are not certain to affect the views of the labor movement, which is likely to continue to regard the one-party state a tyranny and the suppression of free speech, press, and associations as violations of human rights.

Notes

NOTES TO INTRODUCTION

1. Gompers to N. S. Chekheiji, March 21, 1917. He sent several other telegrams, on April 2, April 23, and May 6, 1917, to Chekheiji and the Workmen's and Council of Deputies. They were sent to Petrograd.
2. Samuel Gompers to President Woodrow Wilson, February 9, 1919.
3. Memorandum from Samuel Gompers to the American Commission to Negotiate the Peace, March 12, 1919.
4. Samuel Gompers to Honorable Charles Evans Hughes, July 9, 1923. *Report of the Proceedings of the Forty-Fifth Annual Convention of the American Federation of Labor,* 1925, p. 334.
5. William Green to Albert F. Coyle, June 17, July 8, 1926; Coyle to Green, June 27, July 2, 1926.
6. *Statement of AFL Executive Council,* June 29, 1926.
7. *American Federation of Labor Weekly News Service,* April 22, 1933.
8. Memorandum in Roosevelt Library, OF 142, B1.
9. Statement by William Green, December 21, 1925, issued by the authority of the AFL executive council.
10. Transcript of *Face the Nation,* as broadcast over the CBS Television Network and CBS Radio Network, September 6, 1970; first quote is on p. 3, second on p. 6.

NOTES TO CHAPTER ONE

1. *Report of the First Convention of the Federation of Organized Trades and Labor Unions of the United States and Canada,* 1881, p. 14.
2. *Report of the Second Annual Convention of the American Federation of Labor,* 1887, pp. 26, 29.
3. *To the Officers & Delegates of the Federational Trade Union Congress in London Assembled,* p. 1. In the files of the AFL. October 27, 1888.
4. Gompers to William Liebknecht, November 22, 1888. In the archives of the AFL.
5. Gompers to André Gily, May 20, 1889.
6. *Ibid.*
7. Gompers to Eleanor Aveling and Will Thorne, February 19, 1891.
8. Gompers to International Labor Congress, Brussels, August 4, 1891.
9. *Ibid.*
10. *Report of Proceedings of Twelfth Annual Convention of the AFL,* 1892, p. 15.
11. *Report of Proceedings of Fifteenth Annual Convention,* 1895, p. 65.
12. The quotation is from a letter addressed to members of the executive council asking their approval of allowing the AFL fraternal delegates to the British Trades Union Congress to seek the aid of the British in enlarging international cooperation. The letter to the council is dated September 8, 1896.
13. Gompers to August Keufer, January 23, 1900. Keufer was a conservative unionist by the standards of the French labor movement.
14. Johann Sassenbach, *Twenty-Five Years of International Unionism* (Amsterdam: International Federation of Trade Unions, 1926), pp. 5-9; Walter Schevenels, *Forty-Five Years International Federation of Trade,* (Brussels: International Federation of Trade Unions, 1956), pp 11-20; Georges Lefranc, *Les Experiences Syndicales Internationales* (Paris: Aubier, 1952), pp. 9-10.
15. *American Federationist,* December 1905, p. 938.
16. Philip Taft, *The AFL in the Time of Gompers* (New York: Harper and Bros., 1957), p. 422.
17. Legien was a right wing socialist in his politics, and opposed the advocacy of the general strike by the International Secretariat

because it would keep federations such as the AFL outside. However, in 1920, he led the general strike against the Kapp putsch which tried to overthrow the Weimar Republic. See Theodore Leipart, *Karl Legien: Ein Denkbuch* (Berlin: Allgemeine Deutschen Gewerksschaftsbund, 1949), a short biography by his successor as head of the German trade unions.

18. The resolutions are reproduced in Sassenbach, *op. cit.,* p. 17. The one on the tasks of the conference was unanimously adopted, but the one which excluded consideration of theoretical questions and tactics ran into opposition and the delegates from Belgium, Holland, and Austria voted against it. Hueber, the head of the Austrian trade unions, believed that the resolution would create differences between the trade unions and the political party, and that a discussion of theoretical questions or tactics should not be excluded.

19. Samuel Gompers, *Labor in Europe and America* (New York: Harper and Bros., 1910), p. v-vi. Gompers' description of the personalities among those present at the conference was: "A representative from Roumania, M. Racovsky, was given a seat without a vote, though Secretary Legien had said he was without information as to the status, or even existence, of trade unions in Roumania, or as to whether M. Racovsky lived in that country or in Paris. The gentleman, I am told, spoke French with a Gallic accent." *op. cit.,* p. 131. Racovsky was a professional revolutionary close to the Russian Bolsheviks. He held a number of top jobs after the Russian Revolution of October 1917, including that of Ambassador to France. He was a follower of Trotsky, and was purged in 1937. He died in exile.

20. Sassenbach, *op. cit.,* p. 26; Gompers, *op. cit.,* p. 135.

21. Sassenbach, *op. cit.,* p. 29.

22. Gompers, *op. cit.,* p. 131.

23. Gompers to Karl Legien, December 4, 1909.

24. *Minutes of the Executive Council of the American Federation of Labor,* February 20, 1911.

25. *Report of American Federation of Labor Representative at International Trades Convention,* Budapest, 1911, pp. 15-16.

26. Sassenbach, *op. cit.,* p. 29.

27. *Report of American Federation of Labor Representative at Zurich, Switzerland, World Congress of Trade Unions,* 1913, p. 12.

28. Legien to Gompers, August 27, 1914. The letters between Legien

and Gompers, and Gompers to Appleton and Oudegeest appeared in the *American Federationist,* November 1915, pp. 925-964.

29. Gompers to Legien, September 1, 1914. When Frank Morrison (secretary of AFL) asked whether Legien's letter should be published in the *Weekly News Letter* (Gompers was out of the office), he was told: "It must not be published at this time. It would arouse unfavorable comment and feeling and react injuriously on him and that country." Gompers to Morrison, September 20, 1914.

30. *Report of Proceedings of the Thirty-Fourth Annual Convention of the American Federation of Labor,* 1914, pp. 474-475; Samuel Gompers, "To the labor movements of all countries," March 22, 1916; a leaflet appealing for the meeting.

31. Gompers to President Wilson, December 7, 1914.

32. See Legien's statement to the affiliated national labor centers, November 22, 1914 in Sassenbach, *op. cit.,* pp. 47-48.

33. W. A. Appleton and Léon Jouhaux to Gompers, February 16, 1915. The letter assured Gompers: "There is not the slightest personal feeling against Legien, and it is understood that the arrangement suggested may only be temporary."

34. The resolution of the Scandinavian centers is in Sassenbach, *op. cit.,* p. 54.

35. Gompers to Legien, February 4, 1917; Gompers to Johann Von Bernstoff, February 10, 1917. Joseph Tumulty, secretary to President Wilson told him the President was of the opinion that his letters were "a splendid service . . ."

36. Gompers to Legien, April 2, 1917.

37. Legien to Gompers, February 11, 1917.

38. Samuel Gompers, "American Labor's Position in Peace or in War," *American Federationist,* April 1917, p. 270.

39. *Ibid.*

40. *Report of Proceedings of the Thirty-Seventh Annual Convention of the American Federation of Labor,* 1917, p. 72.

41. *Ibid.,* p. 75.

42. Letters to the prime ministers were sent on April 12, 1917, and are printed in *American Federationist,* May 1917, p. 369.

43. The letter of the Swiss Federation is in *American Federationist,* November 1917, pp. 958-959.

44. Oudegeest to Gompers, May 24, 1917.

45. Gompers to Oudegeest, May 4, 1917 (cablegram).
46. Oudegeest and delegates to June 8 conference to Gompers, June 8, 1917.
47. Gompers to Lindquist, June 27, 1917 (cablegram).
48. Arthur Henderson to Gompers, January 16, 1918; Gompers to Henderson, February 18, 1918. The request of the Socialist Party of the United States was rejected by the organizers of the conference presumably because of Gompers' opposition.
49. Information from a short memorandum (undated) in the file of the AFL.
50. *Report of Proceedings of the Fortieth Annual Convention of the American Federation of Labor,* 1920, pp. 105-106.
51. Gompers to Charles R. Bowerman (Secretary, British Trades Union Congress), December 28, 1918.
52. See O. Piatnitsky, *The Twenty-One Points of Admission to the Communist International* (No date or place), pp. 27-30. Piatnitsky was director of the international communist apparatus. He perished in the 1930 purges.
53. The letter was sent from the Hotel Crillon, in Paris, where the American delegation was housed. It was written by Gompers to E. Van Quaquebeke and J. Roscam, secretaries of the Christian Trade Unions of Belgium, February 19, 1919.
54. Gompers to Henderson, December 19, 23, 1918; Gompers to Charles H. Bowerman, December 28, 1918.
55. Sassenbach, *op. cit.* pp. 68-69, gives part of the statement. The Sassenbach statement and Gompers' resolution are in *Report of Proceedings of the Fortieth Annual Convention of the American Federation of Labor,* 1920, pp. 136-139.
56. *AFL Proceedings,* 1920, p. 137.
57. *Ibid.,* p. 140.
58. Legien to E. Fimmen, September 20, 1919. Fimmen was a Dutch trade unionist and subsequently an officer of the IFTU.
59. *AFL Proceedings,* 1920, p. 155.
60. Excerpts from Gompers' letter: *Ibid.,* p. 167.
61. Schevenels, *op. cit.,* p. 98.
62. *Report of the Proceedings of the Fortieth Annual Convention of the American Federation of Labor,* 1920, pp. 166-167.
63. *Ibid.,* p. 476; Gompers to Appleton, July 15, 1920; Gompers to Oudegeest, July 13, 1920.

64. W. A. Appleton to Edo Fimmen, January 31, 1921.
65. C. W. Bowerman to Gompers, January 31, 1921.
66. *Minutes of the Meeting of the AFL Executive Council,* March 3, 1921.
67. *Document No. 6,* Executive Council Vote Book, March 6, 1923; *Document No. 134,* December 11, 1923; Gompers, *Report to Executive Council,* September 11, 1924 (mimeographed); *Appeal for German Trade Unions,* December 2, 1923.
68. *Document No. 18,* sent by William Green to executive council, May 11, 1926.
69. *Minutes of the Meeting of the AFL Executive Council,* August 26, 1926; *Report of the Proceedings of the Forty-Seventh Annual Convention of the American Federation of Labor,* 1927, p. 23; William Green to Walter Citrine (secretary of the British Trades Union Congress), November 9, 1926.

NOTES TO CHAPTER TWO

1. *Report of Proceedings of the Twenty-Eighth Annual Convention of the American Federation of Labor,* 1908, pp. 259-260.
2. *Report of Proceedings of the Twenty-Ninth Annual Convention of the American Federation of Labor,* 1909, p. 331.
3. Samuel Gompers, "United States-Mexico-Labor: Their Relations," *American Federationist,* August 1916, p. 633.
4. *Report of Proceedings of the Thirty-Second Annual Convention of the American Federation of Labor,* 1912, pp. 256-257.
5. Statement of AFL Executive Council to R. Zuberán, United States Representative of the Mexican Constitutionalists, July 25, 1914.
6. Samuel Gompers to Honorable Woodrow Wilson, September 22, 1915.
7. *Minutes of the Meeting of the AFL Executive Council,* February 26, 1916.
8. The exchange on the religious issue was: Frank Duffy to the Rev. Francis Kelley, April 5, 1916; Kelley to Duffy, April 10, 1916; Duffy to Monsignor Kelley, April 14, 1916.
9. Gompers, *op. cit.,* p. 641.
10. Frank Duffy to Samuel Gompers, May 26, 1916.
11. Samuel Gompers to the Secretary of the *Casa del Obrero Mundial,* May 23, 1916.
12. *Minutes of Meeting of the AFL Executive Council,* July 1, 1916.
13. *Mexican-United States Compact,* A Statement signed by members

of the AFL Executive Council and five representatives of the organized workers in Mexico. *Report of the Proceedings of the Thirty-Sixth Annual Convention of the American Federation of Labor,* 1916, pp. 59-60.

14. Samuel Gompers to General Venustiano Carranza, June 28, 1916; President Carranza to Gompers, June 29, 1916.
15. *Report of Proceedings of Thirty-Fourth Annual Convention of the American Federation of Labor,* 1915, pp. 157-158.
16. *To the Workers of All American Countries,* Statement sent to labor organizations in the Latin American countries, July 6, 1916.
17. *Report of the Proceedings of Thirty-Sixth Annual Convention of the American Federation of Labor,* 1916, p. 57. See Sinclair Snow, *The Pan-American Federation of Labor* (Durham, N.C.: Duke University Press, 1965), which contains material on the origin and growth of the Pan-American Federation of Labor. The volume is marred by lack of knowledge of the views of the AFL on a number of issues.
18. Louis Lorwin, *Labor and Internationalism* (New York: The Macmillan Co., 1929), pp. 288-289.
19. "Report of American Labor Mission to Mexico," *Report of the Proceedings of the Thirty-Eighth Annual Convention of the American Federation of Labor,* 1918, pp. 248-253.
20. Samuel Gompers to President Woodrow Wilson, November 29, 1919.
21. Secretary of State Robert Lansing to Samuel Gompers, December 3, 1919; Lansing to Gompers, January 31, 1920.
22. *Report of the Third Congress of the Pan-American Federation of Labor,* 1921, pp. 37-55.
23. Gompers to Secretary of State Charles E. Hughes, May 28, 1921; Hughes to Gompers, June 18, 1921.
24. Samuel Gompers to Charles E. Hughes, July 1, 1922.
25. Gompers to Secretary of State Charles E. Hughes, September 1, 1923.
26. William Green to Secretary of State Frank B. Kellogg, June 15, 1925.
27. Frank Tannenbaum, *Mexico: The Struggle for Peace and Bread,* (New York: Alfred A. Knopf, 1950), pp. 122-135.
28. *Report of the Proceedings of the Forty-Sixth Annual Convention of the American Federation of Labor,* 1926, p. 61.
29. *Ibid.,* p. 363.

30. *Ibid.*, p. 365.
31. *Report of the Proceedings of the Forty-Seventh Annual Convention of the American Federation of Labor*, 1927, pp. 99-100.

NOTES TO CHAPTER THREE

1. Jan Oudegeest to William Green, September 25, 1925. *Minutes of Meeting of Executive Council of the American Federation of Labor*, October 16, 1925.
2. Green to Oudegeest, March 23, 1926.
3. *Report of Proceedings of the Fifty-Third Annual Convention of the American Federation of Labor*, 1933, pp. 470-471.
4. *Report of Proceedings of the Fifty-Fourth Annual Convention of the American Federation of Labor*, 1934, p. 174.
5. *Ibid.*, pp. 385-390, 570-571.
6. Green to William Willsbyly, January 7, 1935.
7. *Report of Proceedings of the Fifty-Fifth Annual Convention of the American Federation of Labor*, 1935, pp. 385-390.
8. *Report of Proceedings of the Fifty-Sixth Annual Convention of the American Federation of Labor*, 1936, p. 592.
9. William Green to National and International Unions, State Federations of Labor, Central Labor Unions, and Directly Affiliated Unions, November 18, 1938.
10. *Ibid.*
11. *Minutes of Meeting of AFL Executive Council*, January 25, 1938; Green to Citrine, January 25, 1938.
12. *Report of Proceedings of the Fifty-Ninth Annual Convention of the American Federation of Labor*, 1939, p. 421.
13. *Statement of the AFL Executive Council*, February 2, 1940.
14. *Statement of the AFL Executive Council*, May 15, 1940.
15. William Green and George Meany to the Officers of National and International Unions, State Federations of Labor and Central Labor Unions, February 28, 1940.
16. *Daily Proceedings of the Second Constitutional Convention of the Congress of Industrial Organizations*, 1939, p. 5.
17. *Ibid.*, p. 106.
18. *Ibid.*, p. 106-107.
19. *Daily Proceedings of the Third Constitutional Convention of the Congress of Industrial Organizations*, 1940, pp. 227-228.
20. *Ibid.*, p. 106.

21. *Report of Proceedings of the Fifty-Fifth Annual Convention of the American Federation of Labor,* 1935, p. 718.
22. *Minutes of the Meeting of the AFL Executive Council,* October 8, 1936.
23. *Minutes of the Meeting of the AFL Executive Council,* August 31, 1937. The unions in the CIO had not yet been expelled from the AFL. Moreover, the CIO was still the Committee for Industrial Organization, and only became the Congress of Industrial Organizations in the following year. Dubinsky, who was called from Warsaw to judge the dispute, pointed to the fact that the CIO unions were then still part of the AFL.
24. *Minutes of the Meeting of the AFL Executive Council,* February 2, 1938.
25. *Ibid.*
26. Walter Citrine to William Green, December 14, 1938.
27. Citrine to Green, May 2, 1939.
28. Green to Citrine, June 15, 1939.
29. "Eighth International Trade Union Congress," *International Trade Union Movement,* June-July 1939, p. 206.
30. Walter Citrine to William Green, February 25, 1942 (cablegram).
31. Citrine to Green, February 27, 1942.
32. Green to Citrine, March 21, 1942.
33. *Minutes of the Meeting of the AFL Executive Council,* May 20, 1942.
34. *Ibid.*
35. *Ibid.*
36. *Minutes of the Meeting of the AFL Executive Council,* May 21, 1942.
37. *AFL Weekly News Service,* July 28, 1942.
38. Philip Murray, August 6, 1942.
39. A. Johnston, D. R. Robertson, H. W. Fraser, A. F. Whitney, and T. C. Cashen, August 6, 1942.
40. Green to A. F. Whitney, September 22, 1942.
41. *Daily Proceedings of the Third Constitutional Convention of the Congress of Industrial Organizations,* 1942, pp. 364-367.
42. *Daily Proceedings of the Fourth Constitutional Convention of the Congress of Industrial Organizations,* 1941, p. 213. The rest of the resolution expresses a sense of the real danger facing the United States.

43. *Ibid.*, p. 161.
44. Citrine to Green, September 4, 1943; Green to Citrine, September 14, 1942.
45. Statement of Citrine in *Minutes of Meeting of AFL Executive Council,* January 27, 1943.
46. *Ibid.*
47. Statement of Green, *ibid.*
48. *Statement of the Executive Council of the AFL,* January 27, 1943.
49. *Conference Between British Trades Union Delegations and Officers of CIO,* February 14, 1943.
50. Philip Murray's statement is dated March 1, 1945. It is in the Philip Murray papers in Catholic University.
51. International Federation of Trade Unions, *Report on Activities, 1943-1944,* p. 9.
52. *Ibid.*, p. 10.
53. *Emergency International Trade Union Council Summary of the Meeting,* September 24, 1944, p. 3.
54. Citrine to Green, November 2, 1943.
55. Green to Citrine, November 30, 1943.
56. Schevenels to Green, January 14, 1944.
57. *Final Proceedings of the Seventh Constitutional Convention of the Congress of Industrial Organizations,* 1944, p. 299.
58. *Minutes of the Meeting of AFL Executive Council,* January 25, 1944.
59. *Ibid.*
60. International Transport Federation, *News Release,* July 27, 1946.
61. *Trade Union Congress, World Federation of Trade Unions Brief History,* October 27, 1948.
62. *Minutes of Meeting of AFL Executive Council,* October 18, 1945.
63. Trades Union Congress, *World Federation of Trade Unions Brief History,* p. 2.
64. Citrine to Green, October 16, 1945; Green to Citrine, October 19, 1945; Citrine to Green, October 25, 1945. *Report of Meeting of AFL Executive Council,* October 19, 1945.
65. Report of Irving Brown to George Meany, December 4, 1947. It was sent from Paris.

NOTES TO CHAPTER FOUR

1. Green's testimony is in *AFL News Service,* January 21, 1941.

Murray's views are in *Daily Proceedings of the Fourth Constitutional Convention of the Congress of Industrial Organizations,* 1941, p. 41.

2. Green to Breckinridge Long (Assistant Secretary of State), February 7, 1941; Long to Green, March 31, 1941.

3. Matthew Woll to William Green, November 12 and 26, 1943; Green to Woll, November 23, 1943; *Report of the Proceedings of the Forty-Third Annual Convention of the American Federation of Labor,* 1943, p. 557.

4. *Report of the Proceedings of the Sixty-Fourth Annual Convention of the American Federation of Labor, 1944,* pp. 556-557.

5. Matthew Woll to Daniel J. Tobin (president of the International Brotherhood of Teamsters, Chauffeurs, Warehousemen and Helpers of America), March 24, 1949.

6. *AFL Weekly News Service,* March 12, 1946.

7. *Report of the Commission of the World Federation of Trade Unions to Investigate Conditions in Germany,* p. 9. The commission was appointed in accordance with a resolution adopted by the Paris congress, in October 1945. It assembled in Berlin on January 30, 1946, and spent about four days in each zone.

8. *Daily Proceedings of the Tenth Constitutional Convention of the Congress of Industrial Organizations,* 1946, pp. 103-105.

9. *Report of Irving J. Brown,* November 10, 1947.

10. *Ibid.*

11. *Statement of AFL Executive Council,* January 31, 1946.

12. *Ibid.*

13. *Ibid.*

14. Henry Rutz to George Meany, May 31, 1948; Rutz to Jay Lovestone, May 31, 1948 and April 26, 1950.

15. Matthew Woll to Secretary of State George C. Marshall, April 3, 1947. From Advisory and Review Branch, Historical Division, State Department, 862/.008, 3-347.

16. Frank Fenton, Director of Organization, AFL, to Woll, May 15, 1947.

17. Matthew Woll was president of the League for Human Rights. Green sent out periodic appeals on behalf of the above organization.

18. *1948 Proceedings Tenth Constitutional Convention CIO,* p. 135.

19. Green to Secretary of State James F. Byrnes, June 11, 1946.

20. *Ibid.*

21. Dean Acheson to Green, July 9, 1946.
22. General Lucius Clay to Green, July 23, 1946.
23. Woll to Secretary of State Marshall, January 20, 1948. The same letter was sent to Secretary of Defense Forrestal.
24. *Ibid.*
25. The cable for information on the charges made by Woll is in the AFL-CIO archives. It was sent February 25, 1948.
26. *Ibid.*
27. Woll to Secretary of War Kenneth C. Royall, April 27, 1948.
28. Woll to Forrestal, April 6, 1948.
29. William H. Draper, Jr. to Woll, April 29, 1948.
30. Jay Lovestone to William H. Draper, Jr., May 6, 1948.
31. Lovestone to Harvey Brown, April 16, 1948.
32. Woll to James Forrestal, March 17, 1948. The same letter was sent to Secretary Marshall.
33. Lovestone to Henry Rutz, April 16, 1948.
34. Clement Gottwald became president of Czechoslovakia when Eduard Benes was forced out by a *coup d'etat* engineered by the communists.
35. Woll to Marshall, June 22, 1948.
36. General Clay to Woll, January 5, 1949.
37. Woll to General Clay, February 14, 1949.
38. *Ibid.*
39. *Report of the Proceedings of the Sixty-Eighth Convention of the American Federation of Labor,* 1949, p. 126.
40. Jay Lovestone to Secretary of War Kenneth C. Royall, July 8, 1948.
41. Matthew Woll to William H. Draper, Jr., August 23, 1948.
42. *Daily Proceedings of the Ninth Constitutional Convention of the Congress of Industrial Organizations,* 1947.
43. *Ibid.,* p. 46.
44. *Ibid.,* p. 62.
45. *Ibid.,* p. 65.
46. *Report of Proceedings of the Sixty-Sixth Convention of the American Federation of Labor,* 1947, p. 467.
47. *Ibid.,* p. 468.
48. *Ibid.,* p. 469.
49. *Report of the American Federation of Labor Mission to Germany.*

It was submitted to the executive council on January 29, 1947. William C. Doherty, president of the National Federation of Letter Carriers and a vice president of the AFL, and Israel Feinberg, a vice president of the International Ladies Garment Workers Union, were the members of the mission. Anton Jakobs, an organizer for the Meat Cutters' union, acted as interpreter and secretary.

50. *Ibid.*
51. Henry Rutz to General Lucius D. Clay, July 19, 1947; Woll to Clay, July 7, 1947.
52. William Green to Honorable Harry Truman, November 24, 1947.
53. *Ibid.*
54. Foreign Assistance Act of 1948 (Public Law 472), No. 115 (f).
55. Green to Secretary of State Dean Acheson, May 24, 1949 (cablegram).
56. Secretary of State Dean Acheson to Green, May 30, 1949 (cablegram).
57. Statement in *AFL Weekly News Service,* July 5, 1949.
58. Walter Reuther to Honorable Harry S. Truman, May 10, 1949.
59. *Ibid.*
60. *Ibid.*
61. *Statement of AFL International Labor Relations Committee,* January 20, 1949. See also Woll's letter to Willard L. Thorp, Assistant Secretary of State, September 20, 1949.
62. *Eleventh Constitutional Convention, Congress of Industrial Organizations,* 1949, p. 420.
63. *Report to American Federation of Labor* by Henry Rutz, July 1953.
64. Statement by Matthew Woll, on behalf of the Free Trade Union Committee, May 26, 1948.
65. Woll to General Clay, February 13, 1949.
66. George Meany to Walter Freitag, president of the German Federation of Labor, December 4, 1952. There is a tendency of European labor leaders to confuse the attitude held by American union officials on domestic policies with their views on unions in other countries. Gompers once said he would be a nihilist in Russia, a social democrat in Germany, and a member of the Labour Party in England. When George Reuther, the heroic Mayor of Berlin, called on Woll and asked his support for codetermination,

he was told: "Our policy is to support our allies in their undertakings regardless of whether or not we might find ourselves in accord with their point of view or not—in other words, that it was for the German trade unions to decide what they deemed best and that we would help them as best we could." Woll to Rutz, December 15, 1950, describing a visit and conversation with Reuther.

67. *Statement of International Labor Relations Committee* (AFL) June 20, 1949.
68. Woll to High Commissioner John J. McCloy, July 26, 1949.
69. Woll to Secretary of State Dean Acheson, November 26, 1951.
70. *Report to the Labor Department's Trade Union Advisory Committee on International Affairs Concerning Observations and Recommendations by the Mission Sent to Germany to Ascertain Steps to be Taken To Strengthen Free and Democratic Trade Unions in Germany,* p. 3.
71. *Report of the Proceedings of the Sixty-Seventh Annual Convention of the American Federation of Labor,* 1948, p. 483.
72. Woll to General Lucius Clay, February 14, 1949. See also *Memorandum to the Secretary of State, Dean Acheson,* by the International Labor Relations Committee, AFL, March 9, 1949.
73. Rutz to George Meany, May 14, 1947.
74. Woll to Prime Minister Paul Ramadier, May 21, 1947.
75. *Ibid.*
76. *Report of the Proceedings of the Seventy-Second Convention of the American Federation of Labor,* 1953.
77. Philip Taft, *The AFL in the Time of Gompers* (New York: Harper and Brothers, 1957), pp. 339-340.
78. Matthew Woll to Secretary of State Dean Acheson, October 10, 1951.
79. *Ibid.*
80. *Ibid.*
81. *Ibid.*
82. Geoffrey W. Lewis to Matthew Woll, November 6, 1951.
83. *Ibid.*
84. *Ibid.*
85. Matthew Woll to Geoffrey Lewis, November 26, 1951.
86. *Ibid.*
87. Schumacher's speech is in *Report of the Sixty-Sixth Convention of*

the *American Federation of Labor,* 1947, p. 478.

88. Kurt Schumacher to William Green, January 2, 1948.

89. Henry Rutz to Jay Lovestone, February 10, 1953.

90. General W. M. Hodge to Rutz, May 20, 1954.

91. *The Crisis in Europe, Declaration by the AFL Executive Council,* May 11, 1950. See Matthew Woll to H. W. Brown (president of the International Association of Machinists), May 31, 1949.

92. Help Committee for the Austrian Trade Unionists (C. F. Lindahl, Chairman, to AFL, November 23, 1945; Otis E. Mulliken to Robert Watt, December 19, 1945; Watt to C. F. Lindahl, December 20, 1945.

93. Matthew Woll to Secretary of War Kenneth C. Royall, March 7, 1949.

94. Major General Edmond H. Leavey to Matthew Woll, March 30, 1949.

95. Matthew Woll to Secretary of Defense Robert A. Lovett, October 31, 1951.

96. *Ibid.*

97. Secretary of the Army Pace to Woll, December 11, 1951.

98. Woll to Secretary of Army Pace, January 23, 1952.

99. Henry Rutz to General Hays, August 22, 1952.

100. Lieut. General George P. Hays to Henry Rutz, August 7, 1952.

101. Rutz to Jay Lovestone, November 10, 1952; M. J. Kennedy to Matthew Woll, October 21, 1952.

102. Article 16 was published in *The New York Times,* May 5, 1955.

103. *Statement by the Executive Council of the American Federation of Labor,* May 4, 1956.

104. *The New York Times,* April 29, 1955.

NOTES TO CHAPTER FIVE

1. *Report from Irving Brown,* Paris, December 23, 1946.

2. Irving Brown, *Relations with British Trades Union Congress.* This was an undated report made in the summer of 1948.

3. *The TUC and the WFTU, A Statement of Policy on the World Federation of Trades Union Congress,* October, 1948, p. 3.

4. *Ibid.*

5. *1948 Proceedings, Tenth Convention Congress of Industrial Organizations,* p. 228.

6. *Ibid.*

7. *Report of the Proceedings of the Sixty-Sixth Convention of the American Federation of Labor,* 1947, p. 474.

8. *International Free Trade Union News,* January, 1948.

9. *Ibid.*

10. *Ibid.*

11. *Report to CIO Executive Board, 1945-1949,* May 17, 1949.

12. *Free Trade Unions Leave the WFTU: Statement of the British Trades Union Congress, the Congress of Industrial Organizations, U.S.A., and the Confederation of Free Trade Unions of the Netherlands who took part in the meeting of the Executive Bureau of the World Federation of Trade Unions in Paris, January 17-19, 1949* (London: British Trades Union Congress, 1949), pp. 8-9.

13. *Ibid.,* p. 9.

14. *Ibid.*

15. *Ibid.,* p. 6.

16. Matthew Woll, "What Next in Europe," *International Free Trade Union News,* September, 1947. William Green, in an address over the American Broadcasting Co., November 19, 1947, called for approval of the Marshall Plan by Congress. Secretary-Treasurer George Meany spoke in favor of the Marshall Plan over the Mutual Broadcasting System, on December 5, 1947. Kurt Schumacher, the head of the German Social Democratic Party, said "the policy of the American Federation of Labor in favor of the Marshall Plan has become an essential part of social democratic policy in every country of Europe." Kurt Schumacher to William Green, January 28, 1948.

17. William Green to Honorable Harry S. Truman, November 17, 1947.

18. *Ibid.* Subsequent quotations are also from the above letter.

19. *Confidential Report from Irving Brown,* February 18, 1948.

20. Louis Major to William Green, February 1, 1948, also sent to J. H. Oldenbroek, February 1, 1948.

21. J. H. Oldenbroek, February 19, 1948.

22. *Minutes of the Meeting of the AFL Executive Council,* February 3, 1948.

23. Quotation is from a cablegram from William Green to J. H. Oldenbroek, February 18, 1948.

24. J. H. Oldenbroek to David Dubinsky, February 22, 1948.

25. *Ibid.*

26. Irving Brown to Louis Major, February 23, 1948.

27. *Report of the International Trade Union Conference on the European Recovery Program,* March 9-10, 1948, pp. 8-9.
28. *Ibid.*
29. *Ibid.,* p. 9.
30. *Ibid.*
31. *Ibid.,* p. 44.
32. *Report of the Delegates to the International Trade Union Conference on the European Recovery Program.* The report was signed by Frank Fenton, Irving Brown, and Bert M. Jewell who represented the Railway Labor Executives Association, the majority of whose unions were in the AFL. The report was for the AFL executive council and was undated.
33. Matthew Woll to William Green, April 27, 1948.
34. *Minutes of the AFL Executive Council,* May 11-14, August 27, 1948; *Memorandum to President William Green,* May 30, 1948.
35. Irving Brown to William Green, July 1, 1948.
36. David Dubinsky and Irving Brown to Vincent Tewson, General Secretary TUC, July 16, 1948.
37. *Report by Jay Lovestone, Secretary, in Behalf of AFL Delegation to ERP Conference – George Harrison and David Dubinsky,* July 29-30, 1948, p. 2.
38. *Ibid.*
39. *Ibid.*
40. *Ibid.*
41. *Report on Germany by Jay Lovestone in behalf of George Harrison and David Dubinsky AFL Delegates to London ERP Trade Union,* p. 4. The report was written on August 4, 1948, the date the delegation departed from Berlin.
42. *Report on ERP Trade Union Advisory Committee Meeting,* Berne, Switzerland, January 22, 1949, p. 4.
43. *Statement by the International Labor Relations Committee of the AFL,* February 2, 1949.
44. Report of Irving Brown, January 22, 1949, p. 4.
45. *Minutes of the Meeting of the AFL Executive Council,* February 6, 1949.
46. *Ibid.*
47. *Proceedings Twelfth Constitutional Convention, Congress of Industrial Organizations,* 1950, pp. 184-185.

48. *Report of the Proceedings of the Sixty-Ninth Convention of the American Federation of Labor,* 1950, pp. 95-95.
49. *Proceedings Thirteenth Constitutional Convention, Congress of Industrial Organizations,* 1951, pp. 177-178.
50. *Statement of AFL Executive Council,* August 7-10, 1951.
51. *Proceedings Eleventh Constitutional Convention, Congress of Industrial Organizations,* 1949, p. 421.
52. *Report of the Proceedings of the Sixty-Eighth Convention of the American Federation of Labor,* 1949, pp. 450-451.
53. *Minutes of Meeting of AFL Executive Council,* February 6, 1950.
54. *American Labor Looks at the World,* No. IV (New York: AFL International Labor Relations Committee, 1950), p. 47. This volume contained the speeches of several other union officials. The treaty was signed in Washington by ten nations on April 4, 1949.
55. *Proceedings Eleventh Constitutional Convention, Congress of Industrial Organizations,* 1949, p. 420.
56. *Report of the Proceedings of the Sixty-Ninth Convention of the American Federation of Labor,* 1950, pp. 93-94.
57. *Statement of AFL Executive Council,* August 7-10, 1951.
58. *Ratify the Atlantic Pact,* Declaration by Matthew Woll, Chairman, International Labor Relations Committee, AFL, March 15, 1950.
59. *Slave Labor in Russia: The Case Presented by the American Federation of Labor* (New York: The Free Trade Union Committee, 1949), p. 13. For some of the literature on the subject see *A New Slavery: The Communist Betrayal of Human Rights,* edited by Roger N. Baldwin (New York: Oceana Publications, 1949), pp. 154-158.
60. *Report of the Proceedings of the Sixty-Sixth Convention of the American Federation of Labor,* 1947, pp. 624-625.
61. *Slave Labor in Russia,* p. 27.
62. *Ibid.,* p. 32.
63. *Ibid.,* pp. 153-154.
64. Quoted from United Nations, Economic and Social Council, Ninth Session, 319th meeting, *Official Records,* paragraph 512, *Report of the Ad Hoc Committee on Forced Labour* (Geneva: International Labour Office, 1953), p. 429.
65. UN Economic and Social Council, Twelfth Session, 470th meeting, *Official Records,* paragraphs 7-8, *Report of the Ad Hoc Committee.,* p. 438.

66. *Idem,* Tenth Session, 365th meeting, *Official Records,* paragraphs 49-51, *ibid.,* p. 439.
67. *Idem,* Ninth Session, 318th meeting, *Official Records,* paragraphs 510-511, *ibid.,* p. 446.
68. *Ibid.,* p. 447.
69. *Ibid.,* p. 45.

NOTES TO CHAPTER SIX

1. "New Federation of Free Democratic Unions," *Declaration of AFL Executive Council,* May 16, 1949.
2. Ernest Bevin to David Dubinsky, February 14, 1949. Bevin was Foreign Minister at the time, and this was a personal letter, acknowledging a letter from Dubinsky, in which Bevin disclaimed any desire to meddle in trade union matters.
3. *CIO Proceedings 1949, Eleventh Constitutional Convention,* p. 180; William Green to Victor Tewson, May 19, 1949.
4. *Preparatory International Trade Union Conference: First Report of Drafting Committee,* Geneva, June 25-26, 1949, p. 1.
5. *Ibid.,* p. 2.
6. *Official Report of the Free Labor Conference and the First Congress of the International Confederation of Free Trade Unions,* 1949, pp. 34-35.
7. *Ibid.,* p. 35.
8. "The ICFTU and the AFL," A declaration of the AFL Executive Council, February 1950, *American Labor Looks at the World* (New York: International Labor Relations Committee, 1950), p. 42.
9. *CIO Proceedings 1950, Twelfth Constitutional Convention,* pp. 186-187.
10. *Report of Meeting of Interim Finance Committee* (ICFTU), Brussels, January 27 and 28, 1950, pp. 1-5.
11. *Report on Emergency Committee Meeting* (ICFTU), Brussels, March 16-18, 1950.
12. Matthew Woll to William Green, February 7, 1951.
13. Irving Brown, *Report of ICFTU Emergency Committee Meeting,* February 20-23, 1951.
14. William Green to David Dubinsky, April 6, 1951: see also David Dubinsky to J. H. Oldenbroek, April 4 and 20, 1951; Matthew Woll to Oldenbroek, April 5, 1951.

15. *Report of the Proceedings of the Seventieth Convention of the American Federation of Labor,* 1951, pp. 77-78.
16. *Ibid.*
17. *Ibid.,* p. 181; Irving Brown, *Report to AFL Executive Council,* August 22, 1951.
18. *Ibid.*
19. *Ibid.*
20. "AFL and ICFTU," *International Free Trade Union News,* March 1952. The issues are discussed in detail in a letter from Irving Brown to Jay Lovestone, December 2, 1951. See also *Minutes of Meeting of AFL Executive Council,* August 1951. In order that the heads of the ICFTU would understand the basis of the AFL refusal, copies of the minutes of the executive council meeting were sent to J. H. Oldenbroek.
21. *Notes on International Committee Meeting of the AFL,* held at Washington, D.C., June 18, 1952, p. 1.
22. *Notes,* p. 3.
23. *Notes,* p. 5.
24. *Notes,* pp. 5, 9-10.
25. *Notes,* p. 14.
26. *Notes,* p. 15.
27. *Notes,* pp. 15-16.
28. *Report of the Proceedings of the Seventy-First Convention of the American Federation of Labor,* 1952, p. 115.
29. *CIO Proceedings 1952, Fourteenth Constitutional Convention,* pp. 152-153.
30. *Ibid.,* p. 381.
31. *Report of the Proceedings of the Seventy-Second Convention of the American Federation of Labor,* 1953, pp. 254-256; *1951 Proceedings of the Thirteenth Convention of the Congress of Industrial Organizations,* p. 181.
32. *Report by Irving Brown on Emergency Meeting of ICFTU,* March 1-3, 1954, Brussels; *Report of Seventy-Third Convention of the American Federation of Labor,* 1954, pp. 229-30; *Proceedings of the 1954 Sixteenth Constitutional Convention Congress of Industrial Organizations,* pp. 641-642.
33. *First Constitutional Convention American Federation of Labor and Congress of Industrial Organizations,* 1955, p. 105.
34. *Ibid.,* p. 105.

35. George Meany, "The ICFTU: Estimate and Perspective," *AFL-CIO News*, June 12, 1965.

36. International Confederation of Free Trade Unions, *Relations between free trade unions and communist controlled trade union organizations*, October 24, 1967. The letter was addressed "to certain affiliated organizations."

37. "One can readily infer from speeches and other documents that Meany's assessment of communism is one of an utterly evil, expansionist, enslaving, and still basically monolithic force without redeeming qualities of any kind and inherently incapable of transformation or salvation. Communism is epitomized for him by Stalin's terrors and is bound to remain so more or less. Reuther seems to view it in less Dantean terms." John P. Windmuller, *The Foreign Policy Conflict in American Labor* (Reprint Series no. 219, New York State School of Industrial Relations, Cornell University), p. 223.

38. *The New York Times*, January 16, 1971.

39. *To Clear the Record: AFL-CIO Executive Council Report on the Disaffiliation of the UAW* (Washington: American Federation of Labor-Congress of Industrial Organizations, no date), pp. 38-44.

40. "The AFL-CIO and the ICFTU," Statement adopted by the AFL-CIO Executive Council on May 14, 1969, *AFL-CIO Free Trade Union News*, May, 1969, p. 2.

41. Withdrawal was decided by the officers; the staff was not consulted. Some staff members favored remaining in the ICFTU.

NOTES TO CHAPTER SEVEN

1. George Harrison to Green, August 21, 1948.

2. *Minutes of the Meeting of the AFL Executive Council*, August 25, 1948.

3. William Green to George Harrison, August 31, 1948.

4. Dubinsky to William Green, August 30, 1948.

5. P. Neumayer, to Dubinsky, September 14, 1948.

6. Pierre Ferri-Pisani, "The Battle of French Ports," *International Free Trade Union News*, July 1950, pp. 4-5.

7. *National Union of Mineworkers, A Report of Special Sub-Committee Appointed by National Executive Committee to Reply to Statements in Connection with the French Miners Strike and its Visit to 27th Congress of the General Confederation of French Labor and to Define Union Policy;* 1948, pp. 10-11.

8. *Ibid.,* p. 11.
9. M. Balbu, secretary-general of the Department Union *Force Ouvière,* to William Green, March 26, 1948.
10. Daniel L. Horovitz, *The Italian Labor Movement* (Cambridge, Mass.: Harvard University Press, 1963), pp. 181-191. See also *La C.G.I.L. Dal Patto Di Roma Al Congresso Di Genova.* This was issued by the CGIL and has no place or date of publication.
11. Horowitz, *op. cit.*
12. Italo Viglianesi, in *International Free Trade Union News,* February, 1951, p. 8.
13. The letter was signed by 17 members of *Unione Italiana del Lavoro* and sent to Green, July 22, 1950.
14. *The Trade Union Situation in Italy.* This was a mimeographed statement with a covering letter signed by Giovanni Canini, Erico Parri, and A. Claudio Rocchi, May 26, 1951.
15. George Meany to Henry Rutz, June 17, 1952.
16. The statement was drafted by Matthew Woll and issued by Irving Brown for the AFL. It was signed by Elmer Cope, an international representative of the CIO. It was sent by Woll to George Meany, January 16, 1950.
17. Matthew Woll, "AFL for Full Unity," *International Free Trade Union News,* September 1952, p. 1.
18. August Cool, "Christian Unions' Viewpoint," *Ibid.,* p. 1.
19. Woll, "AFL for Full Unity," p. 1.
20. Woll to Meany, January 12, 1950.
21. For the agreement see A. Claudio Rochi to Irving Brown, February 10, 1953. The views of American labor are in *For Free Labor Unity,* a joint statement of the international labor relations committees of the AFL and of the CIO, May 22, 1952.
22. Irving Brown, *Confidential Report on Greece, France and England,* July 7, 1947.
23. Irving Brown, "Crisis in Greece," *International Free Trade Union News,* May 1947, p. 3.
24. *American Labor Looks at the World* (New York: AFL International Relations Department, 1947), pp. 28-35.
25. Matthew Woll to Premier Themistokles Sophoulis, December 26, 1947 (cable in State Department files — 868-504/12-1627).
26. Fotis Makris to William Green, September 26, 1949.

27. *Report of the Proceedings of the Seventy-Third Convention of the American Federation of Labor,* 1954, pp. 235-236.

28. *Proceedings 1954 Constitutional Convention, Congress of Industrial Organizations,* p. 634.

29. "Oppose Junta, Restore Liberty to Greek People," Declaration of AFL-CIO Executive Council, May 31, 1967, *AFL-CIO Trade Union News,* June 1967, p. 1.

30. *Report of the Proceedings of the Fifty-Sixth Convention of the American Federation of Labor,* 1936, pp. 578-580.

31. *AFL Weekly News,* February 5, 1946.

32. *Ibid.*

33. The information on this interview and the quotation were given to me by Jay Lovestone.

34. *Statement of AFL Executive Council,* September 1949.

35. *American Labor Looks at the World* (New York: American Federation of Labor International Labor Relations Committee, 1950), p. 36.

36. *Ibid.,* p. 37. *Proceedings 1951 Constitutional Convention, Congress of Industrial Organizations,* p. 482.

37. George Meany to Dean Acheson, June 5, 1951.

38. Matthew Woll to Secretary of State Dean Acheson, April 26, 1951; also Acheson to Woll, May 25, 1951.

39. Matthew Woll, "Falangist Follies," *International Free Trade Union News,* May 1952, p. 2.

40. Quotation is from *Declaration Adopted by the AFL Executive Council,* February 8, 1954. The CIO's views are in *Proceedings 1954 Sixteenth Constitutional Convention, Congress of Industrial Organizations,* 1954, p. 633.

41. "Statement of the AFL-CIO Executive Council," *Free Trade Union News,* March, 1965, pp. 1-2.

42. Statement of AFL-CIO President George Meany, December 18, 1970.

NOTES TO CHAPTER EIGHT

1. Confidential Memorandum to William Green from R. J. Watt, Sept. 11, 1942.

2. Robert J. Watt to Secretary of State James F. Byrnes, August 17, 1945.

3. *Special Bulletin of the Free Trade Union Committee,* 1945.
4. *Proceedings Tenth Constitutional Convention, Congress of Industrial Organizations, 1948,* p. 143; Victor Alba, *Historia del Movimiento Obrero en America Latina* (Mexico: Libreros Mexicanos Unidos, 1954), pp. 462-471.
5. Serafino Romualdi, *Presidents and Peons: Recollections of a Labor Ambassador* (New York: Funk and Wagnalls, 1967), pp. 30-38.
6. Romualdi, *op. cit.,* pp. 49-63; Matthew Woll, "Argentine Labor is Not Free," *American Labor Looks at the World* (New York: AFL International Labor Relations Committee, 1947), p. 21.
7. Woll's telegram is in Romualdi, *op. cit.,* p. 69.
8. *AFL Weekly News,* November 25, 1947.
9. *Report of the United States Delegation to the Lima, Peru, Inter-American Trade Union Conference,* January 7-10, 1948.
10. *Report of the Proceedings of the Sixty-Seventh Convention of the American Federation of Labor,* 1948, p. 283.
11. *Ibid.,* pp. 492-493.
12. "Infringements of Trade Union Rights in Peru," A memorandum submitted by Matthew Woll and David Dubinsky, AFL consultants to the Social and Economic Council on behalf of the AFL, *American Labor Looks at the World* (New York: AFL International Labor Relations Committee, 1949), Vol. III, p. 2123.
13. Romualdi, *op. cit.,* pp. 91-93.
14. Meany's speech is in Romualdi, *op. cit.,* p. 113.
15. Alba, *op. cit.,* pp. 474-480.
16. Romualdi, *op. cit.,* p. 250.
17. *Statement of AFL Executive Council,* August 1951. Serafino Romualdi to Assistant Secretary of State Edward G. Miller, August 9, 1951; Mann to Romualdi, August 17, 1951.
18. *Report of the Proceedings of the Seventy-Third Convention of the American Federation of Labor,* 1953, pp. 245-246; Romualdi, *op. cit.,* pp. 268-269.
19. *Statement for the Free Trade Union Committee and the AFL International Labor Relations Committee,* January 13, 1955. Woll received a letter of thanks from Antonio A. Facio, Costa Rica's Ambassador to the United States, January 15, 1955. *Report of the Proceedings of the American Federation of Labor,* 1955, pp. 173-174.
20. *AFL-CIO Resolutions on Foreign Policy.* Adopted by the first

constitutional convention of the American Federation of Labor and Congress of Industrial Organizations, 1955, p. 7.

21. *The Trade Union Situation in Latin America,* Statement by the AFL-CIO Executive Council, June 7, 1956.

22. *Military Dictatorships in Latin America,* Statement by the AFL-CIO Executive Council, February 6, 1957.

23. *Proceedings of the AFL-CIO Constitutional Convention,* 1957, pp. 487-490.

24. *Ibid.,* p. 489.

25. Quotation is from *The Struggle for Democracy in the Caribbean Area.* Statement of the AFL-CIO Executive Council, February 22, 1959. See also *Against Admission of Former Dictators to the U.S.,* statement by the AFL-CIO Executive Council, February 24, 1959; Statement by the AFL-CIO Executive Council on Haiti, August 15, 1963.

26. *Latin American Economic Development.* Statement of the AFL-CIO Executive Council, February 24, 1959. *Proceedings of the AFL-CIO Third Constitutional Convention,* 1959, pp. 144-145.

27. *Political Relationship with Latin America.* Statement by the AFL-CIO Executive Council, February 28, 1961.

28. *The Latin American Aid Program.* Statement of AFL-CIO Executive Council, February 28, 1961.

29. *Ibid.*

30. *Punta Del Este 1967.* AFL-CIO Executive Council Statement, May 9, 1967.

31. *The Alliance for Progress.* Statement by the AFL-CIO Executive Council, February 26, 1961.

32. *Proceedings of the AFL-CIO Third Constitutional Convention,* 1957, Vol I, pp. 143-144.

33. *Statement by the AFL-CIO Executive Council on Cuba,* May 4, 1960.

34. *A Report to the AFL-CIO Executive Council on the Cuban Refugee Problem,* February 24, 1961.

35. Statement by AFL-CIO Executive Council on *Aid to Cuban Refugees,* February 25, 1961.

36. *Resolution on Latin America Adopted by 1961 AFL-CIO Convention* (leaflet).

37. "Latin America—Transition and Tasks," *AFL-CIO Trade Union News,* December 1971, p. 5.

38. *Ibid.*

NOTES TO CHAPTER NINE

1. *Disarmament: The American Federation of Labor; Its Declarations in Support of Disarmament and International Peace* (Washington: American Federation of Labor, 1921), p. 2.
2. *Report of Proceedings of Second Annual Convention of the American Federation of Labor,* p. 3.
3. *Report of Proceedings of the Twenty-Sixth Annual Convention of the American Federation of Labor,* 1906, p. 38; *Report of Proceedings of the Thirty-Fifth Annual Convention of the American Federation of Labor,* 1915, p. 48-52.
4. *Report of Proceedings of the Eighteenth Annual Convention of the American Federation of Labor,* 1898, pp. 86-91.
5. *Report of Proceedings of the Nineteenth Annual Convention of the American Federation of Labor,* 1899, p. 148.
6. "Statement of AFL Executive Council on the Crisis in the Far East," *International Free Trade Union News,* December 1949, p. 5.
7. *CIO Proceedings 1949, Eleventh Constitutional Convention,* p. 421.
8. Woll to Honorable George C. Marshall, June 22, 1948.
9. *Ibid.*
10. *Report of the Proceedings of the Sixty-Seventh Convention of the American Federation of Labor,* 1948, p. 488.
11. *Ibid.*
12. *CIO Proceedings 1951, Thirteenth Constitutional Convention,* p. 487.
13. *Declaration by AFL Executive Council,* February 1952.
14. *Ibid.*
15. *AFL-CIO Free Trade Union News,* April 1971, p. 7.
16. *Ibid.*
17. Woll to Secretary of Defense Johnson, June 24, 1949. The same letter was sent to Secretary of State Dean Acheson. Johnson acknowledged Woll's letter in Johnson to Woll, July 1, 1949.
18. Secretary of State Dean Acheson to Woll, July 13, 1949.
19. *Report of the Proceedings of the Sixty-Ninth Convention of the American Federation of Labor,* 1950, pp. 53, 485, 507.
20. *CIO Proceedings 1950, Twelfth Constitutional Convention, Congress of Industrial Organizations,* p. 389.
21. *CIO Proceedings 1951, Thirteenth Constitutional Convention,* p. 483.

22. "No Forced Repatriation of Korean War Prisoners," *International Free Trade Union News,* May, 1952, p. 3.
23. "Against Forced Repatriation in Korea," *American Labor Looks at the World* (New York: Free Trade Union Committee, 1953), p. 20.
24. *Memorandum for President William Green from W. C. Roberts,* undated.
25. *Memorandum for President William Green from W. C. Roberts,* March 12, 1927.
26. *Ibid.*
27. William Green to Walter Citrine, January 23, 1938.
28. *Ibid.*
29. *Report of the Proceedings of the Sixty-Eighth Convention of the American Federation of Labor,* 1949, p. 437.
30. *Report of the Proceedings of the Seventy-First Convention of the American Federation of Labor,* 1952, pp. 543. *Statement of Executive Council,* February 4, 1955.
31. *Proceedings 1954 Congress of Industrial Organizations,* p. 637.
32. Matthew Woll, "An Historic Declaration," *American Labor Looks at the World* (New York: AFL International Labor Relations Committee, 1953), p. 55.
33. *Ibid.,* p. 56.
34. *Report of the Proceedings of the Seventieth Convention of the American Federation of Labor,* 1951.
35. "Declaration of the AFL Executive Council on the Crisis in Asia," *International Free Trade Union News,* July 1954, p. 1.
36. *Report of the Procedings of the Seventy-Third Convention of the American Federation of Labor,* 1954, p. 203.
37. *Ibid.,* p. 203.
38. *Ibid.,* p. 204.
39. *Proceedings of the AFL-CIO Constitutional Convention,* 1963, Vol. II. p. 103.
40. *AFL-CIO Free Trade Union News,* September 1964, p. 1.
41. *Proceedings of Sixth Constitutional Convention of the AFL-CIO,* 1965 (fifth day), p. 4.
42. *Ibid.*
43. *Ibid.,* p. 7.
44. "Statement of AFL-CIO Executive Council," *AFL-CIO Free Trade Union News,* March 1966, pp. 1-2.
45. *International Affairs Policy Resolutions.* Adopted December 1967, at AFL-CIO Seventh Constitutional Convention, 1967, pp. 8-9.

46. *AFL-CIO Free Trade Union News,* March 1968, pp. 1-2.
47. *Proceedings of the AFL-CIO Eighth Constitutional Convention,* 1969, Vol. I, pp. 444-449.

NOTES TO CHAPTER TEN

1. Woll to Secretary of State Dean Acheson, April 7, 1952; *International Free Trade Union News,* June 1952, p. 1.
2. *International Free Trade Union News,* June 1952, p. 1.
3. *Statement of George Meany,* December 8, 1952; Matthew Woll to Ambassador Henri Bonnet, April 27, 1953.
4. Matthew Woll to Ambassador Henri Bonnet, December 10, 1953, and Ambassador Bonnet to Woll, December 15, 1953; *International Free Trade Union News,* March 1954, p. 7.
5. *Declaration by Matthew Woll,* September 2, 1953.
6. Information from George Meany and Jay Lovestone.
7. "Toward a Reappraisal of American Foreign Policy and a Program of Action," *Report of the AFL Executive Council to the Seventy-Third Convention,* 1954, p. 31.
8. *AFL-CIO Resolutions on Foreign Policy.* Adopted by the First Constitutional Convention of the American Federation of Labor-Congress of Industrial Organizations (AFL-CIO), 1955, p. 6.
9. *Proceedings of the AFL-CIO Constitutional Convention,* 1957, Vol. I, pp. 422-423.
10. *Statement of the AFL-CIO Executive Council on Apartheid in South Africa,* May 1, 1958.
11. *Statement of AFL-CIO Executive Council,* February 20, 1959.
12. *Statement of AFL-CIO Executive Council on Boycott of South Africa,* February 1960.
13. *Proceedings of the Fifth AFL-CIO Convention,* 1963, pp. 265-266.
14. *Proceedings of the AFL-CIO Sixth Constitutional Convention,* 1965, p. 45. Resolution #175.
15. *Statement by the AFL-CIO Executive Council on National Freedom and Free Labor in Africa,* February 1960.
16. *Proceedings of the AFL-CIO Fourth Constitutional Convention,* 1961, p. 306.
17. *Statement by the AFL-CIO Executive Council on the Trade Union Situation in Africa,* March 1, 1965.
18. *Proceedings of the AFL-CIO Seventh Constitutional Convention* 1967, Vol. I, pp. 305-307.

19. *Report of the Proceedings of the Seventy-Third Convention of the American Federation of Labor,* 1954, p. 600.
20. *AFL-CIO Resolutions on Foreign Policy Adopted by First Constitutional Convention,* 1955, pp. 7-8.
21. *Statement by AFL-CIO Executive Council,* February 12, 1956.
22. *Statement by the AFL-CIO Executive Council on the Middle East,* February 1957.
23. *Proceedings of the AFL-CIO Seventh Constitutional Convention,* 1967, p. 311.

NOTES TO CHAPTER ELEVEN
1. *A Proposal for a Comprehensive Educational Program for Leaders of South American Unions,* August 1960, p. 1.
2. *Resolution on a Fund for Union Leadership Development in Latin America,* June 29, 1961.
3. Serafino Romualdi, *Presidents and Peons: Recollections of a Labor Ambassador in Latin America* (New York: Funk & Wagnalls, 1967), p. 420.
4. Romualdi, *op. cit.,* p. 427, quotes from the *Memo: AIFLD: Aims, Objectives and Program.*
5. Romualdi, *op. cit.,* p. 420.
6. *Survey of Labor Policies and Programs.* A study prepared by R. H. Dockery for the staff of the Senate Committee on Foreign Relations, Ninety-First Congress, First Session, p. 31.
7. *American Institute for Free Labor Development. Hearings Before the Senate Committee on Foreign Relations,* Ninety-First Congress, First Session, August 1, 1959, p. 5. Testimoney of George Meany.
8. *Survey of Labor Policies and Programs,* p. 31.
9. *Ibid.*
10. *Ibid.,* p. 35.
11. *Ibid.,* p. 36.
12. *Report of AIFLD to AFL-CIO Executive Council,* February 1971.
13. Testimony of George Meany, *American Institute for Free Labor Development,* p. 9.
14. *Ibid.,* p. 9.
15. *Ibid.,* p. 82.
16. *Ibid.*
17. *Ibid.,* p. 83.
18. *Ibid.*

19. *Ibid.*, p. 84.
20. Testimony of George Meany in *Ibid.*, p. 48.
21. *AFL-CIO Free Trade Union News,* March 1956.
22. *Ibid.*, p. 49.
23. *Annual Progress Report,* 1969, American Institute for Free Labor Development.
24. *Ibid.*
25. *Survey of Labor Policies and Programs.* A Study prepared by Robert H. Dockery for the staff of the Committee on Foreign Relations, United States Senate, Ninety-First Congress, First Session, p. 10. The data for the 1967-1969 are from AIFLD audited financial reports.
26. *Report to the Committee on Foreign Relations: United States Senate Follow-Up Review of Activities Under Contracts with the American Institute for Free Labor Development,* Comptroller General of the United States, April 23, 1970, pp. 9-10.
27. *Ibid.*, p. 11.
28. *Ibid.*
29. *Ibid.*, p. 12.

NOTES TO CHAPTER TWELVE
1. Irving Brown, "New African-American Labor Center Concentrates on Aiding Economic Independence of African Nations," *International Free Trade Union News,* February, 1965, pp. 5, 8.
2. *African-American Labor Center,* 1965-1970, p. 2.
3. *Ibid.*, p. 3.
4. *Ibid.*
5. *Ibid.*, p. 5; *Minutes of the Board of Directors of the African-American Labor Center,* September 16, 1968, p. 2.
6. African-American Labor Center, p. 5.
7. *Ibid.*, p. 6.
8. *Ibid.*
9. *Ibid.*, p. 7.
10. *Ibid.*
11. *Ibid.*
12. *Ibid.*
13. *Ibid.*, p. 8.
14. *Ibid.*
15. *Ibid.*, p. 9.

16. *Ibid.*
17. African-American Labor Center, *Summary of Impact Projects,* May 12, 1966 – March 15, 1970, p. 1 (unpublished).
18. *Ibid.,* p. 1.
19. *Ibid.,* p. 17.
20. *Ibid.,* pp. 19-20.
21. Funds were provided by the ILGWU, the IBEW, and the Brother-hood of Locomotive Enginemen and Firemen.
22. *Ibid.,* pp. 23-24.
23. *Ibid.,* pp. 30-31.
24. *Ibid.,* p. 30.
25. *Ibid.,* p. 32.
26. *Ibid.,* pp. 48-49.
27. Material for the table taken from a detailed description in *Ibid.,* pp. 5-10.
28. One project was divided into two parts. Part of the grant was for the purchase of a vehicle and the other was to support training of leaders.
29. *Ibid.,* pp. 11-12.
30. Russell Warren Howe, "The Mobutu Style Taming of the Congo," *The New Republic,* August 1, 1970, p. 16.

NOTES TO CHAPTER THIRTEEN
1. *AAFLI News,* October, 1970.
2. *Report to AFL-CIO Executive Council,* February, 1971 in *AAFLI News,* January/February, 1971.

NOTES TO CHAPTER FOURTEEN
1. Samuel Gompers to President Woodrow Wilson, December 7, 1914; *Report of the Proceedings of the Thirty-fourth Annual Convention of the American Federation of Labor,* 1914, pp. 474-475.
2. The proposal was approved at the AFL conventions of 1915 and 1916. See *Report of the Proceedings of the Thirty-Sixth Annual Convention of the American Federation of Labor,* 1916, p. 55; *The Origins of the International Labor Office,* edited by James T. Shotwell (New York: Columbia University Press, 1934), Volume II, pp. 88-91.
3. *The Official Bulletin,* Volume I, published by the International Labor Office, contains the discussions of the commission. See also Shotwell, *Op. Cit.* Vol. II, p. 142.

4. The *Official Bulletin,* Vol. I, p. 261.
5. *Report of the Proceedings of the Thirty-Ninth Annual Convention of the American Federation of Labor,* 1919, pp. 399-400; "Minutes of the Meeting of the American Federation of Labor Committee on International Labor Conference," Shotwell, *op. cit.,* Vol. II, p. 539.
6. *Report of the Proceedings of the Fifty-Fourth Annual Convention of the American Federation of Labor,* 1934, p. 85.
7. William Green to President Franklin D. Roosevelt, March 13, 1944; *Report of the Proceedings of the Sixty-Fifth Convention of the American Federation of Labor,* 1946, pp. 574-575.
8. *Toward a Reappraisal of American Foreign Policy and a Program of Action* (Washington: AFL, 1954), p. 53.
9. "Report of the Committee on Freedom of Employers' and Workers' Organizations," *Official Bulletin,* Vol. XXXIX, p. 478.
10. *Ibid.,* p. 478.
11. "International Labor Organization," *American Labor Looks at the World* (Washington: AFL, 1955), Part IX, p. 19.
12. *Statement by the AFL-CIO Executive Council,* February 11, 1956.
13. *Statement of the AFL-CIO Executive Council on the ILO,* February 6, 1957; *Proceedings of the AFL-CIO Constitutional Convention,* 1957, Vol. II, p. 179.
14. *Proceedings of the AFL-CIO Constitutional Convention,* 1959, Vol. II, p. 124.
15. *Resolution on The Trade Union Situation in the USSR – Report of a Mission from the International Labor Office,* February 21, 1961.
16. A comparison of the treatment accorded the Soviet unions and those in the United States is in *Crisis in the International Labor Organization* reprinted in *Hearings Before a Subcommittee of the Committee on Appropriations, House of Representatives,* Ninety-First Congress, Second Session, Part 5, Additional Testimony on the International Labor Organization, especially pp. 24-29.
17. *To Clear the Record: AFL-CIO Executive Council on the Disaffiliation of the UAW,* p. 6.
18. *Ibid.,* p. 9.
19. *Ibid.,* p. 10.
20. *Ibid.,* p. 11.

21. *Remarks on Director General's Report by Rudolph Faupl, United States Workers' Delegate to 51st International Labor Conference,* June 21, 1967, p. 2.
22. *Address of AFL-CIO President George Meany at an International Labor Conference in Celebration of the Fiftieth Anniversary of the International Labor Organization,* Temple University, May 8, 1969, p. 3.
23. *Ibid.,* pp. 59, 76. In an interview on July 16, 1971, President Meany said he never favored withdrawal from the ILO.
24. *The ILO, Statement of the AFL-CIO Executive Council,* August 4, 1970.
25. *President George Meany's Press Conference,* May 11, 1971.
26. *The International Labor Organization, Statement by the AFL-CIO Executive Council,* May 11, 1971.

NOTE TO CHAPTER FIFTEEN

1. The late William Green faced such a dilemma when the convention endorsed a resolution of Andrew Furuseth on the limiting of the labor injunction.